Go to the Ark

A Modern-Day Allegory on
How the Animals Got to the Ark

CHRISTOPHER A. MURRAY

ISBN 978-1-0980-2876-3 (paperback)
ISBN 978-1-0980-2878-7 (digital)

Christian Faith Publishing, Inc.
832 Park Avenue
Meadville, PA 16335
www.christianfaithpublishing.com

Printed in the United States of America

A special thanks to God.
I would like to thank God for making this book happen.
This book took thirteen years to write.
The reason I wrote this book is because I believed the
whole time that God wanted me to write it.
It was God who gave me the idea for this story.
It was God who motivated me to write this story.
It was God who caused me to finally finish this story.
This book is dedicated to God.
Thank You, God.

CONTENTS

INTRODUCTION

Our culture today treats the Genesis flood as a myth.[1] There are also many children's books with cute little smiling animals on a small boat giving the impression that the Genesis flood is a fairy tale. The Genesis flood is not a myth, nor is it a fairy tale. Jesus Christ referred to the Genesis flood as a historical fact.[2] Secular research is often discovering evidence of a global flood, but they refuse to attribute it to the Genesis flood.[3] The surface of the earth is filled with beautiful and majestic mountains, landscapes, waterfalls, canyons, and all kinds of other breathtaking scenery. But underneath all the beauty, buried beneath the surface, is a global graveyard known as the fossil record.[4] The Genesis flood is the stark reality of the judgment of God on an ungodly world full of violence,[5] where the wickedness of man was so great that people wanted to do evil all the time.[6] The evil and wickedness was so normal that Jesus said that before the flood, everyone was preoccupied with everyday life and unconcerned about God's impending judgment.[7] While building the Ark, Noah was preaching God's righteousness to this ungodly world.[8] After Noah finished building the Ark, the Bible says that God made the animals go to the Ark.[9]

What if Noah was alive today and preaching righteousness and warning the world of God's coming judgment? What would that look like? How would the world respond? How would God make the animals go to the Ark?

This story aims to answer these questions in an allegorical way. Every chapter is created from historical and modern-day current events, books, philosophies, articles, belief systems, etc. I have provided references where applicable to help you see how the subject matter was formulated.

In today's culture, animals are often used in books and animated movies to convey a moral message or other lesson to children. Although this book uses animals, this story is intended for adults to hopefully cause you to think about what you believe in light of God's judgment. The Ark was the only way to escape God's judgment in the Genesis flood. The Ark was symbolic of Jesus Christ who was better than the Ark because He not only saves us from God's future judgment but He also changes our heart so that we desire the righteousness of God.[10] For this reason, you will see the *A* in *Ark* always capitalized to cause you to think of Jesus every time you read the word *Ark* in this story.

There are a lot of animals in this story so to help eliminate confusion, only the animals that are going to the Ark will be identified as Mr. and Mrs.

Please resist any temptation to jump ahead and read a chapter out of order. This story is designed to flow from start to finish and jumping ahead may cause confusion and disturb the flow of the story.

Join me now in this fascinating story of how the animals got to the Ark...

CHAPTER 1

The Rainbow

As the rain was tapering off, the clouds began to part and reveal a beautiful blue sky. One by one the sun's bright rays poked their way through the parting clouds until they lit up a fully formed perfect rainbow. Little Joey Kangaroo was the first to notice the full rainbow arcing across the cloudy sky. It was the first time he had ever seen a rainbow.

"Mom! Dad! Look! Look over there!" shouted Joey.

Mom and Dad hurried to where Joey was. "Look at what?" they asked as they looked in the direction that Joey was pointing.

"What is that?" asked Joey.

"That's a rainbow!" Mom and Dad answered together in one voice.

"It's beautiful and amazing!" announced Joey.

"Yes, it is!" Mom agreed. "I love how they are so colorful."

There was much that Dad wanted to teach Joey about God and the rainbow, but Joey was very young and not ready to understand the deeper things of God. But Joey was growing fast, and Dad decided this was a good time to teach his son about the true meaning of the rainbow.

"Son, the rainbow has a special meaning," Dad began.

"A special meaning?" inquired Joey. "What special meaning?"

Dad continued, "Son, the rainbow is a sign from God to the humans and every living creature that He will never again destroy the earth by a flood."[1]

"Destroy the earth by a flood?" Joey asked confused. "God destroyed the earth?"

"He sure did," Dad replied. "God caused rain to come down on the whole earth for forty days and forty nights until everything was underwater."[2]

After the recent rain, Joey saw how puddles and streams drained away or dried up, but he could not imagine how much rain it would take to flood the earth until everything was underwater.

"It rained for forty days and forty nights straight?" asked Joey to be sure he heard his dad correctly.

"Yes, it did," Dad confirmed.

"Why did God do that?" asked Joey.

"Because God saw that the wickedness of everyone was great on the earth, and that all of the thoughts of their heart were only evil,"[3] answered Dad. "God decided to put an end to all the evil and violence by destroying all living flesh in a flood."

"Did everybody drown?" asked Joey.

"Not everybody," answered Dad. "Sit down, Joey, and I'll explain the whole story from the beginning. After I'm finished, I'm sure that all your questions will be answered."

Joey sat next to his dad, intently staring at him with his full attention. Dad always told Joey how much God loved him, so Joey was eager to know why God would destroy everybody in a flood. That didn't sound like love to Joey.

Dad began the story by going back to a time before the flood and before Joey was born when God first spoke to his dad, also known as Mr. Kangaroo.

CHAPTER 2

God Speaks to Mr. Kangaroo

Mr. Kangaroo was minding his own business eating a shrub when he was suddenly hit in the head with a rock.

Whack!

"Ouch!" Mr. Kangaroo groaned. He looked down at the rock as it rolled to a stop. He looked up just in time to dodge another rock coming at his head. It was that pesky bully kangaroo again. The bully and all his kangaroo friends turned on Mr. Kangaroo ever since he asked them if they believed in God. They have been mean to him ever since. They kicked him out of their mob but the bully continues to hassle, torment, and mock Mr. Kangaroo every time he sees him. This time the bully was throwing rocks at him.

"Why did you do that?" Mr. Kangaroo asked while rubbing his head. "Why are you throwing rocks at me?"

"Because I feel like it!" the bully shouted as he was throwing another rock.

"God is watching you!" he shouted even though he knew the bully didn't believe in God.

"What God? I don't see any God," the bully replied with sarcasm.

Mr. Kangaroo just hopped away from bully as fast as he could, but not before being hit in the back with another rock.

Thump!

"Ouch!" he groaned again.

The bully chased after Mr. Kangaroo until he caught up to him and yelled at him, "That is some God you have, He doesn't even protect you! Ha ha ha ha ha ha ha."

Mr. Kangaroo continued to hop and hop until the bully finally stopped chasing him. He found a place to hide in some bushes while he caught his breath. He thought that he was the only one around that believed in God. Nobody cared about God. Whenever he asked others about God, they just mocked him or laughed and made fun of him. And now they even bullied him.

Why does God allow all this evil? he thought to himself. *How come nobody else believes in God?*

The more he thought about it, the more saddened he would get. He felt very lonely and depressed. He looked up to the sky and asked, "God, I know You're there, and I believe in You, but how come I'm the only one who believes in You?"

Mr. Kangaroo sighed as he wondered why God was so silent. Why did God make it so difficult to believe in Him sometimes? He prayed from a desperate heart, *"O God, where are You?"*

He became overwhelmed with sadness. He felt all alone in an evil world full of unbelievers while God remained silent. He sat in silence feeling very sad and lonely.

Suddenly a bright light shown all around him.[1] The light was so bright that he couldn't see anything. Then a voice from the light said, "Mr. Kangaroo, Mr. Kangaroo."

"Here I am… I can't see. Who are you?" he asked trembling with fear.

"Do not be afraid, for I am God," the voice proclaimed.

Mr. Kangaroo bowed to worship, trembling with fear, "Why are You speaking to me? What do you want?"

"Do not be afraid, Mr. Kangaroo," God declared. "I have seen all the violence, and I see that there is continually evil in everyone's heart. I see that no one seeks after me, and they never will. I am going to destroy all flesh, and I have chosen to save you because of your faith in Me. Do not be afraid. I have heard your prayers. Mr. Kangaroo, I want you to go to the Ark."

"What's an Ark?" he asked.

"You'll know it when you see it," God said. "When you get to the Ark, you must enter it."

"Where is this Ark?" he asked.

"I will lead you to it," God promised. "Do not fear or lose heart, for I will be with you, I will not leave you nor forsake you."[2]

The light went out, and the voice stopped.

Mr. Kangaroo looked around, but the light was gone.

What just happened? he thought with excitement. *Did God really just speak to me? Yes, yes, He did! God just told me to go to the Ark. What's an Ark? Where is this Ark? God said I would know it when I see it and He would lead me to it. What does that mean? Where do I go from here?"*

Mr. Kangaroo was no longer sad. He was excited…yet fearful.

CHAPTER 3

The Mongooses (Apostasy)

"Excuse me!" came the sound of another voice.

"Yes, God, here I am," Mr. Kangaroo replied.

"Excuse me, but you're on my tail," the voice said.

"What?" Mr. Kangaroo asked confused.

"Look down here, you're on my tail," the voice said.

He looked down and saw that he was standing on the tail of a mongoose. "Oh, I'm so sorry!" Mr. Kangaroo apologized as he stepped off his tail. "God was just speaking to me, and I thought you were Him."

"God was just speaking to you?" the mongoose asked with sarcasm. "Oh no, not another god-freak who hears from God. What did He say? Is He the One Who told you to step on my tail?"

"He said I need to go to the Ark because He is going to destroy all living flesh by flooding the earth," answered Mr. Kangaroo.

"God told you He is going to destroy all flesh?" the mongoose replied. "It sounds more like you've been talking to the devil."

"No, really," Mr. Kangaroo insisted. "God just told me that He sees all the evil and He knows that nobody seeks after Him and He is going to destroy all living flesh. Why don't you come with me to the Ark?"

"Whoa, slow down there, Mr. Tail Stomper," the mongoose replied. "God just told you…like…just now?"

"Yes," answered Mr. Kangaroo. "A bright light shone on me, and God spoke to me through the light and—"

"A bright light?" asked the mongoose. "It's midday. How can you see a bright light with the sun shining so bright?"

"It was brighter than the sun," Mr. Kangaroo answered. "I know it sounds weird, but it's true. It just happened a few minutes ago."

"I've been here the whole time, I didn't see a bright light," the mongoose answered.

"I don't know why you didn't see it," he replied. "Did you hear God speaking to me?"

"No," the mongoose answered. "But even if I did hear a voice, it definitely wouldn't be God's voice."

"Do you believe in God?" asked Mr. Kangaroo.

"No, no, not me," the mongoose replied. "I don't believe in God. I've already tried that god thing. I prayed and did all that religious stuff, but everything just stayed the same. Actually everything is getting worse. I realized that God was just something that I imagined."

"You did not imagine God," Mr. Kangaroo insisted. "He is real."

"If God is real, then why is He so hidden?" the mongoose asked.

"God is not hidden," Mr. Kangaroo replied. "His attributes are revealed in all His creation.[1] Just look at all the different kinds of animals, plants, stars, and so on."

"If God created everything, then where is He?" the mongoose replied.

"God is hidden to those who have been blinded by their unbelief,"[2] Mr. Kangaroo answered. "God also hides Himself from those who don't repent of their sin but continue in their sin as if God is okay with it."[3]

"God is hidden because He isn't real, and blaming it on my sin is just a way to make an excuse for God," the mongoose replied. "I tried to believe, but my life just got worse and worse. God is not real."

"It sounds like things didn't go your way so you gave up on God," Mr. Kangaroo answered. "Maybe things didn't go your way because you wanted God to conform to your will rather than you conforming to His will. God is not hidden to those who trust Him."

"Go my way?" the mongoose replied. "I lost a relative to sickness, and my brother was eaten. I have been through all kinds of abuse. I didn't ask for things to go my way. I just wanted to know why God wasn't there for me when I needed Him. I've tried the god thing. Been there, done that. God is not real. I asked God to speak to me many times, but He never did. It was just a bunch of false hope."

"No, no, it's not false hope!" Mr. Kangaroo insisted. "I'm sorry about your brother and your relative. I too have lost loved ones to evil and sickness. But God is real, and I'm telling you that He just told me that He sees all the evil and violence and His judgment is coming. Please come with me to the Ark!"

"What's an Ark?" the mongoose asked.

"He didn't tell me," answered Mr. Kangaroo. "He told me that I will know it when I see it."

"God told you to go to an Ark because He's going to judge the world and He didn't tell you what an Ark is?" the mongoose asked while holding his laughter. "Where is this Ark?"

"He didn't tell me where it is," Mr. Kangaroo answered as he realized how silly this all must sound. "He told me that He would lead me to it and I must enter it before the flood comes."

The mongoose did everything he could to control himself from bursting out with laughter. After suppressing his laughter, he asked, "So God is going to guide you to something you've never seen and you don't know where it is because He is going to judge the world of evil by flooding the earth?"

"Yes! Yes!" Mr. Kangaroo shouted with excitement.

The mongoose couldn't take it anymore, and he laughed out loud, "Ha ha ha ha ha ha ha ha. This is too funny. Can you hear yourself? Is this really how God spoke to you? This is so absurd that I'm glad He didn't speak to me. The only thing God has led you to is my tail."

"I know it sounds silly, but—" Mr. Kangaroo replied but was interrupted.

"I think someone must've hit you in the head with a rock or something," the mongoose said with sarcasm.

"I know it sounds silly, but it's true," Mr. Kangaroo said as he remembered being hit in the head with a rock by that bully kangaroo.

"God is not real, which is why this judgment talk is nonsense," the mongoose replied. "You're better off staying in the real world rather than getting caught up in a false hope of a nonexistent God who wants to flood the world."

"Please come with me," Mr. Kangaroo pleaded again.

"No, no, definitely not, I have already tried God," the mongoose replied. "And I certainly don't want to follow a god who wants to kill everyone."

Mr. Kangaroo began to turn and go his way when the mongoose said one last thing, "Wait, come to think of it, there is a couple of mongooses in our gang that have been talking about God, and they were babbling something about a flood too. Maybe they will go with you to your Ark. Why don't you tell them how God talked to you?"

"I would love to, where are they?" asked Mr. Kangaroo.

The mongoose turned and pointed to a pair of mongooses that were kneeling down. "They're over there. In fact, you can see them praying together right now. They're always praying. It hasn't helped them a bit."

"Thank you. I'll go talk to them right now," Mr. Kangaroo said as he began hopping over to them.

As Mr. Kangaroo was hopping toward them, he was thrilled to finally get to speak to someone else who believes in God. He hadn't met anybody who believed in God in a very long time. He was eager to know if they heard from God too. Did God speak to any other animals about the coming flood? Did God tell anyone else to go to the Ark? As Mr. Kangaroo approached the two mongooses, he was able to hear them praying…

"God, we don't know where to go from here. Everybody is against us. Please help us. Amen."

When the mongooses opened their eyes, they were startled to see Mr. Kangaroo standing right next to them.

"What do you want?" the irritated Mr. Mongoose asked. "Why are you bothering us? Can't you at least leave us alone while we pray?"

"I'm sorry for interrupting your prayer, but I was told by another mongoose that you believe in God," Mr. Kangaroo replied. "I overheard your prayer, did God speak to you about His coming judgment and the Ark?"

"Yes, He did. Why are you asking?" Mr. Mongoose asked as he was expecting more ridicule for his faith in God.

"God spoke to me too," Mr. Kangaroo answered happily. "He told me to go to the Ark and enter it when I get there and—"

"That's what He said to us!" Mr. Mongoose replied with excitement.

"Praise the Lord!" Mr. Kangaroo exclaimed. "I was sure that I was the only one left who believes in God. What a blessing it is to meet the both of you."

"We thought we were the only believers left too," Mrs. Mongoose said. "We get hassled about our belief in God by almost everybody. Now that God spoke to us, it's even worse."

"Tell me about it," Mr. Kangaroo replied. "I was kicked out of my mob of kangaroos, and I just got bullied by a kangaroo before God spoke to me. Then that mongoose over there laughed at me when I told him how God spoke to me. He said he used to believe in God but he doesn't anymore."

"That mongoose stopped believing in God when life didn't go his way," Mrs. Mongoose said. "He went through some very difficult trials and gave up on God."

"That's what I thought," Mr. Kangaroo said. "Sounds like the problems of this world choked out any belief that he had."[4]

"Yeah, his faith was very shallow anyway," answered Mrs. Mongoose. "He never really was a true believer. True believers don't give up on God."[5]

"I tried to get him to come with me to the Ark, but he wanted nothing to do with God now that he doesn't believe anymore," Mr. Kangaroo said.

"None of the mongooses around here believe in God anymore," Mr. Mongoose answered. "They abandoned their faith years ago when they fell prey to false teachers and their lies."[6]

"Thank God we still believe," Mr. Kangaroo said.

"Amen to that!" answered Mrs. Mongoose. "Do you know where the Ark is?"

"No, but God told me that He would lead me to it," answered Mr. Kangaroo. "Did God tell you that too?"

"Yes, but we don't know what that means, how is He going to lead us?" Mr. Mongoose asked.

"I don't know how He is going to lead us, but I trust Him," Mr. Kangaroo answered. "What do you say we all go to the Ark together?"

"That's a great idea," answered Mr. Mongoose.

"Let's pray right now before we go any further," Mr. Kangaroo insisted.

"Okay," Mr. And Mrs. Mongoose replied at the same time.

The three of them closed their eyes and bowed their heads, and Mr. Kangaroo prayed, *"Dear God in heaven, we thank You for saving us from Your coming judgment. We are so grateful, but we don't know which way to go from here. You promised to lead us to the Ark, and we trust You. Please make it known to us which way to the Ark. Amen."*

CHAPTER 4

The Hyenas
(Terrorism)

After the three of them prayed, they opened their eyes and looked around…nothing.

They stood up in the middle of a grassy field and looked around to see only brush and trees a short distance away.

"Which way do we go from here?" Mr. Mongoose asked.

"I don't—" Mr. Kangaroo started to answer but was interrupted.

"Look at all these paw prints on the ground," Mrs. Mongoose said.

"Those are hyena prints!" Mr. Mongoose declared. "We are in a no-go zone."

"A what?" Mr. Kangaroo asked.

"A no-go zone," Mr. Mongoose answered. "Hyena armies control large areas of land, and by the looks of these prints, they have expanded their territory."

"Why do they call it a no-go zone?" asked Mr. Kangaroo.

"I've never been in one, but I've heard terrifying stories of others who have wandered into them," Mr. Mongoose said. "Most animals just know not to go near them."

"We need to get out of here, and fast," Mrs. Mongoose insisted.

Suddenly some hyenas came through the brush with their eyes fixed on the three of them.

"Let's get out of here!" Mr. Kangaroo shouted.

The three of them turned around to run only to immediately stop as there were several more hyenas standing right behind them.

"Freeze, infidels!" the leader hyena ordered.

"We're surrounded," Mr. Mongoose muttered.

"Yes, you are," answered the leader hyena.

"This is not good," Mrs. Mongoose said while trembling.

"Actually, it's very good," leader hyena said. "This land is controlled by the religion of peace."

"What a relief," Mr. Kangaroo said. "We heard stories of—"

"I love torturing infidels," an excited hyena said.

"That doesn't sound like peace," Mr. Kangaroo said while he trembled in fear.

The hyenas began giggling and cackling as the excitement made them laugh uncontrollably. "He he he ha ha ha he he he." Then the hyenas began to drool.

"Silence!" the leader hyena shouted. All the hyenas immediately stopped laughing but continued drooling.

The leader looked at the three animals and asked, "What are you infidels doing on our land?"

"We didn't know this was your land," Mr. Kangaroo said while shaking with fear. "We were just passing through."

"Just passing through?" another hyena angrily answered. "Nobody just passes through our land." Then the hyena looked at the leader hyena and asked, "Don't you know who he is?"

"No, I don't," Mr. Kangaroo answered. "I'm sorry, who is—"

"He's god's holy messenger!"[1] the hyena answered angrily.

"Hey, that's great," Mr. Kangaroo answered as he trembled with fear. "We have a message from God too. God said He sees all the evil in the world and that it will never end so He's going to bring His judgment and destroy all flesh by flooding the earth. The only way to escape God's judgment is to go to the Ark before the flood comes. Do you want to come with us to the Ark?"

"That's ridiculous!" the messenger hyena answered angrily. "You have corrupted god with your own imaginations. Our god is all-mer-

"A choice?" asked Mr. Kangaroo.

"Yes, a choice," messenger hyena said. "You can renounce your faith in your flood God and join the religion of peace and help us spread the message of peace, or you can keep your faith in your flood God and we will slowly torture you and watch you scream before we eat you. Infidels taste so much better when they're screaming."

Mr. Kangaroo boldly declared, "Our God Whom we serve is able to deliver us from you, and He will deliver us out of your hand. But if not, know this, that we will not serve your god or join your army of terror."[6]

"So be it. You have made your choice," the messenger hyena said. Then the messenger hyena gave his attention to Mr. and Mrs. Hyena and said, "First, we are going to tear you and Mrs. Hyena to shreds right in front of Mr. Kangaroo, and then we are going to finish the job on your new friends."

Again all the hyenas started laughing hysterically. "He he he he he he he he he."

The hyenas began drawing closer to the five of them as they laughed and drooled through their teeth. The five surrounded animals backed up close to each other as the hyenas closed in on them.

"Lord, help us!" Mr. Kangaroo shouted. The others called out for God's help too.

"Your flood God can't save you now…you're mine!" shouted the messenger hyena. "First, I'm gonna bite your throat, then I'm gonna—"

"*Roar!*" came the sound of a mighty lion.

All the hyenas immediately stopped laughing, and everyone turned to see the mighty Mr. and Mrs. Lion staring at them with their large teeth showing. Mr. Lion leaped over to the messenger hyena and stared down at him with his face only inches from the face of the messenger hyena. The messenger hyena was crouching back and trembling as he looked straight up into the face of the mighty lion.

"Leave them alone!" Mr. Lion growled at the messenger hyena.

Shaking and trembling, the messenger hyena responded, "I was just testing their faith to see if they truly believed in their God. They did good, I was about to let them go."

"I'm feeling kinda merciful today," Mr. Lion announced. "Normally I just tear apart hyenas and eat them. But since I hate the taste of hyenas, today I think I will give you a choice."

"A choice?" asked leader hyena.

"Yes, a choice," Mr. Lion said. "You and your hyena friends can leave now, or I will make it obvious to all your army that you are a false messenger of god."

"I choose option number 1," the leader hyena said.

"Leave!" shouted Mr. Lion.

The entire herd of hyenas took off running as fast as they could into the brush—all except Mr. and Mrs. Hyena.

"Don't be afraid," declared Mr. Lion. "Mrs. Lion and I heard all the laughter and shouting, so we came over to see what was going on. When we heard you talking about the Ark, we knew we had better stop them from hurting you."

"Thank you so much for saving us!" Mrs. Mongoose announced.

"All glory goes to God," Mr. Lion answered. "He's the One Who caused us to be here at the right time."

"So you know about the coming judgment?" asked Mr. Kangaroo.

"Yes, God spoke to me and Mrs. Lion too," answered Mr. Lion. "We heard you talk of going to the Ark, do you mind if we go with you to the Ark?"

"After saving us from the hyenas, why would we mind if you go with us?" Mr. Kangaroo asked rhetorically.

"Well then, we are very glad to join you," Mr. Lion said.

"What was with those hyenas and their terror tactics?" Mrs. Lion asked.

"The messenger hyena said an angel visited him in a dream, but an angel of God would never give a message of violence and terror to force others to believe," Mrs. Hyena answered. "All the other hyenas believed him and joined his army."

"It just goes to show that we need to beware of anyone who claims to be a messenger of God," Mr. Hyena said.

"Especially when they do things that contradict God's righteousness," Mrs. Hyena added.

"I'm glad they're gone," Mr. Kangaroo said. Then he looked at Mr. Lion and asked, "Do you know where the Ark is?"

"No," Mr. Lion answered. "God told us the same thing He told you, that He would lead us to it."

"Which way do we go from here?" Mr. Hyena asked.

"I don't know, but let's pray before we make any decisions," Mr. Lion answered.

They all agreed and bowed their heads and prayed.

CHAPTER 5

The Lions (Pride)

After the seven animals prayed, they looked at each other, not knowing where to go or what to say or do. After a few moments, Mr. Lion said, "Well, God just spoke to me and Mrs. Lion today, so why don't we go tell the other lions about the coming flood, and maybe God spoke to them too and maybe they will want to go with us to the Ark."

"Sounds good," answered Mr. Kangaroo.

They followed Mr. and Mrs. Lion to their pride of lions. As they approached their pride, the lions appeared to be fighting with each other as if they were in a huge brawl.

"*Roar! Growl! Roar!*" were the sounds coming from the brawl. They were clawing and biting each other, but none of them were bleeding.

Mr. Kangaroo became very afraid and said, "I don't like the looks of this, Mr. Lion. They're fighting, and who are we to try and break it up?"

"Relax, Mr. Kangaroo," Mr. Lion said with a laugh. "They're play-fighting. Lions are the king of the jungle, and they know it, so they're always roughhousing to show their dominance."

"W-w-why don't we come back after they're done playing?" Mrs. Hyena asked with a slight stutter.

"No, no," answered Mr. Lion. "They're always roughhousing, so now is as good a time as any."

The leader male lion noticed the animals approaching and shouted, "Hey, you guys, where have you been? You missed out on some serious rumble!"

"Who are your five friends?" another lion asked. "Do they want to rumble?"

"Ha ha ha," all the other lions laughed at the idea of wrestling the other animals.

"Hey, Mr. Kangaroo, you want to wrestle?" asked another lion. "If you win, we'll crown you king of the jungle."

All the lions laughed at the challenge.

Another lion chimed in, "I've never eaten a kangaroo before. Will he be sticking around for dinner?"

All the lions laughed again.

"Ha…ha…ha," answered Mr. Lion with a fake laugh. "Very funny. Actually we want to talk to you about something serious."

"Like what?" asked a lioness.

"Yeah, what could be so serious to interrupt our rumble?" another lion asked.

"God spoke to me and Mrs. Lion today," Mr. Lion stated.

"Really," a skeptical lion said.

"Yes, really," Mr. Lion answered. "God spoke to Mrs. Lion and me with a clear message. God said that He has seen all the evil and violence, especially the humans, and He is going to destroy all flesh by flooding the earth. We have to go to the Ark and enter it before the flood comes."

"Whoa!" answered leader lion. "That's a whopper!"

"It's true," answered Mrs. Mongoose as she pointed to the other four animals. "God spoke to each of us too."

"Well, if the little mongoose says it's true, then by golly it must be true!" another lion answered sarcastically.

All the lions laughed again.

"Don't you believe in God?" asked Mrs. Hyena.

"I don't have time for God," the leader lion answered. "I live in the real world. God doesn't bring me food, I have to go get it. I have to feed my young. I'm in charge of my life. I work hard and make the decisions that guide my future."

"God's in control, and He created the real world, and God provides the food for you to get,"[1] answered Mr. Mongoose.

"You're right, Mr. Mongoose," the leader lion answered sarcastically. "Normally I have to go hunt for food, but today it looks like God provided a mongoose for dinner."

All the lions laughed again.

"Calm down," Mr. Lion said. "Find something else for dinner. These are my friends, and we're going to the Ark."

"What are you lions doing hanging around with these weak little animals?" leader lion asked. "How can you call yourself a lion? You'll never become great like us if you keep resisting your rightful role as king of the jungle."

"You all think too highly of yourselves," Mrs. Hyena said.

"What's not to love," the leader lion replied confidently. "We're not afraid of any other animals. We are stately in our walk, which displays a swag that clearly shows our self-confidence.[2] We are beautiful and fearful in our appearance."

Then leader lion turned to the other lions and asked, "Which animal is the king of the jungle?"

"Lions!" shouted the entire pride in one loud voice.

"Your God obviously favors lions over all other animals," another lion announced.

"Ha ha ha," all the lions laughed.

"God created all animals for His glory," Mr. Lion answered. "He doesn't favor any animal over another."[3]

"Mr. Lion, your poor self-esteem is showing," the leader lion declared. "You and Mrs. Lion always were the weak ones in our pride. You never did embrace your rightful role as king of the jungle. You always quit when we rumble, or you don't even try. You don't even eat meat.[4] It's no wonder you need God as a crutch. I wouldn't be surprised if the rest of your little friends have poor self-esteem and need God too."

"We aren't concerned about self-esteem," answered Mr. Lion. "We are confident in our belief in God, and we are certain of His coming judgment. Just because we are the king of the jungle does not mean we will escape His coming judgment."

"Let me make myself clear," replied leader lion. "We are lions! We are the king of the jungle! Your God made us this way. We can take care of ourselves even if this judgment were true."

"Shouldn't you be thankful to God since He is the One Who created you?" Mr. Kangaroo asked.

"I am thankful that I'm a mighty lion and not a kangaroo or a hyena or a tiny mongoose or a lion with poor self-esteem,"[5] the leader lion answered confidently.

"Ha ha ha ha," all the lions laughed again.

"God's judgment is coming, and God does not favor the proud,"[6] Mrs. Mongoose replied.

"A tiny little mongoose preaching God's judgment doesn't have much of an impact," the leader lion answered. "Even if your God were real, it makes no sense that He would create us as the greatest of all animals and then destroy us in some kind of judgment."

"God's judgment is coming because He sees all the evil and violence and He sees that it will never end because the heart continues to be evil," Mr. Lion answered.

"That's nonsense," answered another lion. "We're behaving the way lions are supposed to behave. It's who we are. It doesn't mean we're evil. And besides, other animals are far worse than us."

"Everybody has an excuse for their evil behavior, and comparing yourself to other animals will always deceive you into thinking you're not that bad,"[7] Mrs. Hyena answered. "You will never have a proper view of yourself until you compare yourself to the righteousness of God. Compared to God, we all fall short of His righteousness."[8]

"You believe whatever you have to believe to build your self-esteem and confidence," leader lion answered. "As for us, we don't need God."[9]

Mr. Hyena whispered to Mr. Lion, "They seem to be pretty confident in their pride. I don't think they're going to change their minds."

Mr. Lion nodded in agreement and asked the lions again, "One last time, judgment is coming. Do you want to come with us to the Ark and escape God's coming judgment?"

"For the last time, WE DON'T NEED GOD!" the leader lion exclaimed.

"Okay, but just remember that pride comes before the fall,"[10] Mrs. Lion answered.

"Hey, I get it, we're a pride of lions. How funny... Ha ha ha how dumb!" the leader lion answered sarcastically. "Lions are supposed to be prideful. HELLO! It's who we are! Now take your crutch God and go. There is no room in our pride for timid vegetarian lions with low self-esteem."

"So be it," answered Mr. Lion. "Come on, guys, let's go."

The seven of them turned and walked away.

"Well, that didn't go well," Mr. Lion said.

"Wow," Mr. Hyena replied, "that was a serious display of pride and arrogance."

"Yeah, when you are the most powerful animal in the kingdom, pride tends to be a problem," Mrs. Lion answered.

"Although their pride was obvious, we must all be on guard because pride infects all of us," Mr. Lion replied. "It is very difficult to deal with since as soon as we think we've cut it from our lives, it instantly grows back, and quite possibly even worse than before."

"Pride is deadly because it inevitably sets us in direct opposition to God," Mr. Kangaroo stated. "No one can ever boast about conquering pride."[11]

Mr. Hyena smiled and said, "Look at me, I have overcome pride!"

They all laughed at the thought of being prideful about overcoming pride.

"Hey, I'm curious," Mr. Kangaroo said as he interrupted. He looked at Mr. Lion and asked, "Why don't you eat meat?"

"I don't know," Mr. Lion answered. "Me and Mrs. Lion just don't like the taste of meat."

"That's comforting," Mr. Mongoose said with a smile.

"There used to be a lot of vegetarian lions, but as time went on, they all eat meat now,"[12] Mrs. Lion said.

"It's pretty clear the other lions wanted to eat us," Mr. Mongoose said.

"Yeah, let's get out of here before they get too hungry," Mr. Kangaroo insisted.

"So which way do we go from here?" asked Mrs. Hyena.

"The lions definitely won't let us pass through them after that nasty discussion," Mr. Lion answered.

Pointing in another direction, Mr. Kangaroo said, "We can't go that way because Mr. and Mrs. Mongoose and I just came from there. I don't want to deal with that bully kangaroo again."

"We can't go that way because the hyenas went that way," Mr. Hyena said as he pointed in the direction where the army of hyenas went.

"Well, that leaves us with only one way to go," Mr. Lion said as he pointed in the only direction left to go. "Let's go that way."

Mr. Lion led the way as the others followed.

"Wait!" shouted Mrs. Mongoose. "Let's stop and thank the Lord and pray for His protection and guidance."

They all agreed and huddled together and thanked the Lord and worshipped Him and prayed for continued guidance and protection. Then they continued on in the direction that they all agreed upon.

CHAPTER 6

The Monkeys (Evolution)

After a long while of traveling, trees and vegetation began to steadily increase as the seven animals entered into a jungle. Soon after entering the jungle, several monkeys up in the trees began squealing as they jumped from tree to tree and came down and gathered in front of the group of animals headed for the Ark. The first monkey to arrive spoke first, "You guys look lost. Where ya headed?"

"We're not lost," Mr. Kangaroo answered. "We're going to the Ark to escape God's coming judgment because of all the evil and unbelief."

"What do you mean the coming judgment, and what's an Ark?" the monkey asked.

"We don't know what an Ark is, but God said we will know it when we see it," Mr. Lion answered. "And when we see it, we are supposed to enter it to protect us from the coming flood over all creation. Do you want to come with us to the Ark?"

"Did you just say something about creation?" a monkey asked. "I thought the world was rid of all you creation freaks. You guys are like some sort of cult."

"We want to go with you to the Ark!" shouted Mr. Monkey from a nearby tree. "God spoke to me and Mrs. Monkey about the

35

coming judgment. What a relief to meet you animals. I thought we were the only two animals left who believed that God created everything."

"Oh no, it's you two creationists again," another monkey announced. "I thought we were done with you two."

"Why do you have a problem with creation?" asked Mr. Lion.

"Creationism died out many years ago when science proved that evolution was a fact,"[1] an evolution monkey said. "Yet no matter how much evidence debunks the creation myth, you still continue to believe in some sky god who created everything."

"What evidence do you have that debunks creation?" Mr. Mongoose asked.

"They don't have any evidence," Mr. Monkey declared. "They just have a wild theory."

"You two creationist monkeys never learn," evolution monkey replied. "Even after showing you the evidence, you still cling to your creation myth."

"What evidence?" asked Mr. Hyena.

The evolution monkey turned to another monkey and said, "Go get the skull."

"Go get the skull?" asked a confused Mrs. Hyena. "What are you going to do with a skull?"

"You asked for evidence, so evidence you will get," the evolution monkey answered. "The skull will totally debunk your creation myth."

The other monkey came back with a skull in his hand and handed it to evolution monkey and said, "Here it is."

The evolution monkey took the skull and held it up so the group could see it. "Look at this skull. Do you see how similar it is to a monkey skull?"

"Yeah, so what?" asked Mr. Hyena as the others looked and wondered what the skull meant.

"This skull is evidence that millions of years ago, our skulls were shaped different," answered evolution monkey.

"It looks like a human skull," Mrs. Lion stated.

"It's not a human skull," answered evolution monkey. "The similarities of this skull to a monkey skull are much too great for it to be a human skull. This monkey skull is millions of years old, and when compared to our current monkey skull, it is clear evidence that we evolved over millions of years to our current form."[2]

"So you believe that monkeys evolved over time to what you are today?" asked Mr. Mongoose.

"The evidence confirms evolution as I will explain," evolution monkey answered.

"How do you know it's a monkey skull?" asked Mr. Hyena

"They don't," Mr. Monkey answered.

"It looks just like a human skull," Mrs. Lion stated again.

"It's not a human skull," answered an irritated evolution monkey as his tone began to change because the animals didn't see the obvious evidence of evolution. "We know it's a monkey skull because of the similarities. Look at the jawbone, the eye sockets, the nose cavity, and the shape and size of the cranium. All are very similar traits that are too similar to ignore."

"How do you know the skull is millions of years old?" asked Mr. Kangaroo.

"They don't," answered Mr. Monkey.

"Be quiet, Mr. Monkey," answered another monkey. "Just because you refuse to see the facts doesn't mean these animals will."

Evolution monkey turned to the animals in the group and said, "Ignore Mr. Monkey while I explain the skull. We know the skull is millions of years old because we found the skull near some rocks that are millions of years old."

"Rocks?" asked a confused Mrs. Hyena. "How do you know how old the rocks are?"

"We can determine how old rocks are by measuring the rate of decay in their elements," answered evolution monkey.

"Rate of decay of nearby rocks?" questioned Mrs. Hyena. "You determine how old a skull is by measuring the rate of decay of a nearby rock? Why not measure the rate of decay in the skull?"

Evolution monkey was losing his patience. "Because the skull does not have the right kind of measurable elements. The skull elements don't date back far enough, so they can't be used to determine the accurate age of the skull. We have to measure the age of nearby rocks."[3]

"Huh?" Mr. Hyena wondered out loud. "Maybe the skull elements don't date back far enough because it's really not that old."

"We know that the skull is millions of years old, so we have to measure the age of nearby rocks to determine how old the skull is," evolution monkey answered. "The rate of decay determines the age of the rock. Once we know how old the rock is, we can then determine how old the skull is."

"How can you have an accurate formula for the age of a skull by measuring a rock?" Mr. Hyena asked. "It sounds more like you came up with a formula that fits your belief in evolution."

"It sure seems that way," Mrs. Monkey agreed. "And not only that, but we studied the skull and found soft tissue in it with cells that are translucent and flexible. It's impossible for this skull to be millions of years old because soft tissue does not last millions of years."[4]

"Something preserved the soft tissue over millions of years, but we don't know what it is yet," evolution monkey answered. "The beauty of science is that we are always learning, and we will eventually learn why the soft tissue was able to survive over millions of years."

"Wow, your explanation of the skull isn't scientific at all," Mr. Mongoose said. "So this is what happens when you try to explain creation without the Creator."

"The scientific proof of evolution is right before your eyes, but you insist on closing your eyes to the facts," evolution monkey replied.

"Let's assume what you say is true, how does a skull get from that old shape to your current skull shape?" Mr. Kangaroo asked.

"Through random mutations over millions of years, monkeys adapted to their various environments leading to the current shape of our skull today," evolution monkey answered. "In a million more years, it will look vastly different as we continue to adapt to our changing environment."[5]

"The odds of random mutations causing improvement over millions of years are mathematically impossible,"[6] Mrs. Lion answered.

"Just to be clear," Mr. Mongoose asked, "you believe monkeys became monkeys by random chance?"

"It's not random chance," answered evolution monkey. "Natural selection through random mutations causes desirable traits to overcome undesirable traits over time."

"What about other animals?" asked Mr. Lion. "There are so many other species of animals with no similarities to monkeys."

"Oh yes, there are," answered evolution monkey. "We all have many similarities, including heads, bodies, various kinds of hands and feet, hearts, lungs, blood, and so on. I could go on and on, but the point is that all these similarities show that we have common ancestors dating back millions of years. Basically we are each like a different branch that evolved from the same tree."

"How do you know that we all evolved from a common ancestor?" asked Mrs. Lion. "I mean, you weren't there to see any of this."

"You're right, none of us was there in the beginning," answered evolution monkey. "So those of us who are experts at studying the evidence have come up with a clear scientific explanation for the evidence."

"I told you, they have no proof," Mr. Monkey answered. "All they have is a wild theory that they call science. The similarities point to a common Designer, not common ancestry."

"Your explanation of the evidence is that a god did it, now that's a wild theory!" evolution monkey answered. "We prefer real scientific answers instead of just saying a god did it."

"Evolution is not a fact," answered Mr. Lion. "It's just a story you made up for the evidence."

Mrs. Monkey chimed in, "They teach us evolution from the moment we're born, so it becomes ingrained in our thinking at a very young age, making creation seem absurd."

"Not only that, but anybody who brings up creation is considered to be antiscience and shunned," Mr. Monkey added.

"I just gave you scientific facts of evolution, and you reject it in favor of creationism, that makes you antiscience," evolution monkey said.

"Facts of evolution!" Mr. Hyena replied. "That's absurd! God was there in the beginning. He is the only eyewitness, and He created every creature after their own kind for their own purpose and His glory."

"Creation is absurd!" declared evolution monkey. "Look at what your belief in God and creation is doing to you. You're all running away to some fantasy Ark. That is one crazy god you follow!"

"This discussion is starting to get heated up," Mr. Lion announced. "We're not going to waste any more of your time. I just want to ask you for the last time, do you or any of the other monkeys want to come with us to the Ark and escape God's judgment?"

"Don't be ridiculous," evolution monkey replied. "You can take Mr. and Mrs. Monkey with you. We would never follow anybody who is antiscience, and we don't need creationists rejecting the clear evidence of evolution. Now take your creationism and go find your fantasy Ark."

"Very well," Mr. Lion said as he motioned to the group. "Let's get moving."

The whole group continued into the jungle with the addition of Mr. and Mrs. Monkey.

"Welcome to our group," Mr. Lion said.

"We are glad to join you on your way to the Ark," answered Mr. Monkey.

"They totally reject God as the Creator, but they will be without excuse in God's judgment because everyone intuitively knows that God created everything,"[7] Mr. Lion said. "In their sinful nature they suppress this truth in unrighteousness so their minds are darkened."

"Isn't it interesting how we all see the same thing but interpret it totally differently?" Mrs. Lion said. "I saw what looked like a human skull, and they saw a million-year-old monkey skull."

"They will only accept an explanation that excludes God," Mr. Monkey said. "For all we know, that could very well have been a human skull."

"Creation versus evolution is a battle between worldviews,"[8] Mrs. Monkey declared. "If you reject God, then evolution is how you interpret the evidence. If you believe in God, then you interpret the evidence through God's creation."

"Whatever kind of skull it is, one thing is for sure," Mr. Monkey said, "the soft tissue proves it's not millions of years old."

"And like I said before, they have no evidence, just a wild theory," Mrs. Monkey insisted. "Evolution is just a story taught as fact."

Mr. Mongoose insisted that they all pray before continuing on.

They all paused to pray before they continued their journey to the Ark.

Mr. Kangaroo couldn't help but notice that he was the only one without a female partner. He wondered if he should mention it to the others. Why did everybody have a female except him? Did God forget about him? Did God make a mistake? For now, Mr. Kangaroo decided to wait it out.

CHAPTER 7

The Cow and the Bull (Addiction)

After a while of making their way through the forest, the nine animals finally cleared the jungle and came to a large grassy meadow with cows and bulls lying around. Mrs. Mongoose wanted to rest, so she said, "These cows look like they're resting peacefully, let's stop and rest with them for a little while."

"Sure," answered Mr. Lion. "While we're resting, I'll see if they want to go to the Ark."

As they approached the resting herd of cows and bulls, one of the bulls looked over and said, "Hello there, animals, you're just in time. We just grazed on some goofy grass, and now we're as high as the sky. Do you want some?"

"Goofy grass?" asked Mr. Monkey. "What is that?"

"It's kind of like regular grass except it gets you high," a stoned cow answered. "It almost looks like regular grass, but when you look close, you can see that the grass blades are wider. Those are the ones that get you high."

Another stoned bull chimed in, "Eat some. You'll be glad you did."

"No thanks," answered Mr. Lion. "We just want to rest before we continue on. What is so great about getting high anyway?"

"It takes away the stress of all the evil in the world and makes you feel good," a stoned bull answered,

"And it helps you to be more creative,"[1] a stoned cow added.

"It also opens up your mind and allows you to think about things you normally would never think about,"[2] another stoned bull said.

Mr. Lion was about to say something, but he was interrupted when a stoned bull randomly announced, "I was just thinking, what if we uprooted a tree and turned it upside down and buried the branches in the ground so the roots were on top, would the roots become branches and grow leaves and would the branches become roots in the ground?"

"Whoa, that's deep," the stoned bull replied. "Why wouldn't the tree still grow?"

"It has to grow, right?" a stoned cow asked. "I mean, a tree is nothing but a trunk with branches on the top and branches on the bottom, seems to me it would grow either way, right?"

Another stoned bull randomly asked, "Is infinity minus one still infinity?"

"Whoa, that's beefy," a stoned bull said. "Just thinking about it hurts my brain."

The stoned bull continued, "Infinity never ends, but if you subtract one it still never ends. It's still infinity with one less. Am I right?"

"How would you prove it?" another stoned bull asked. "Seriously, if you subtracted one from infinity how would you prove it? It's still infinity."

"Whoa!" the entire herd gasped. Then they all completely froze while trying to process the thought.

After a few moments a stoned bull said, "That was a little too beefy for me. My mind almost got stuck in an infinite thought loop."

"Ha ha ha ha," the entire herd laughed.

Mr. Lion was about to say something again, but then another stoned bull randomly asked, "What if God grazed on some goofy grass? Would He be more creative?"

"Whoa!" the entire herd gasped again as they thought about how creative God would be if He were stoned.

"God created everything, but imagine if He were stoned when He created everything!" a stoned bull said.

"Whoa! That's even beefier!" another stoned bull declared. "It seems like God has already created everything so the only thing left for Him to do would be to use His creativity to mix and match what He already created."

"You mean, like mixing a monkey and a mongoose together to make a mongoomonkey!" another bull said while looking at Mr. Monkey and Mr. Mongoose.

"Ha ha ha ha ha!" the entire stoned herd laughed.

Then another stoned bull randomly said, "I can feel the earth rotating under my hooves. Seriously, I can feel it moving."

"Did you eat those mushrooms again?" a stoned bull asked. "I told you to stay away from the mushrooms!"

"I found them under a cow patty," the bull answered while tripping out. "I saw fresh mushrooms, and I couldn't resist, so I ate them... Hey, check it out, my hide is turning blue!"

A stoned bull burst into laughter and couldn't stop laughing. "Ha ha ha ha, I think I'm going to die if I don't stop laughing! Ha ha ha ha ha ha."

"Hey, I have a question," chimed another stoned cow. She looked at Mr. and Mrs. Mongoose and asked, "If two gooses are called geese, then does that mean that two mongooses are called mongeese?"

"Ha ha ha ha ha!" the entire stoned herd burst into hysterical laughter.

"I'm serious," she said. "Are they mongooses or mongeese?"

"Ha ha ha ha," came more and more laughter.

"I think this is the highest I've ever been," announced a stoned bull.

"Me too," another stoned bull replied. "What an amazing graze."

"Ha ha ha ha ha!" came more laughter.

"Amazing graze, how sweet the ground," added a stoned cow.

"Ha ha ha ha!" they all laughed uncontrollably.

Then a certain Mr. Bull interrupted and said, "I can't take this anymore. Shame on all of you for dishonoring God with your dumb jokes. God is holy. He would never engage in sinful behavior. Every day it's the same thing. You all get stoned and babble about nothing and think you're intelligent."

"Stop the buzzkill," a stoned bull replied. "I've had a long day, I deserve to get high."

"This is not the time to complain," another stoned bull said. "Have some goofy grass and join the conversation."

Then Mrs. Cow joined in, "I don't want to get high. God's judgment is coming, and we need to get to the Ark to escape God's judgment."

"Ever since you two stopped getting high, it's been nonstop talk about God's judgment," a stoned bull replied. "I think you ate too much goofy grass, and now you're paranoid."

"They're not paranoid," announced Mr. Lion. "What they say is true. God sees that nobody seeks after Him and He sees all the evil and violence, and He is going to judge the world in a flood."

"You know about God's coming judgment?" Mr. Bull asked as he looked over at Mr. Lion and the animals.

"Yes, we know about the Ark," Mrs. Lion answered. "We're going to it. Do you want to come with us?"

"Yes!" they both answered together.

A stoned bull interrupted, "What do you mean nobody seeks after God? We seek after God all the time even when we're high. In fact, it enhances our worship."[3]

"Not only that but getting high puts me in a reflective state to consider the questions of the universe,"[4] another stoned bull added.

"God wants us to worship Him with a sober mind, not get high off goofy grass,"[5] Mr. Kangaroo replied.

"Didn't God give us every herb that yields seed for food?" a stoned bull asked. "What is wrong with eating what God told us to eat?"[6]

"You clearly aren't eating it for food," Mr. Hyena answered. "You eat it to get high. Besides, God made that statement before the curse of sin when all creatures including humans were vegetarians."

"Twisting God's Word to justify getting high is a serious sin," Mrs. Mongoose answered. "To say that God wants you to get high goes against His righteous character."

"The world is a mess," a stoned bull replied. "What is wrong with a little goofy grass to ease the tension? It's not like we're addicted. We can quit anytime we want, we just don't want to."

"God wants Him to be our supreme joy and pleasure," Mr. Monkey replied. "You are finding your joy and pleasure in goofy grass."

"Slow down there, preacher," answered a stoned bull. "The whole world is full of evil and violence, and we have found a way of keeping the peace. Why would God care if we ate what He created if it keeps us from acting like the rest of the world?"

"God does not want us eating goofy grass to cope with life," answered Mrs. Lion. "God wants us to trust Him because He's in control."[7]

"If God was in control I wouldn't need to get high," a stoned bull said.

"God is in control and His judgment is coming," Mrs. Monkey replied. "You're all slaves to goofy grass, which is a form of idolatry because you desire something created more than the Creator."[8]

"I am having trouble believing in a god who doesn't want us to enjoy what he created," a stoned cow replied.

"I used to eat the goofy grass and get high," Mr. Bull answered. "I finally quit, and it wasn't until I was sober for a long time that I began to see what it was doing to all of us. The conversations are great if you're stoned, but if you're sober, they are shallow and dumb. We also ignore the long-term effects that lead to mental illness and more violence."[9]

"Not only that, but they spend more and more time just eating and lying around," Mrs. Cow added. "They have no desire to get up and work. The only god they believe in is the god that is okay with getting high."

"They created their own god, which again is idolatry," Mr. Bull declared.

"Y'all have taken your belief in God too far," a stoned bull answered. "Lighten up already."

"There's no time to lighten up," Mr. Bull answered. "God's judgment is coming very soon."

"They gather to worship once a week, but you would never know they worship God by their lives,"[1] Mr. Bear answered.

"Lighten up, Mr. Bear," another bear said. "Don't start with that #&!$% judgment talk again. We're not going to an Ark, and there is no #&!$% flood coming. We're cool with God."

"What's with the foul language?"[2] Mr. Bull asked.

"I like to keep things real," the bear replied. "No sense in pretending I'm perfect. God knows I believe in Him."

Another bear joined in, "By keeping things real, we advance our ministry by reaching more animals, newcomers need to feel welcomed, not judged."[3]

"Puh-leeze," Mrs. Bear groaned. "They have foul mouths all week long. The only time they don't use foul language is when they are at their worship service. For one hour a week they have good behavior."

"God's not going to reject us just because of a little salty language," a bear replied.

"From the abundance of the heart the mouth speaks,"[4] Mr. Bear answered. "Salty language is just a symptom of the true condition of your heart. You say you believe in God, but there is no repentance,[5] no changed behavior, no desire for righteousness,[6] no sense of grief over your sin,[7] nothing."

"Who are you two to judge us anyway?" a bear asked as he looked at Mr. and Mrs. Bear. "You both used to have foul mouths worse than all of us. Mr. Bear used to tell the filthiest jokes, and they were really funny too. You used to hang out with us and make us laugh. We miss the old Mr. and Mrs. Bear. Now you just preach about judgment."

"That's because God spoke to us about His coming flood," Mrs. Bear answered. "God showed us that our worship meetings were just empty religious behavior because we made no effort to honor God or allow Him to change our heart. We were just like you till God opened our eyes. We thought we were good with God because we went to worship service once a week, but we lived a life totally contrary to God's holiness. We worshipped God with our lips, but our hearts were not with God."

"Excuse me?" a bear said angrily. "Are you saying that we're not spiritual? My parents are religious. My grandparents were religious. All of our ancestors were religious. We are descendants of the first bears God created on day 6 of creation week.[8] We have been religious from the beginning."

"We were believers in name only,"[9] Mr. Bear answered. "We were hypocrites."

"Hypocrites? How can you say that?" asked another bear. "We go to worship service once a week, and we help those in need when we can. Now you come along telling us it all means nothing and the only way to escape His judgment is to go to this Ark thing."

"God sees your heart and He sees that you worship Him with your words but your heart is far from Him," Mrs. Bear said. "You speak about God once a week when you're at the worship meeting, but then you go back to your sinful living the rest of the week. All week long you hang out with unbelievers, you live like unbelievers, you use the same foul language as unbelievers, you enjoy entertainment that glorifies sin. The only time you mention God is when you use His name as a swear word, the only time you want to change is when you feel bad about the way you treated someone but the change really never happens. You go to worship service as if it makes you right with God and then you go back to living without Him the rest of the week. There's literally no difference between you and unbelievers except that you go to a worship meeting once a week and claim to believe in God. God sees your heart and your hypocrisy and that your heart is far from Him."

"Oh, I get it now," a bear announced. "You and Mrs. Bear are holier than thou because God spoke to you."

"No, no, you have it all wrong," Mrs. Hyena replied. "We're not better than you. We have the same problems as you. We struggled with the same truth about our sinful nature, and we realize that we are just as deserving of God's judgment. It grieves our heart knowing that we sin against God. Thankfully, He has offered us a way to escape His judgment by going to the Ark before the flood comes."

Fire and Faith

Fortunately for me, the people that lived in the home were in the back yard. I truly believe now when I think about it, someone above was watching out for me. I could see the people through the living room window in the backyard doing work. I quietly opened the front door and stepped out and made my way home. My heart was racing, and I was out of breath by the time I got home. My mother was worried about how I was acting and, asked what happened. I told her the whole story and she told me that everything was going to be ok. I continued to walk to and from school, but with a group of kids. Safety in numbers is how my folks looked at it.

It was not long before I heard the words that we would be moving again. This time we were moving back east again. We were moving to Merrimack, New Hampshire. Only this time there would be something very different about the new house we were going to. Bob had an 18 year old daughter named Jackie. Jackie lived with Bob's ex-wife and she was too much for his ex-wife to handle. Jackie flew in to Phoenix, Arizona and, we picked her up to take her with us to Merrimack. I will never forget the first time I saw her. Being a boy at my age and due to my sexual dysfunctions, all I could do is stare at her large chest. I remember that she had the biggest well you know what I saying. She had a fowl mouth and, she smoked cigarettes constantly. It seemed like

Fire and Faith

every other word was the "f" bomb. She had a lot of silver rings on her

fingers, and she smelled weird. I don't think she liked me very much

judging by the way she looked at me. She was totally fake when she

talked to my mom. Jackie would kiss my mom's butt for everything

and, while my mother was not looking stole cigarettes from my

mother's purse.

Chapter 5

If I ever thought that the seven hour trip from Arizona to California was long, the trip back east took seven days. Once again Bob said I was not allowed to take my cat and this time he won. My grandmother agreed to keep the cat, so that when I visited her, the cat would be there for me. The trip back east was pretty much a blur. I slept most of the way there. We would stop at rest areas and my mother would go straight to work making lunches. While we would eat she would go and clean out the car in preparation for the next four hundred mile journey. The funny thing was that (with the exception of my mother being a Hebrew slave) we all got along pretty good. I think when you pile a bunch of people in a car and travel over two thousand miles in seven days; you tend to get "slap happy". All the little quarks are overlooked. It is just a shame that things could not have stayed that way.

When we got to the new place things started going downhill fast. There were plenty of arguments over petty crap. Bobs' main priority was to plug in the television so he would be able to watch the football game or, any other sporting event. Things went right back to the way they were. My mother in the kitchen and Bobs butt planted on the couch for the game. My new step-sister spent most of her time in her

Fire and Faith

bedroom except at dinner time. Dinner time was not any fun at all. The only thing Jackie ever did was scream and yell at me about the way I chewed my food. Sometimes I would argue with her, and Bob would come to her defense. I was always (according to Bob) in the wrong.

One night at the dinner table, she was picking on me. Over and over again she would pick and pick. I finally had enough and I stood up and screamed at her at the top of my lungs. She immediately reached across the table hitting me, and split my lip. Even then according to Bob, I was at fault. I really hated living there. We lived in a rough part of town, and I hated the new school. The only thing I enjoyed about it was that they played marbles in the morning before class. I had always played marbles. And not tooting my own horn, I was pretty good. It was not long before Jackie started showing more of her true colors. My mother's jewelry turned up missing, and Jackie knew nothing about it. Jackie was into drugs, and was selling my mother's jewelry to keep her supply of drugs coming in.

One day my mother and Bob went to see some friends, and I was left alone with Jackie. For some reason or other she was being nice to me, instead of beating me up. I went outside to shoot some hoops and when I returned she was on the front porch smoking something. I was only nine years old and not familiar with drugs of any kind. She asked me to sit down with her. As I sat there watching her smoke and cough over and over again, my curiosity was building up. I don't think I really wanted to smoke it. I think I just wanted to be able to get along with her and, if that meant me smoking it, then I was going to. I finally said "What is it that you are smoking?" She handed to me and said, "Try it." I took a big hit off of it and just about choked to death. Right about that time my mother and Bob pulled up in the driveway. They did not catch us but, it was close. From that point on my step sister and I were friends. She had something on me and had something on her.

My mother's jewelry kept disappearing, and she finally got so mad that Bob had to take action. There was a massive fight in the house. Bob was yelling at Jackie, and my mother was yelling right along with them. My mother was in the kitchen when the fight broke out. I remember Jackie throwing a pot of boiling water at Bob. The fight continued for what seemed like hours to me, and it eventually moved into Jackie's bedroom. All three of them were screaming at the top of their lungs, and I needed to see what was going on. The house that we lived in had the old style doors with the key hole that you could look through. I ran from my bedroom down the hallway to Jackie's door to watch the excitement. I remember seeing her jump up off the bed with a fully closed fist and punching Bob straight in the face. He then came at her with his hands flying hitting her multiple times in the head. My mother did not know whose side to take. One minute she would say "Hey don't talk to your father that way" and, then yell "Hey Bob! Stop it! You're hurting her!"

I watched all the shoving, hitting and, screaming. It just would not end. For a brief moment I thought this was the greatest day of my life. I was not getting hit or yelled at this time. It was someone else. Every time it looked like it was coming to an end, Jackie would say something stupid, and it would start all over again. The fight finally came to an end as I ran back to my room and pretended to sleep. Jackie eventually moved out with her boyfriend, and started her own life. The funny thing about that episode (I probably should not say funny) but, she is currently serving a several-year term in a penitentiary. I guess she just could not stop stealing or, keep her mouth shut.

I used to have a friend there named Shane, and we were both into a song from Pink Floyd called "Another Brick in the Wall." We just had to have this album. One day we set out to go downtown with our bikes, and go buy this new album. On the way down there we had fun but, it was a long way. Unfortunately, the return trip was not as much fun. On our way back, we ran into some older kids carrying pipe wrenches. They wanted my bike and, they were not taking no for an answer.

Fire and Faith

Shane was safe because he took his sisters bike and, they did not want a pink girl's bike. There was a little scuffle and, I lost. They took all the parts off my bike. I ended up walking home with the bike frame in one hand and the new Pink Floyd album in the other, sporting a nice, fat lip.

When I came home, Bob was pretty mad at me as if it were my fault. He was upset that I did not beat them up. I explained that these kids had to have been sixteen or seventeen years old and, that I was only nine, not to mention that they had pipe-wrenches in their hands for weapons). Soon after, my mother put me in a karate class and, I was on my way to being a "full-fledged butt kicker". That did not happen either. I think I was in the class for about a month before I was taken out. I was taken out for good reason though, we were moving again. (I bet you didn't see that coming.) We were moving back to California. Once again, I was put on a plane to my grandmother house, and I was told that they would be there in a couple of weeks. Then we were going to go to California from there.

I was ten at that point, and on my way back to Arizona for two weeks during the summer. I was glad to see some familiar friends and, of course, my grandmother and grandfather. My grandfather was a craftsman. He could build anything and, he showed me the trade. To me, my grandfather was more than a craftsman. He was a true

Fire and Faith

definition of a man, father, grandfather and husband. I have often said that any worldly good in me, came from him. When I was a little boy, I got to stay at their house on rare occasions. My grandfather used to sit with me and draw Mickey Mouse pictures. He also used to play a game with me called pic-up-sticks. I would often think to myself that if I lived with them during my childhood years, I would have turned out fine. My grandfather's idea of discipline was a lot better as well. He did not believe in groundings and beatings. He would walk up, give you a swift kick in the butt and, tell you to get outside and play. I respected him enough when I was young to not get into trouble. He had a wonderful way of teaching a person a lesson using a calm voice, and displaying patience. He also believed that learning a good trade or skill was one of the most important things in life to learn. By the age of 15, I could build a house from the ground up. I really enjoyed hanging out with my grandfather.

My friends were important as well, and for the next two weeks, I surrounded myself with them. As the end of the trip grew near, I expected my mother to arrive from New Hampshire. I truly expected my somewhat stable life in Arizona to come to an end. I knew that Bob and my mother were on their way. One night just before I was getting ready to go to bed, my grandparents called me out to the living room.

Fire and Faith

They told me that my mother and Bob felt it would be better for me to stay with them indefinitely. It may not sound like a big deal, but to a ten year old child, it is abandonment. I felt like my mother did not want me around anymore, because it made it easier to get along with Bob.

When my grandparents told me, I tried to be tough and replied, "Its ok. I like it here." The truth was I wanted to be with my mother. I loved her, and wanted to be with her. The summer days passed by, and before I knew it, it was time to start school again. I thought for sure I would be attending school in Arizona. About two weeks before school started, my grandmother explained that I would be going to California to stay with my mother and Bob. She told me that she would be driving us there, and that we were going to be bringing my cat Tiger. It was a quick goodbye to my friends, because we left the next morning.

When we arrived in California, there was not much to do where they lived. My mother and Bob had chosen an apartment in a small town in Ramona, California. It was pretty much a rodeo town, and as a city kid, I did not fit in well. Needless to say, I did not like living there. I started school there and it took me forever to fit in. The kids were different than what I was used to. For some reason though, I found myself pretty good at football and so did the other kids. I remember

Fire and Faith

schools prior to this I used to have a fear of being picked last for any

the teams during P.E... At this time however that was not the case. I

was usually picked first, because I could run very fast and catch a ball.

In fact just about the time when I started to fit in, we were on the move

again.

I know at the time Bob was going to school to get his teaching

credentials. As for my mother she stayed at home while I was at

school. They decided to put me in boy scouts. That was okay I guess,

but still there was some strain there as well. Remember, I was a city

kid and really had no idea about camping, fishing, making knots, and

earning badges. Never the less I went to the functions and found them

to be rather boring. This time we moved because Bob could not find a

job. We had a neighbor that worked at a local grocery store, as a meat-

wrapper. She would bring us home steaks, ground beef and pork

chops. We had no money, but we had the best of the best when it came

to food. Bob used to say that "we were the richest poor people."

because of the great food.

We said our goodbyes to our neighbors and went back to Arizona.

It is a little fuzzy for me as to what took place next. I do know we went

back to California to the small town of Ontario. I actually liked this

town, and we actually stayed there for a couple of years. I made

Fire and Faith

friends quickly with the neighbor kids and life seemed pretty good for me. Living in the house however got much worse. It seemed to me that my relationship with my mother was growing more distant. Bob was slowly winning the battle for my mother's attention. And, of course, when I child does not get the attention they need, they start looking for bad attention. I started smoking at the age of eleven and smoking a little pot at as well. Bob's youngest daughter was sixteen, and she came to stay with us during this time. Her name was Karla.

Chapter 6

Karla and I got along great. In fact she was my saving grace with Bob. I started not caring about the good, warm, and fuzzy attention I wasn't getting from my mom anymore. I was wrapped up in swearing, smoking cigarettes, and the occasional pot smoking. Karla smoked cigarettes and pot, so things were great for me. Karla and I had each other's back. If she did something wrong I would try and cover for her.

I remember one night she came home really late. Our parents were out for the evening, and she planned on getting back before they did. I was sitting in the living room, when I saw the headlights from our car pull in the driveway. I knew it was not Karla, because her boyfriend would park down at the end of street. I quickly jumped up and ran to the bathroom and turned on the shower. When my parents walked in they asked where she was. I had told them that she was in the shower. It was late, and I knew my mother and Bob would go straight to bed without checking on her. Karla came home about a half an hour later. I went and turned the shower off and she made it to her room.

During the summer months she would send me to go and buy cigarettes at the local corner store. Karla would take the money from Bobs change jar he had hidden in his room. (Years ago all a person

Fire and Faith

needed was a note from a parent approving the cigarette purchase, if you were under age.) This came at a cost to Karla though. She had to give me half of the pack. This was a great deal for me because I always had smokes. One weekend my mother decided to go and put my laundry away, and she found three smokes on my dresser. I thought for sure I was in trouble, but Karla had my back. She told our parents that she had been in my room the night before and must have left them there. Like I said we had each other's back. The problem was that things started to get a little out of control with stealing the change...

Bob usually had about thirty to forty dollars in the change jar. One night I heard Bob yell from the living room for Karla and me to come see him. On the way down the hallway Karla asked me, "You got my back right?" I remember walking out to the living room and seeing the empty jar sitting on the coffee table. She had taken every dime of it. I could not believe it. Bob said he wanted an answer to where the change went. I immediately said "I did it." He said well then where is it? I told him that I blew it on video games. I couldn't believe it, but he bought the lie. The truth was Karla had stolen it to go to the river with her friends the following day. I took a serious butt whipping on top of being grounded for two weeks.

Fire and Faith

Karla felt as if she really needed to make it up to me. One night when our parents went out for the evening, we had a small party at the house. I had two of my friends over, and she had a couple of her really cute girlfriends over. I can't remember too much of that night, because I was pretty high. My motto used to be "if you can remember last weekend then you did not have a good time." What I do remember was that Karla had some really good weed, and I smoked a lot of it. The last thing I remember was sitting on the kitchen table eating a bag of cookies. Then I woke the next morning in bed. I had no idea how I got there. These kind of nights happened just about every time our parents went out.

Karla did not stay too much longer after that summer and ended up going back to Texas. After she left I started hanging out with a different type of friends and it was going great for a while. One of these friends lived on the other side of town. My mother had met him a couple of times but she did not like him. His name was Gregory. Gregory was a couple of years older than me. My mother had told me that I was not allowed to hang around him. But, I was not taking orders from her anymore.

One day I decided to walk all the way to Gregory's house. He lived in crappy apartment in South Ontario. Back in those days there were a

Fire and Faith

lot of Mexican gangs that ruled the area. I was graced in because I knew Gregory. When I got to his apartment, I could hear Gregory's mother yelling at him. Her language towards him was extremely foul, and his was to her as well. I did not even knock at the door before Gregory came out swearing at his mother over his shoulder. I asked him if he was ok and said "Yes, let go get some weed." This was normal for us and I agreed. We went to a different apartment complex which I had never been to. I asked where we were going and he said "It's cool, don't worry." Something just did not sit well with me. The one thing I had going for me, was my gut instinct. I still have it to this day. The problem was, I completely ignored it, and decided to go anyway.

I remember climbing the stairs to the second level, and my stomach just kept bugging me. I kept getting a cold flash across my forehead. As I walked up the stairs I tried to think of an excuse as to why we should not go to this apartment. It was about 2:00 p.m. and I was thinking I could use the "I am hungry" excuse. I asked Gregory if he was sure this guy was cool. He kept telling that everything was fine. He said we are going to score a little weed and then we would be on our way. Something still did not sit right with me, but I still went to the door. Gregory knocked at the door and there was no answer. He

67

Fire and Faith

knocked again only louder and harder, and yet no reply. I told Gregory

that he must not be home and that we should come back later. Gregory

said, "Hang on." as he banged on the door harder. At that moment a

man yelled from inside saying "Who is there? What do you want?!" I

could hear the man's heavy footsteps as he came closer to the door.

He opened the door fast and hard as looked out side to side to see

who was there. He was a large, fat man, and I immediately got the

chills as I flashed back to my old baby sitter. He had a zippo lighter in

his left hand, and he kept opening and closing the lid as he stared at

Gregory and me. I could smell something in the apartment that smelled

like trash, which had not been taken out in a few weeks. Finally, after

what seemed like ten minutes he said to come in. As we walked in, I

looked around and there was clutter everywhere. Every part of the

room had some type of decoration or some type of object piled up. The

place was cluttered beyond belief. Every part of the place had some

type of object or clutter.

As I looked around I had seen that he had a porno on the television

but the volume turned all the way down. To the left of me was the

dining room with a bunch of newspapers, and penthouse magazines on

the table. He told us to come into the dining room and sit down. As I

walked into the dining room I looked to the right of me to the kitchen.

"That's your opinion," the bear answered. "Just because we don't worship perfectly doesn't mean God doesn't forgive us."

"It's not about being perfect," Mr. Monkey answered. "God does not forgive us so that we can go on living the same as if forgiveness means nothing. God is glorified when our forgiveness results in a changed life."

"We glorify God all the time," answered another bear. "We praise His name all the time."

"You praise Him out of one side of your mouth while the other side of your mouth uses His name as a swear word," Mr. Bear said.

"It's just a part of the normal language of our society," a bear insisted. "God knows we don't mean anything by it."

"Hello!" exclaimed Mr. Bear. "That's the problem, you don't mean anything by it. You don't mean anything when you use His name because you take His name in vain. God's name is never to be meaningless. God is to be honored, not cheapened to a swear word because it's the normal language of our society."

"Enough!" shouted a bear. "You #&!$% overzealous believers are too much. We can't do anything without you judging us. We are fine with God. We will continue worshipping Him, and you can go to your Ark thing."

"We are warning you because judgment is coming, and the only way to escape is to go to the Ark before the flood comes," declared Mrs. Bear. "Now is the time to repent and come with us to the Ark."

"Yeah, yeah, we know," another bear said. "You've told us about the flood and the Ark a thousand times, and we've told you a thousand times that we believe in God and we are fine with God."

"I'll just ask you all one more time before we go," Mr. Lion announced. "Do any of you bears want to come with us to the Ark to escape God's coming judgment?"

"No," a bear answered firmly.

All the other bears nodded in agreement.

"There you have it," Mr. Lion concluded. "Let's get going."

Mr. Lion turned and started walking, and all the animals turned to follow Mr. Lion. They left the bears and continued their journey to the Ark.

After the bears were out of sight, Mrs. Bear stopped and said, "I need to calm down after all that."

Let's pray together right here before we continue on," Mr. Lion said.

They all bowed their heads and prayed.

CHAPTER 9

The Sheep (The False Prophet)

After the thirteen animals finished praying, Mrs. Lion asked, "I'm thirsty, where can we get some water?"

"There's a river down this hill," Mr. Bear answered. "Follow me."

They all followed Mr. Bear as he led them to the river. As the animals approached the river, they noticed a flock of sheep grazing and drinking from the river.

"Thankfully, it's just sheep," Mrs. Hyena said. "They are usually friendly, and who knows, maybe all of them will come with us to the Ark."

Then one of the sheep from the flock noticed the animals coming toward them and started walking toward the animals. Then another sheep noticed, and eventually the rest of the sheep noticed and started walking toward the animals.

The first sheep spoke up, "Hey, all you animals, welcome. Come on down and have some water."

"Yeah, it's good to see you," another sheep said. "Come on down."

"Welcome, welcome," all the other sheep joined in.

"Thank you for the nice greeting," Mr. Bear said. "We are very thirsty."

All the animals were grateful for the warm welcome, but they were so thirsty that they all drank some water without saying much.

While the animals were drinking, the sheep kept talking, "Oh, it's so wonderful for you all to join us."

"You all look like you have been traveling for a while, you must be thirsty," another sheep said.

"You came to the right place," another sheep said. "This water is very refreshing."

Mr. Mongoose finished drinking first, and he said, "Thank you for the warm and friendly welcome. Why are you so outgoing and friendly?"

The other animals paused from drinking water to hear why the sheep were so friendly.

The sheep answered, "God has sent us a prophet, and he has been leading us and giving us hope."

"A prophet?" Mr. Lion asked.

"Yes, a prophet," another sheep answered. "He has been our shepherd and our protector. He looks out for us."

"Your shepherd?" Mr. Kangaroo asked.

"Yes, our shepherd," another sheep replied. "With all the evil and violence in the world, we were always being harassed. We were lost and helpless sheep without a shepherd.[1] We were afraid, weary, and scattered with nowhere to go. We couldn't do anything right. We had no hope until God brought this prophet into our flock, and he encouraged us and gave us hope by showing us how to shape our future with positive words."[2]

"Shape your future with positive words?" asked Mr. Monkey. "What do you mean?"

"Before the prophet came, we were afraid, depressed, and always talking negative," a sheep answered. "The prophet showed us that we could change our life through positive confession."[3]

"How does positive confession change your life?" Mr. Hyena asked.

"We used to constantly have negative thoughts about ourselves," another sheep answered. "We believed we were hopeless and dumb sheep because that's all we ever thought or heard. Now we speak to ourselves only positive things. Our own words have more of an impact than the words of others, so we constantly speak positive words to ourselves."

"We no longer believe we are dumb sheep," a sheep confessed. "We are smart, strong, and victorious."

"We will live and not die, and everything we touch will prosper," declared another sheep.

All the other sheep agreed enthusiastically.

"Your positive talk isn't even based on reality," Mr. Bear replied. "Everyone dies at the appointed time, and everything you touch will not prosper.[4] God's purpose in our suffering is to build our character.[5] God wants us to be content in all circumstances."[6]

"We don't need to be content with suffering or bad circumstances," a sheep replied. "We can speak into existence things that don't exist."[7]

"We cannot speak things into existence," Mr. Monkey replied. "We must learn to be content in all situations."[8]

"Nothing is impossible with God," a sheep declared. "Our prophet also has the gift of healing."

"Your prophet can heal?" asked Mr. Bear.

"Yes," another sheep answered. "One of our fellow sheep had a leg that was shorter than the others, our prophet performed a miracle and caused his leg to grow."[9]

"He made his leg grow?" asked Mr. Monkey.

"Yes," another sheep answered. "His leg grew a half inch, it was a miracle."

"That seems like a questionable miracle," Mrs. Cow said. "How do you know his leg grew?"

"We all saw it," announced another sheep. "The prophet held his legs as he called out to God, and slowly but surely his leg grew a half inch right before our very eyes."

"I need something more convincing than that if you want me to believe that your prophet has the gift of healing," Mr. Mongoose said.

"If someone doesn't get healed, it's because they don't have enough faith,"[10] another sheep said.

"God decides who will get healed,"[11] announced Mr. Lion. "God sometimes uses sickness to bring about His sovereign purpose and to glorify Himself."[12]

"If someone doesn't get healed, it's not because of God," a sheep said. "It's because of their lack of faith."

"Faith is trusting God even if He doesn't heal us," Mr. Monkey said.

"Don't put God in a box,"[13] a sheep said.

"Hey, wait a second." Mrs. Bear said. "You just suggested that God doesn't heal those who lack faith. You're the one who put God in a box by deciding who He won't heal."

"Are you aware of God's coming judgment?" Mr. Monkey asked.

"No, we're not aware of it, and it sounds negative," a sheep answered.

"You mentioned all the evil and violence in the world," Mr. Monkey replied. "Well, God sees it all, and His judgment is coming. He's going to flood the world and destroy all living flesh. The only way to escape His judgment is to go to the Ark and enter it before the flood comes. Do you want to come with us to the Ark?"

"You still don't get it," a sheep insisted. "That's why we were miserable. We were dwelling on all the evil, and it brought us down. God sent us a prophet to be our shepherd and encourage us."

"Judgment is coming, and neither your prophet nor your positive speaking will stop it," Mr. Kangaroo said.

"What is all this end-of-the-world talk?" a sheep asked. "You sound just like us before God sent us a prophet. You just need to hear him speak, and he will convince you to put away all the doom and gloom talk and begin speaking positive. We can change our world through positive thoughts and words."

"He sounds like a false prophet," Mr. Mongoose said.

"Touch not God's anointed!"[14] a sheep angrily declared. "Don't you dare speak negative about our prophet! If you don't have anything nice to say, then don't say anything at all."

"Our great prophet will be back shortly," a sheep said. "You can hear him speak for yourself. He will inspire hope in you and show you how to speak to yourselves with positive words that will change your life."

"We don't need to hear your prophet speak because God spoke to each one of us directly, and He told each one of us that His judgment is coming," Mrs. Lion answered.

Then a certain Mr. Sheep spoke up and asked, "How did God speak to you?"

"He spoke to each of us individually and told us to go to the Ark because He is going to judge the world with a flood," Mr. Lion answered.

"God spoke the same thing to each of us!" Mrs. Sheep exclaimed.

"We would like to go to the Ark with you!" Mr. Sheep said.

"Okay!" all the animals replied. "We would love for you to join us."

"I don't believe it," a sheep replied. "You're going to go back with them even after the prophet convinced you that all that judgment talk was just negative self-talk in your head?"

"After God spoke to us, we weren't sure what to do," Mr. Sheep replied. "The prophet started to make us feel good with his prophesying, and we began to doubt what God said because the prophet made it sound like we were just being negative. But now we know God really did speak to us, and now we're going to the Ark with them."

"You're letting all this negative talk of evil and judgment corrupt your mind and bring you down again," another sheep said.

Just then another sheep shouted, "Here comes the prophet!"

"Now you can see for yourself that he is from God," claimed another sheep.

"Yeah," another sheep chimed in.

All the sheep called for the prophet to come to where the animals were. They all separated and made a clear path for the prophet to walk to the animals.

As the prophet arrived, he said, "Greetings, animals. Welcome to our flock."

"Greetings to you as well," answered Mr. Kangaroo.

Mrs. Mongoose leaned over and whispered into Mr. Mongoose's ear, "His voice sounds different."

"It sure does," Mr. Mongoose replied.

"I trust the flock treated you all to some water," the prophet said. "Why are you here?"

Before any of the animals could answer, a sheep said, "They keep talking negative talk about how God is going to judge the world."

"Why don't you prophesy the Word of God over these animals so they can see what God has in store for them?" another sheep asked.

The prophet shepherd agreed and looked at all the animals and began to prophesy. "By the power of the Holy Ghost, I declare to you the Word of the Lord. God says He is raising up a new generation, and this coming year is going to be a year of victory, a year of plenty, a year of health, a year of prosperity, saith the Lord.[15] By the power of the Holy Ghost, I bind the devil and his stronghold on your life. God says this will be the year that you take every negative thought captive and replace them with positive thoughts. This will be the year that your words will change your future as you speak positive things and declare the promises of God on your life. This will be the year of breakthrough, declares the Lord. By the power of the Holy Ghost, I impart God's anointing on the lives of these animals so they can live victoriously by the power of God. Amen!"

"AMEN!" shouted all the sheep except Mr. and Mrs. Sheep.

"He can be very persuasive with his prophetic talk," Mrs. Sheep said.

"I can see how his words can lure you in if you didn't know better," Mrs. Hyena replied. "Who doesn't want to hear such positive uplifting words?"

"That all sounds positive and hopeful, but it's false hope because it's not from God," declared Mr. Lion. "God has made it clear that His judgment is coming, which means this coming year will not be prosperous or victorious but will instead be full of destruction as God destroys all living flesh in a flood."

"What nerve you have to reject the Word of the Lord and speak lies and destruction," the prophet declared. "You are a demon, and I rebuke you."[16]

"How about that," Mr. Lion said. "First he prophesied great things, now he says we have a demon."

"Clearly this is a false prophet who does not speak for God," Mrs. Kangaroo declared.

"Well, if you all want to remain negative, that's your problem," the prophet hastily answered. "Some animals will never change even if God were to speak to them Himself."

"God did speak to us, and He said His judgment is coming," Mr. Bear said.

"The prophet's voice is weird," Mrs. Mongoose stated.

"Yeah, what's wrong with your voice?" asked Mr. Monkey. "Why do you sound so different from the other sheep?"

"I am a prophet of God," he replied with a nervous tone. "My voice is different so that the sheep will know my voice. Since all of you are so negative, you are not able to hear my voice, and now you are cursed. Such negativity is not welcome here, so we will let you go your way." The prophet turned around and summoned all the sheep to follow him. "Come on, sheep, forget them. They will just bring you down again."

All the sheep turned to follow the false prophet.

Mr. Hyena and Mrs. Monkey both noticed that the prophet had a different tail than the other sheep.

"Look at his tail," Mrs. Monkey shouted.

"It's a wolf!" Mr. Hyena shouted. "It's a wolf in sheep's clothing!"

"Hey, sheep, you're following a wolf," Mr. Lion warned. "You've been deceived by a wolf in sheep's clothing."

"I don't care if he's a wolf," one of the sheep said while looking back. "He's God's anointed, and he is our shepherd. He changed our life."

All the sheep kept following the wolf in sheep's clothing.

"Don't follow him!" Mr. Kangaroo shouted. "He's tricked you. He's going to hurt you!"

"You've let all the evil in this world blind you of the good that God is doing among us," another sheep said as he looked back. "Now take your negativity and go to your Ark and leave us alone."

"We've tried to speak to them," Mr. Sheep said. "There's no changing their minds. But thank God He brought you animals to us because that wolf in sheep's clothing had us deceived."

"Thank God we are out of his deception," Mrs. Sheep said. "Let's go to the Ark."

"Indeed," Mr. Lion agreed.

They began to walk, but then Mrs. Monkey said, "Before we go any further, let's pray."

They all agreed and huddled in a circle and prayed for God's protection and guidance.

Then they began to walk again.

But now with Mr. and Mrs. Sheep joining the group, Mr. Kangaroo took notice again that he was the only one by himself. All the other animals were male and female. He couldn't stand it anymore, so he decided that he would mention it as soon as the time was right.

CHAPTER 10

The Beavers
(Earning God's Grace)

The group has now grown to fifteen animals. They left the sheep and their positive-thinking false prophet and continued their journey to the Ark, not sure if they were going in the right direction. But they were confident that God would lead them in the right direction just as He had promised.

Mr. Bear made the first suggestion, "I think we need to cross this river. Let's follow the river and see if we can find a place to cross over."

"I agree," answered Mrs. Mongoose. "We've done all our traveling on this side of the river. It only makes sense to cross over."

All the other animals nodded in agreement as they started walking down the river.

Mr. Kangaroo noticed something and announced, "Look, I see something in the distance, it looks like we might be able to cross over on it."

"Yeah, I see it too," Mr. Bear said. "I hope it's strong enough to hold us so we can all cross over."

As the animals got closer, they noticed that it was a makeshift dam running all the way across the river. There were several beavers maintaining it.

Mr. Lion shouted toward the beavers on the dam, "Hey, beavers, can we cross over the river on your dam? Is it strong enough to hold us if we cross over on it?"

"Yeah, you can cross over on it," answered a beaver from on top of the dam. "And yes, it will hold each of you no problem."

"Thank you so much," answered a grateful Mr. Lion.

The animals gathered to the edge where the dam looked the strongest and began stepping on it one by one.

"Hey, this dam is pretty strong and sturdy," Mr. Bear said. "Nice work, beavers."

"Thank you for the compliment," answered a beaver. "We always work hard at building our dams."

"Why do you want to cross the river?" another beaver asked. "Where y'all headed?"

"God spoke to each of us and told us He sees all the evil and violence and He is going to destroy all flesh by flooding the earth," Mrs. Sheep answered. "In order to escape God's judgment, we have to go to the Ark before the flood comes. We're all going to the Ark. Would you like to go with us to the Ark and escape God's judgment?"

"What's an Ark?" asked another beaver.

"We don't know," answered Mr. Lion. "God said we will know it when we see it and we are to enter it when we get to it."

"All you have to do is enter it to escape God's judgment?" asked a beaver. "That doesn't sound right, it sounds too simple."

"Yes, it is right, and, yes, it is simple," answered Mr. Bull. "The only way to escape God's judgment is to enter the Ark."

"Are you saying that any animal can enter the Ark even if they're a sinner?" asked a beaver.

"We're all sinners, yet God provided an Ark to escape His judgment as a demonstration of His grace," Mrs. Hyena answered.

"God's grace must be earned by living righteously,"[1] a beaver replied.

"God's grace can't be earned, that's why it's called grace,"[2] answered Mr. Monkey. "We are saved by grace alone through faith alone.[3] All we have to do is trust God and go to the Ark."

Then Mrs. Beaver spoke up, "We want to go to the Ark with you and escape God's judgment, can we come with you?"

"Of course you can come with us," answered Mrs. Hyena.

"God spoke to us too, but the other beavers made it sound too simple," Mr. Beaver explained. "We began to question the Word of God because the beavers insisted we must prove to God that we are worthy of His salvation. Then we heard you say that grace can't be earned, and that made a lot of sense. We've been trying to earn God's grace our whole life, but we never really felt like we were doing enough."

"That's because it's impossible for sinners to do enough to please a perfect and holy God," Mrs. Mongoose answered. "God's grace is available by going to the Ark to escape His judgment."

"God's grace is available providing we do our part," a beaver chimed in. "We must pray regularly, gather together for worship, help others, live righteously, and many other things to prove we are worthy of His grace. Heaven is for those who do their part and earn it."[4]

"No, no," replied Mr. Lion. "Heaven is for those who trust in God alone. You are in a spiritually dangerous place if you think you are going to earn God's grace by living righteously. Because of our sinful nature, there is none who is righteous.[5] In fact, our righteousness is so corrupted by our sinful nature that God sees our righteousness as filthy.[6] Our only hope is His grace, not our righteousness."

"It's not that simple," a beaver replied. "It doesn't make sense that God would save us from judgment without having to do anything to earn it. That would mean that all my effort to please God all my life was of no use. That's not right."

"That is right," answered Mrs. Beaver. "We need His grace because no matter how much we try to live up to God's righteousness, we will always fall short."[7]

"We have to partner with God,"[8] another beaver declared. "We know that it is by grace we are saved, after all we can do.[9] We must pray as though everything depends on the Lord and work as though everything depended on us."[10]

"You can't help God save you," Mr. Mongoose pleaded. "You can't earn your way to heaven. We are saved entirely by His grace by going to the Ark. Please come with us to the Ark."

Mr. and Mrs. Beaver and all the animals pleaded with the other beavers to come to the Ark.

"We have spent our whole life earning God's grace," a beaver replied. "Even if there were judgment coming, I would rather face God knowing that I did everything I could to earn His grace."

"You don't have a chance if you face God in your own effort," Mr. Lion declared. "God has provided the Ark as a demonstration of His grace to escape His coming judgment. We have to go now, so I must ask you for the last time, do you want to go to the Ark with us to escape His coming judgment?"

"No, we don't want to go," a beaver answer with all the other beavers nodding in agreement. "We spent our whole life earning God's grace, we're not about to stop earning His grace now."

"We must obey the righteousness of God to earn His grace," another beaver stated. "We do our part, and He does His part."

"No, no, no," pleaded Mr. Kangaroo, "relying on your own righteousness separates you from God."

"They will not listen," answered Mr. Beaver. "We know how deceiving it is to think that somehow we can contribute to our salvation."[11]

"Nobody on that Ark will be able to boast about how they earned salvation from God's judgment," declared Mr. Hyena.

"It is what it is," Mr. Lion said. "C'mon, let's go."

They all finished crossing the dam, and after they got to the other side of the river, Mr. Lion looked back at the beavers and shouted, "Are you sure you don't want to come with us to the Ark?"

"Positive," answered a beaver.

"Thank you for allowing us to cross your dam," Mr. Hyena shouted. "You do good work."

"You're welcome," answered a beaver.

After the animals crossed the dam, they gathered together to pray before continuing their journey to the Ark.

CHAPTER 11

The Giraffes
(Everybody Is Born Good)

It had been awhile since the group of seventeen animals crossed over the beaver dam.

As they traveled they were discussing the coming judgment and all that had happened up to this point. While they were talking, a voice from above and behind them asked, "Hey, you guys...where are you going?"

Everyone looked around and up to see a giraffe following behind.

"We're going to the Ark because God's judgment is coming and He's going to flood the whole earth," Mr. Kangaroo replied reluctantly, hoping to avoid another difficult discussion about God.

"I thought I heard you talking about the coming flood!" Mr. Giraffe exclaimed. "I just wanted to make sure I heard you right."

"You heard us right," Mr. Monkey answered. "Why are you—"

"Can we go with you?" Mr. Giraffe asked as he interrupted.

"Who's we?" asked Mrs. Mongoose.

"Me and Mrs. Giraffe," he answered. "She's over there eating off that tree." He looked over at her and shouted, "Mrs. Giraffe, come over here quickly!"

Mrs. Giraffe came over to the group. "What's going on?" she asked.

"They're going to the Ark, and—" Mr. Giraffe began to speak.

"Can we go to the Ark with you?" Mrs. Giraffe eagerly asked. "Do you know about the coming judgment? Did God speak to you too?"

"Yes, God spoke to each of us the same way He spoke to you," Mr. Lion answered. "And yes, of course, you can go with us."

Mrs. Giraffe turned to Mr. Giraffe and said, "Now maybe the other giraffes will believe us and come with us to the Ark."

"Oh, I don't know," Mr. Giraffe replied. "They're pretty firm in their beliefs. Remember how we used to believe all that same stuff until God spoke to us?"

"Yes, but now we can all go talk to them together," Mrs. Giraffe said. "All of us together will convince them that we weren't dreaming."

"You might be right," answered Mr. Giraffe. He turned to the rest of the animals in the group and said, "We have been trying to tell the other giraffes about God's coming judgment, but they think we saw it in a dream and that it was all too gloomy to be real. Will you all come with us so we can show them that we weren't dreaming and that God's coming judgment is real? Then maybe they will come with us."

"Sure, we'll go with you," Mr. Bull replied. "The more we can get to come to the Ark, the better."

The whole group followed Mr. and Mrs. Giraffe as they led the way to the other giraffes.

As they approached the tower of giraffes, one of them spoke up and said, "Hey, you two came back and brought some friends. Did they help you understand that you were only dreaming about all that flood and judgment stuff?"

"No, no, actually we brought them with us to show you that we weren't dreaming because each of them also heard from God," Mr. Giraffe answered. "God told each of them the same thing He told us, that He is going to flood the earth in judgment because of all the evil, especially the humans."

Another giraffe from the tower spoke up, "So you want us to believe that all [he began counting the animals] one, two, three,

"Maybe we should get going to the Ark?" Mrs. Hyena said.

Mr. Bull and Mrs. Cow agreed heartily, and Mrs. Cow said, "We have tried and tried to convince them of God's coming judgment, but they would rather get stoned and not stress over it."

Mr. Lion looked at the stoned herd and asked, "We're going to the Ark to escape God's coming judgment, do any of you want come with us?"

"No thanks," answered a stoned bull. "Going with you would ruin our high. And besides that, you're all in too much of a hurry. Just remember, you can always come back here and eat some goofy grass and mellow out."

"Thanks for the offer, but we prefer to go to the Ark and escape God's coming judgment," Mr. Lion answered.

With that all the animals left the herd behind and headed for the Ark.

"Wow. Addiction really is a form of idolatry," stated Mr. Monkey.

"Yeah, when I was getting high, my desire to be high was greater than my desire for God," answered Mr. Bull. "I was never sober long enough to find any pleasure in God. I also wasn't sure how to find pleasure in God since goofy grass gave me pleasure instantly. Unfortunately that pleasure deceived me into believing that God was fine with me getting high. In the end, getting high was one big rip-off. It promised a better life, but instead it left me addicted and unable to cope with life without it."

"Faith in God is far more rewarding than the high from goofy grass," added Mrs. Cow.

"We are grateful that you got sober and are headed to the Ark with us," declared Mrs. Lion.

All the animals nodded in agreement.

"Let's pray before we continue on," Mr. Kangaroo stated.

All the animals gathered together and prayed for God's protection and guidance to the Ark.

CHAPTER 8

The Bears
(Believers in Name Only)

There are now eleven animals in the group headed for the Ark. After traveling for a couple of hours, Mr. Hyena noticed that they haven't seen or met anybody in a while, and he asked, "Is it just me, or has it gotten pretty quiet around here?"

"Yeah, I noticed it too," Mrs. Mongoose agreed. "How odd that it's so quiet."

"Where do you suppose all the other animals are?" asked Mrs. Monkey.

"Did you feel that?" asked Mr. Kangaroo. "Shhhhh, stop talking and listen and feel the ground."

Thump.

"I felt it that time!" shouted Mr. Mongoose. "The ground just shook!"

Thump.

"I felt it again!" Mr. Kangaroo shouted. "But this time the ground shook harder!"

Thump. Thump.

"It must be a dinosaur," Mrs. Mongoose said. "No wonder it's been so quiet"

Thump, thump.

"*ROOOOAAAAR!*" came the sound from just beyond the bushes.

"Run for your life!" shouted a scared Mrs. Cow.

They all took off running away from the dinosaur.

Thump, thump, thump, thump. The dinosaur started chasing them. It was a large Tyrannosaurus Rex. The T-Rex broke through the bushes, and it was now visible to the animals, making them run as fast as they could. The T-Rex was just too fast, and it was gaining on them.

Each animal was praying as they ran, "God, save us!"

As the T-Rex got closer, it focused on Mrs. Cow, and it was about to nab her when suddenly a tree fell down right in front of the T-Rex and it tripped over the tree and tumbled head over feet, coming to a stop with a *thud*.

The animals looked back to see what happened, and they saw Mr. Bear next to a tree stump and the T-Rex lying on the ground in a cloud of dust.

"Keep running!" Mr. Bear shouted. "I'll take care of this beast!"

Mr. Bear took a vine and quickly wrapped it around the T-Rex's legs before it could even figure out what just happened. Then he grabbed Mrs. Bear, and they started running to catch up to the other animals. After catching up with the other animals, they all ran together until they were completely out of breath.

"Stop here," announced Mr. Bear. "I think we are safe now."

"The ol' tree in the path of a T-Rex works every time," boasted Mrs. Bear.

"You've done this before?" asked Mr. Lion.

"Yeah," answered Mr. Bear. "Normally I just push a tree down in front of the T-Rex, making him trip and fall, it usually gives us enough time to run or hide. But this time there was some vine handy, so I tied his feet real quick. The T-Rex will break free, but we are safe now. When the T-Rex breaks free, he won't even know what happened or which way we went."

"Thank you for saving us!" shouted a grateful Mrs. Cow. "We thought we were T-Rex food for sure. Why did you save us and risk your own life?"

"I heard the T-Rex roar and we saw you all running toward us," Mr. Bear answered. "I looked at Mrs. Bear, and she looked at me, and we knew the tree-tripping trick was the only way to help since the T-Rex was just a tooth away from getting Mrs. Cow."

"Oh, you saved my life," declared Mrs. Cow. "How can we ever thank you?"

"Don't even worry about it," Mr. Bear answered. "God would expect nothing less of us."

"God? Did you say God?" asked Mrs. Monkey. "Do you believe in God?"

"We sure do," answered Mrs. Bear. "Do you all believe in God too?"

"Yes, we do, and we were on our way to the Ark," said a hesitant Mr. Mongoose, not knowing if he should mention the Ark.

"We want to go to the Ark too," Mrs. Bear said. "God told us that He is going to flood the world because of all the evil and unbelief. Is that what God told you?"

"Yes!" they all answered in one voice.

"God said the same thing to each of us," Mr. Hyena said. "Would you like to join us on our way to the Ark?"

"Of course," answered a happy Mrs. Bear.

"That was a close call," another voice said.

"What?" asked Mr. Lion as all the animals turned to see who said that.

There were several bears gathered together, and one of the bears repeated what he said, "That was a close call, that T-Rex nearly got you."

"Yes, it did, but thank God for Mr. Bear who saved my life," Mrs. Cow replied.

"The ol' tree-in-the-path trick," the bear stated. "I taught Mr. Bear that trick. We finished our worship service just in time to see the T-Rex take a tumble."

"You finished your worship service?" Mr. Mongoose asked. "You worship God?"

"Of course we worship God," the bear answered. "We gather together once a week to worship God. You just missed it."

four, five…um…all nineteen of you had the same dream about God destroying the earth?"

"Yes!" Mr. and Mrs. Giraffe answered at the same time. "And we weren't dre—"

"Nineteen of you having the same dream doesn't mean it's from God," the leader Giraffe said.

"We weren't dreaming," Mrs. Mongoose said.

Leader giraffe ignored Mrs. Mongoose and continued talking, "We have fourteen giraffes in our tower who understand the nature of life. Even the two of you used to understand the nature of life until you started telling us about your dream of God's judgment, which is the opposite of the nature of life."

"We weren't dreaming," Mrs. Giraffe said.

"The nature of life?" Mr. Bear asked. "What does that mean? What are you talking about?"

"Yeah, what is the nature of life?" asked Mr. Mongoose.

"The nature of life is that all living creatures, including humans, are born good,"[1] the leader giraffe answered. "It is society that makes us bad. Bad behavior is learned.[2] We are born good, but society teaches us to be bad.[3] This is the nature of life. It is our duty to teach our children to remain good and not let society or circumstances make us bad."

"Wow!" exclaimed Mr. Kangaroo. "You have the nature of life the exact opposite of what God says it is. God says we are born with a sinful nature.[4] Sin is not learned, it is inherent within us."[5]

"How can you say that?" asked leader giraffe. "That would mean that a child is born evil. All you have to do is observe a baby, and you will see that a child is born innocent and they learn evil from society. We become evil when we are oppressed by bad individuals or groups, or overcome by starvation, or something else causes us to commit evil behavior. We would remain good if it was not for the evils of society causing us to become bad."

"Don't let a cute little baby fool you," answered Mr. Hyena. "The sinful nature in their heart is just waiting for the opportunity to express itself. Every child comes into the world with an insatiable faculty for evil. That means that left to themselves, children will pursue a course of sin. And left entirely to themselves, there is no evil of which they are incapable."[6]

"And guess where they got their sinful nature?" Mr. Bear asked. "They got if from their parents who passed it on to them at birth. Unfortunately, it's gotten so bad that the adults are now worse than the children, and because of all the evil, God's judgment is coming."

"That's ridiculous," another giraffe answered.

"If we are born good, as you say, then why do we make laws?" Mrs. Bear asked. "And why do we keep breaking our laws?"

Mr. Lion chimed in, "All of creation breaks their own laws, and they rebel against God's law continually. They have brought God's judgment on to themselves by ignoring God and His righteousness. They lie, steal, cheat, and kill each other continually. They clearly are not good. Society didn't make them bad. Their evil behavior is what made society so bad. God knows their heart will not change, so His judgment is coming."

"I don't know how you could come to such a crazy way of thinking," leader giraffe replied angrily. "It's animals like you who prevent change from happening. How can society ever get better if we teach our kids that they are born bad?"

"The best way to make society better is to teach children their true sinful nature and how they must deny themselves,"[7] Mr. Bear answered. "We must teach them to battle daily against their sinful nature by learning self-control and seeking God and His righteousness."

"I've had enough of this nonsense," answered leader giraffe. "You can all take your doomsday dreams and go your way before your crazy way of thinking infects the rest of us and causes us to behave evil."

"We weren't dreaming!" answered Mrs. Mongoose.

"Your lunacy is already infecting me and giving me evil thoughts," another giraffe said.

"Evil thoughts come from an evil heart," answered Mr. Monkey.

"Enough!" shouted leader giraffe. "Get out of here!"

"So be it," answered Mr. Giraffe. "We will leave."

Mr. Giraffe turned to the rest of the group and said, "Thank you guys for trying to convince them of the coming judgment. Sadly, they reject it. Let's go to the Ark before the flood comes."

"It is sad," Mr. Mongoose replied, "especially how they blame evil behavior on everything except the individual. The problem is in the heart because the heart is sinful and deceptive."[8]

The animals turned and started walking away, and Mrs. Giraffe said, "Why is it that nobody sees when they are deceived?"

"Our sinful nature deceives us into believing what's right in our own eyes,"[9] Mrs. Hyena answered. "Only God can open our eyes to the truth about our true sinful nature."[10]

The group started walking, but then Mr. Mongoose reminded them that they needed to pray for God's guidance before they went any farther. So they stopped and prayed then continued on.

CHAPTER 12

The Rabbits (Spiritual but Not Religious)

With the addition of Mr. and Mrs. Giraffe, there are now nineteen animals in the group headed for the Ark.

"Welcome to our group," Mr. Bear said.

"Thank you," answered Mrs. Giraffe. "We are grateful to be going to the Ark with you."

Mr. Giraffe was about to say something else, but he suddenly tripped and began to teeter on his right legs, nearly falling over. As he struggled to gain control, he overcompensated and teetered all the way to the other side on his left legs, nearly falling over again. He came back down on all four legs and stumbled for a few more steps before he finally caught his balance.

"Whoa!" Mr. Hyena expressed. "What a ride! You almost fell, and it's a long way down from way up there."

"What happened?" asked Mr. Monkey. "Why did you stumble?"

"I think I stepped in a hole," answered Mr. Giraffe.

"He can be clumsy sometimes," Mrs. Giraffe jokingly said. "He landed on his head when he was born, and that's a six-foot drop to the ground at birth."[1]

"Ha ha ha ha ha," all the animals laughed at that.

"She loves telling that joke," answered Mr. Giraffe. "But it is true, we giraffes fall six feet to the ground and land head first when we're born."

"That was when you were a baby," Mr. Beaver said. "It looks like it's a lot farther to the ground now that you've grown."

"Ha ha ha ha ha," all the animals laughed again.

"I think you tripped in a rabbit hole," Mrs. Hyena said. "Check it out, there are rabbit holes all over this area."

Just then some dirt started flying up from where Mr. Giraffe tripped. All the animals looked to see a rabbit digging his way out of the ground. The rabbit finished digging out his hole and looked at the animals and said, "Which one of you stepped on my hole and covered it up?"

"That was me," Mr. Giraffe answered. "I'm sorry, I didn't see your hole, and I stepped on it and tripped and nearly fell to the ground."

"There are rabbit holes all over the place," the rabbit replied. "How could you not see them?"

"I don't know, I guess we were busy talking about God," Mr. Giraffe said. "What about you rabbit? Do you believe in God?"

"No, no, not me," the rabbit replied. "Wait, I take that back... I believe in god, but I don't believe in religion. I'm spiritual but not religious."

"Spiritual but not religious?" asked Mr. Kangaroo. "What does that mean?"

"I'm spiritual because I believe there is a god or higher power that has a purpose for me, and I'm not religious because I reject organized religion,"[2] the rabbit answered.

"Why do you reject organized religion?" Mrs. Cow asked.

"I reject religion because of all their doctrines, rituals, beliefs, institutions, and so on," the rabbit answered. "I don't need a religion with rules telling me how to live."

"How do you decide what to believe if you reject religion?" Mrs. Beaver asked.

"My heart guides me," the rabbit answered. "I do what gives me inner peace. I'm not bound by religious rules."

By this time other rabbits gathered around to hear the conversation.

"It sounds like being spiritual but not religious means anybody can believe anything they want," Mr. Kangaroo said.

"Yes, that's exactly right," another rabbit replied. "We have freedom to pursue our own spiritual life apart from burdensome religious rules or doctrines."

"How do you have any spiritual unity if you all believe something different?" Mrs. Sheep asked.

"We are united by our freedom to believe whatever we want," another rabbit answered.

"You said you believe in God, what role does God have in your life?" Mr. Kangaroo asked.

"For me, god is loving, forgiving, and understanding," the rabbit answered. "He's not full of commands and condemnation. He loves me just the way I am."

"We are energy beings," another rabbit declared. "Our challenge is to learn how to harness, channel, and increase that energy.[3] I believe in a positive universal energy that surrounds me when I meditate. It gives me balance. Would you like me to give you an energy reading?"

"No, thank you," answered Mr. Kangaroo.

"I believe we are all god," another rabbit announced.

"We're all god?" asked Mr. Beaver. "What does that mean?"

"A heightened spiritual consciousness enlightens us to discover the god within us,"[4] the rabbit answered. "Once you discover the god within you, you will have inner peace beyond explanation."

"What do you mean by a heightened spiritual consciousness?" Mr. Bull asked.

"When we meditate, we are able to focus and allow our conscious and unconscious minds to come together in harmony," the rabbit explained. "This allows something magical to happen: the creation of a third mind, or higher consciousness."[5]

"So this higher consciousness is called a third mind?" asked Mr. Monkey.

"Yes," the rabbit answered. "The third mind is like a spiritual eye that gives us perception beyond what we can see. It gives us greater feeling and understanding."

"When thoughts and feelings come into our consciousness, it's up to us to choose to empower the positive ones and release the negative ones,"[6] another rabbit answered. "We need to release bad memories in order to be happy so our inner potential can be released."[7]

Then a certain Mr. Rabbit came forward and said with sarcasm, "Welcome to our spiritual-but-not-religious community where god and spirituality is whatever you want it to be."

"You can mock us all you want," another rabbit answered angrily and abruptly. "But it doesn't change the fact that we all have different paths of spirituality. All your negativity is just creating bad vibes in all of us."

Another rabbit joined in, "Once you release your mind you will be able to find your true self."

This time Mrs. Rabbit interrupted and spoke up, "*Spiritual but not religious* is nothing more than an unorganized religion based on self. It's the religion of me."

"There you go again judging us," an irritated spiritual rabbit replied. "Are you going to start talking about your Ark and preaching God's judgment again?"

Mr. Lion looked at Mrs. Rabbit and asked excitedly, "You know about God's judgment and the Ark?"

"Yes, God spoke to me and Mr. Rabbit," she answered. "We tried to warn the other rabbits, but they reject it because it sounds like religious talk."

"We're going to the Ark," Mr. Lion answered. "Would you and Mr. Rabbit like to join us on our way to the Ark?"

"We would love to join you!" Mrs. Rabbit answered happily.

"Do you know where the Ark is?" Mr. Rabbit asked.

"No, we don't," answered Mr. Lion. "God has been leading as we travel, and He led us to you."

"Praise the Lord because we have been praying on what to do and where to go, and here you are," Mr. Rabbit said.

"God answered our prayer!" Mrs. Rabbit declared.

An irritated spiritual rabbit chimed in, "So you all think you're going to escape judgment and the rest of us are condemned because we don't believe what you believe? This is why we reject religion."

"From what I hear, it sounds like you reject any authority outside yourself," Mr. Bull answered. "To think that you can navigate the realities of eternity, life, death, and life after death by looking inside yourself is insanity.[8] Unfortunately, your belief system is focused on self under the cloak of spirituality."

"Yep," Mr. Rabbit agreed. "Being spiritual but not religious is all about self,[9] self-development, self-transformation, self-realization, and self-actualization. That's why I call it the all-about-me religion."

"There are so many religions to choose from," a spiritual rabbit said. "Even if we did decide to be religious, how are we supposed to know which one to follow?"

"God is righteous," Mr. Sheep answered. "Go with the religion that teaches our true sinful nature and exalts God and His righteousness. Go with the religion that promotes God's moral goodness and rejects evil and violence. Go with the religion that worships the Creator, not His creation. We need God to save us from ourselves and free us from our sinful nature."

"There's evil and violence all over the world, especially the humans," another rabbit answered. "Every religion is full of hypocrites who preach goodness but they live evil and violent lives."

"You don't judge a religion by its abuse,"[10] answered Mr. Mongoose. "The fact that others abuse religion doesn't mean the religion is false. We are all sinners, so you judge a religion by what they teach. The reality is that we can't appease God because we are far worse off than we ever imagined.[11] God sees all the evil, violence, and hypocrisy, and His judgment is coming."

"God has provided an Ark to save us from ourselves," Mrs. Bear said. "Our only hope is to trust God and go to the Ark to escape His judgment."

"We are going to the Ark to escape God's judgment," Mr. Lion declared. "Mr. and Mrs. Rabbit are coming with us. Do any of you other rabbits want to come with us?"

"No thanks," a rabbit answered. "You are too religious for us, and we are content with peace in our hearts."

Mr. Lion turned to the other animals and said, "You heard them. They don't want to come. Let's get going."

With that, all the animals moved on from the rabbits and continued on to the Ark. They stopped briefly to pray then continued on their journey.

After walking for a while, it began to get dark.

"I need to rest," Mrs. Mongoose said.

"Me too," Mrs. Cow replied.

"Yes, indeed," Mr. Lion agreed. "We've been through a lot since we began our journey to the Ark. Let's pray and rest here for a while."

After they prayed all twenty-one of the animals settled down for the night. Each got as comfortable as possible. They were all asleep within minutes.

CHAPTER 13

The Pigs
(Mother Gaia)

All the animals were sound asleep as the morning sun began to peek on the horizon.

Mrs. Hyena was the first to wake up to the sound of a calm voice giving calm instructions. Mrs. Hyena quietly looked over and saw a group of pigs sitting in a circle with their eyes closed and their legs crossed. There was a nature pig giving calm instructions to the other pigs.

"Before we connect with Mother Gaia, we must prepare ourselves through grounding and centering.[1] Close your eyes, and focus your body's energy centers so that you can connect smoothly with all parts of yourself, those around you, and Mother Gaia."

All the pigs were intently focused as they meditated with their eyes closed.

The nature pig continued, "Now pull in as much energy from the universe as you need. If you get too much energy, you can just ground it back to the earth."

The nature pig paused to let the other pigs meditate.

The nature pig continued, "Keep your eyes closed, and let go of all your concerns… Feel your heartbeat… Feel the space around your heart… Now become aware of the space all around you… Notice, the space inside you is the same as the space all around you.[2] This is because the molecules in our body are interconnected with the molecules in the air... We are all connected with Mother Gaia."[3]

The nature pig paused again for a few seconds, then she continued, "Now, feel Mother Gaia all around you... Feel your connection to Mother Gaia."

"It's wonderful," another pig declared.

"It's peaceful," another pig said.

"Yes, yes," the nature pig continued. "Feel the ground under your feet... Feel the consciousness of the trees, plants, flowers, rocks, and sky.[4] They are speaking to you... Listen to their voice... What are they telling you?"

"The trees and plants are telling me they're all sad by the way they are being treated by animals and especially the humans," a pig answered.

"I hear the plants telling me that we all need to work together for the good of Mother Gaia," another pig answered.

At this point, all the other animals were awake and listening to the pigs.

The nature pig continued, "What else is Mother Gaia telling you?"

From among the pigs, a certain Mr. Pig spoke up and said, "I can't hear anything from Mother Gaia, but I did hear God speak to me. He said we need to go to the Ark before the flood comes."

"Now why would you disrupt our connection to the universe like that?" the nature pig angrily asked. "Especially after we've already discussed this? This judgment talk has got to stop."

"We're supposed to listen to the Creator, not the trees," Mr. Pig replied.

"AMEN!" shouted Mr. Monkey.

All the pigs turned to see Mr. Monkey and all the other animals staring at the circle of pigs.

"I'm sorry," answered Mr. Monkey. "I should not have blurted out like that."

"What are you all doing over there?" the nature pig asked.

"We were sleeping for the night, and we woke up to the sound of your meditations," answered Mrs. Rabbit. "We're on our way to the Ark to escape the flood just like Mr. Pig said."

"You're all going to the Ark?" Mrs. Pig excitedly asked. "Can we come?"

"Of course!" answered Mr. Bear.

"What are you all doing over there sitting like that with your eyes closed?" Mrs. Bear asked.

"We were getting connected to Mother Gaia," answered nature pig. "That was before Mr. Pig rudely interrupted us."

"Who is Mother Gaia?" asked Mrs. Bear.

"Mother Gaia is the single living entity in which all of nature exists," the nature pig answered.

Before the nature pig could continue, Mrs. Hyena picked an apple from a tree and began to eat it.

"Put that apple down!" demanded an irritated nature pig. "Who gave you the right to infringe on Mother Gaia?"

"What?" asked Mrs. Hyena not sure what to make of the question.

"Who gave you the right to infringe on Mother Gaia?" the nature pig asked again.

"Infringe on who?" asked a thoroughly confused Mrs. Hyena.

Mr. Hyena came to the aid of Mrs. Hyena and asked, "What are you talking about?"

"Your lady friend infringed on Mother Gaia and picked an apple from her tree and started eating it," an irritated pig said.

"Infringe on Mother Gaia? Huh?" a confused Mr. Hyena asked. "It's an apple. You have to pick it to eat it. They look good. I want one too." Mr. Hyena picked an apple and took a bite.

"How dare you pick an apple and violate Mother Gaia after we just told you that your lady friend did it!" the irritated pig shouted.

"Apples!" shouted Mr. Kangaroo. "Breakfast is served." He picked an apple and started eating it.

Then the entire group of animals started picking apples and eating them.

"*Oink! Oink! Oink!* What are you doing!" shouted another very troubled pig. "Leave that tree alone."

All the pigs started oinking uncontrollably as if they were being personally attacked.

"Oink! Oink! Oink! Oink! Oink! Oink!"

Another angry pig grabbed Mr. Kangaroo's tail and yanked it and asked, "How do you like it when someone picks at you? How do you think the tree feels when you pick its fruit?"

"I never thought about it," Mr. Kangaroo replied. "I have been eating apples all my life."

"It's not that difficult to understand," an angry pig said. "Nature needs to be preserved. Every time you pick from a tree, you're infringing on Mother Gaia and violating her right to exist without interference."

"Her right to exist?" Mrs. Mongoose asked. "Who...how... what are we supposed to eat?"

"You eat what falls from the trees," a pig replied. "This is how we know that Mother Gaia is okay with us eating her fruit."

"But I'm hungry now, and no fruit is falling to the ground," answered Mrs. Hyena.

A pig responded by putting his nose to the ground and sniffing and saying, "You put your nose to the ground and rummage through the ground foliage, sniffing like this, until you find something edible." He sniffed for a few feet and found a piece of something and ate it. "Yummy! That was tasty. Do you see how easy it is to eat without infringing on nature?"

"That's easy for you to say with your pig snout," Mrs. Sheep replied. "I am not dragging my nose along the ground looking for who knows what's on the ground."

"Hey! Look up here!" ordered Mrs. Giraffe.

The pig looked up at Mrs. Giraffe, "What?"

"Do I look like I can walk around dragging my nose through the ground looking for food?" asked Mrs. Giraffe. "I have enough trouble stooping down just to get a drink of water!"

"Stop already!" Mr. Bear declared. "This conversation is getting ridiculous. You mentioned Mother Gaia. Who is that? What does that mean?"

"There is consciousness in everything from tiny microscopic organisms to plants, trees, water, rocks, animals, humans, stars, and everything in between," the nature pig explained. "All matter has a spark of intelligence,[5] and everything consists of a single living entity.[6] This living entity is known as Mother Gaia."

"God created life," Mrs. Giraffe replied, "not Mother Gaia."

"Nobody can prove God exists, but there is circumstantial evidence for Mother Gaia,"[7] the nature pig answered. "Just look at the air we breathe, regardless of what we do to the air, including the constant pollution from humans, the right mixture of molecules in the air always remains just right to support life."

"The circumstances prove the genius of God Who created the earth to support life for His glory," Mrs. Beaver answered.

"You mean the same God you say is going to destroy everything?" another pig answered sarcastically. "That doesn't make sense. The reality is that Mother Gaia maintains the conditions favorable for life in all circumstances."[8]

"Without Mother Gaia, we would not even be able to exist," another pig replied. "Mother Gaia evolved first, so we must honor her by respecting nature and allowing nature to flourish without our interference."

"So you think nature is controlled by an evolved entity called Mother Gaia?" Mr. Kangaroo asked.

"It's obvious," an irritated pig replied. "All we animals do is fight with each other, and don't even get me started on those evil and violent humans. They not only fight but they destroy nature by polluting it, and they even tear up the ground to grow things their own way. Humans and animals live and die, but Mother Gaia never dies, and she is able to repair herself even after we and the humans damage her. If there were no animals or humans, Mother Gaia would continue flourishing without interference."

"Mother Gaia has given us special permission to live on earth,"[9] another pig said. "But instead of living in harmony with Mother Gaia, the animals and humans are the bacteria and cancer on the earth's skin."[10]

"So you think the problem with the earth is animals and humans?" Mr. Bear asked.

"Mother Gaia knew what she was doing when she designed the earth's surface to be mostly water," the nature pig replied. "Otherwise, the human and animal populations would grow too big for Mother Gaia to regulate the environment faster than we can destroy it.[11] If the earth was mostly land, there would be way too many useless eaters, and Mother Gaia would have to send more famines to reduce the population and restore balance on the earth."[12]

"Nature was created by God,[13] and He is in control of everything,"[14] Mr. Kangaroo replied. "You mentioned all the violence, well, it turns out that God is very aware of all the violence, and He sees that everyone is continually evil. The problem is in the heart. That's where the evil is coming from."

"Stop with the flood-and-judgment talk," a pig replied. "We don't want to hear it anymore. Notice how nice and unaffected Mother Gaia is around here, except for the apple tree that you violated."

"Everything is a part of the same living organism under the control of Mother Gaia," another pig replied. "Like it or not, no matter what we do to the environment, Mother Gaia will continue to draw us into her process of regulation."[15]

"A rat is a pig is a dog is a boy,"[16] another pig joined in. "We are all of equal value under the control of Mother Gaia."

"Your Mother Gaia is going to be covered in water when God floods the earth in His judgment," Mr. Pig replied. "God has given us a way to escape the flood by going to the Ark before the flood comes."

"Even if your God were going to destroy the earth, the animals and humans will destroy it before He does," a pig replied.

"You have exalted your Mother Gaia above God," answered Mr. Giraffe. "You have exchanged the truth of God for a lie, and you are worshipping the creation rather than the Creator.[17] The whole face of the earth is going to be underwater very soon, and the only escape is to go to the Ark."

"God created everything for His glory," Mrs. Cow said. "You have turned your back on Him, but it's not too late to repent and trust God by going to the Ark."

"There will be no flood or judgment," the nature pig angrily answered. "The goal is to find common ground so we can reharmonize life on earth under Mother Gaia.[18] If you're going to keep ranting about judgment, then just leave."

"Okay, we'll leave," answered Mrs. Lion. "But we will ask all of you one last time before we go if any of you want to come with us to the Ark to escape God's coming judgment?"

"No," the nature pig answered. "Mother Gaia is very resilient, but she is also fragile. She doesn't need judgment, she needs healing. We will stay here and use our energies to heal the planet."

With that the group of animals turned from the pigs and began to leave but stopped to watch as they saw the pigs again form a circle among themselves.

"What are they doing?" asked Mrs. Bear.

"They are getting ready to connect with Mother Gaia," Mr. Pig answered. "They sit in a circle, cross their legs, close their eyes, and begin meditating until they feel they are one with Mother Gaia."

"How long do they do this?" asked Mrs. Monkey.

"It can last a few minutes to several hours, depending on how connected they feel with Mother Gaia," Mrs. Pig answered.

"Wow. They actually worship creation over the Creator," Mr. Kangaroo said.

"Yep," Mr. Pig agreed. "We tried to warn them, but as you saw for yourselves, they won't listen."

"So which way to the Ark?" asked Mrs. Pig.

"We don't know," answered Mr. Hyena. "We just know that God promised to lead us to it. And it seems that we keep adding more and more animals as we head to the Ark."

Mr. Kangaroo became very troubled that he was the only one without a female, and he said, "We aren't just picking up more animals, we're picking up a male and a female of each. Except for me, I'm the only male without a female. Why does everybody have a female except me?"

Mrs. Hyena answered, "I know this must be very hard for you, we don't understand either. All we do know is that God is in control, and He obviously has a plan in place."

All the animals agreed with Mrs. Hyena and gave Mr. Kangaroo a big hug.

"Let's pray for God to bring you a female as He leads us to the Ark," Mr. Lion said.

"Okay," answered Mr. Kangaroo.

They all bowed their heads and prayed for Mr. Kangaroo and for continued protection and guidance on their journey.

Mr. Kangaroo was very encouraged now that they prayed over it.

CHAPTER 14

The Sloths
(Karma)

A few hours had passed since the group of twenty-three animals left their encounter with the pigs. As they traveled, the animals were discussing all their different encounters with other animals.

"This journey to the Ark has brought a lot of difficult problems," Mr. Kangaroo said.

"Yeah, I'm getting more worn out from the encounters with other animals than with the physical part of this journey," Mrs. Mongoose said.

"I hope there are no more problems along the way," Mrs. Hyena said.

"Sounds like you're working out your karmic debt from a past life,"[1] a new voice said.

"What? Who said that?" asked Mrs. Sheep as all the animals looked around to see who said that strange statement.

"It was me. I said it," answered a sloth in a tree. "I'll say it again, it sounds like you're working out your karmic debt from a past life."

"What's that supposed to mean?" asked Mr. Bear. "Who are you?"

"I am a karmic guru sloth," answered the guru sloth. "Karmic debt means you were not a very good animal in your previous life, and that's why you're having so many problems in this life. It's called karma."

"You think our problems are from a past life?" asked a confused Mr. Giraffe.

"Yes," answered guru sloth. "It may be that you have accumulated karmic forces stored up from a past life that have to be worked out in this life.[2] You can reduce suffering by creating good karma in this life that will be transferred over to your next life."[3]

"What?" asked Mrs. Bear. "Past life…? Next life…? What are you talking about?"

"It's called reincarnation," answered another sloth. "When we die, it's only our physical body that actually dies while our soul along with our mind, intellect, senses, and vital energy are reincarnated and born with another body.[4] Our karma determines how we will be reincarnated and how long we will live."[5]

"If you live a good life now, then after you die, you will be reincarnated to a better life in the future," the guru sloth said. "If you live a bad life now, then your next life will be difficult."

"I've never heard of this karma thing," stated Mrs. Cow.

"Karma is not a thing," guru sloth replied. "It has no fixed nature, and it's not a reality, but yet it is very real. Karma is a phenomenon."[6]

"Don't you believe in God?" Mrs. Pig asked.

"Of course," answered guru sloth. "God is the giver of the fruits of karma.[7] He makes sure everyone gets their own karma and not someone else's. Karma enables all paths to lead to God."[8]

"Reincarnation…um…so what did you do in your previous life to come back as a sloth?" asked a sarcastic Mr. Lion.

"Being a sloth means I lived a good previous life," the guru sloth answered. "My life is great now. I love everybody, I'm never in a hurry, I have no cravings or desires, my soul has been liberated."

"Your soul is liberated?" asked Mr. Mongoose.

"Karma is about attaining freedom from a variety of karmic hindrances and constraints,"[9] the guru sloth explained. "When we reach the peak of spiritual progress through God-realization, and we no longer have any desires, we become free from karmic hindrances and our soul is liberated."[10]

"I hate to disrupt your liberated soul, but we have an urgent message from God," declared Mr. Hyena.

"Since karma is continually evolving, I would love to hear your message from God,"[11] the guru sloth answered. "We are always open to new insights."

"God sees all the evil, especially from the humans, and He sees that our hearts are continually evil, so God is going to flood the entire world in judgment and destroy all flesh," Mr. Hyena answered. "The only way to escape God's judgment is to go to the Ark before the flood comes."

"I don't like that message," answered the guru sloth. "I reject it. That kind of hateful talk will produce very bad karma and bring you back as a human in your next life. Humans are so bad that you can tell they are storing up a lot of karmic debt for their hateful living. Once you come back as a human, it's difficult to have a liberated soul because it takes several rebirths to overcome so much bad karmic residue."[12]

"You only get this one life,"[13] Mr. Monkey replied. "You will not be reincarnated. There is no karma. God says you will reap what you sow in this one life for all eternity. If you reject God's plan for salvation in this life, He will reject you for all eternity. You must come with us to the Ark if you want to escape God's judgment."

"That is a very troubling message, which is why we reject it," another sloth said.

"We don't reject it!" a certain Mr. Sloth announced. "God spoke to me and Mrs. Sloth about the same coming judgment, and we want to go with you to the Ark."

"You know that if you follow them and their terrible message, you can expect bad karma in return," another sloth answered. "Reincarnation is a fact.[14] There are plenty of us who remember past lives, plus we have the testimony of liberated souls. There is no way to escape karma."[15]

"We don't believe in karma anymore," Mrs. Sloth said. "God spoke to us clearly about His coming judgment, and we believe Him, so we are going to the Ark."

"Suit yourself, but every time I see a bug or a human, I will wonder if they are actually you reincarnated working out your very bad karmic debt for following after that terrible message from a terrible God,"[16] the guru sloth replied.

Mr. Lion asked the other sloths, "Do any of you want to come with us and escape God's coming judgment?"

"No, thank you," the guru sloth replied. "We'll stay here and continue creating good karma while you stress out over some terrible judgment."

"Let's go," Mrs. Sloth said.

The guru sloth said to the animals as they were leaving, "As you go your way, remember the rule of karma is that this will all come back on you in your next life."

"There is no karma," Mr. Mongoose declared. "There is no reincarnation, there is only this one life. The world is morally corrupted by sin, and so God's judgment is coming."

"We are not morally corrupted by sin,"[17] the guru sloth replied. "Each of us does good and bad things because our karma is mixed.[18] It's up to us to overcome bad karma with good karma. By continually practicing good karma and spiritual discipline, we will transform our mind and manifest the inherent divinity in us, and then we can become all-knowing."[19]

"Inherent divinity and all-knowing?" Mrs. Sheep asked. "Only God is divine and all-knowing."

"It does you no good to resist because sooner or later, your true self, your divinity, must manifest itself,"[20] the guru sloth replied.

"We are not God, and we don't have divinity," Mr. Lion replied. "We are not like God at all. We are His creation, and He is bringing judgment on His creation. The only escape is to go to the Ark. One last time, do you want to come with us to the Ark?"

"No, we don't," guru sloth replied. "Your judgment talk is accumulating bad karma."

"So be it," answered Mr. Lion as he motioned the other animals to move on.

All the animals, including Mr. and Mrs. Sloth, turned from the karma sloths and continued on their journey to the Ark.

"I don't see how anyone could find peace through reincarnation and karma," Mrs. Monkey said. "And to think their whole belief system is about being reincarnated over and over. Sounds more like an endless nightmare."

"You got that right!" exclaimed Mrs. Bear. "And not only that, but they have no personal relationship with God either."[21]

"What they don't understand is that our sinful nature cannot be overcome by karma or anything else," Mr. Sloth stated. "The only hope for our sinful nature is God's grace to save us from His coming judgment."

"Wow, they have totally come up with a way to water down our true sinful nature," Mr. Bull said.

"Yes, they have," Mrs. Sloth answered. "And we used to believe all that karma stuff till God opened our eyes and spoke to us."

"Praise the Lord for His grace on all of us," Mr. Lion replied.

"Amen!" all the animals agreed.

The animals left the other sloths behind and continued their journey to the Ark, but Mr. and Mrs. Sloth were lagging behind because they were so slow.

"Come on, Mr. and Mrs. Sloth, speed up," Mr. Lion said. "You're falling behind and slowing us down."

"We're walking as fast as we can," Mr. Sloth said.

"Mr. Sloth, you ride on my back," Mr. Bear said. "And, Mrs. Sloth, you ride on Mrs. Bear's back."

"I don't want to weigh you down and be a burden," Mrs. Sloth said.

"Yeah," Mr. Sloth agreed. "You guys go ahead. We'll find our way to the Ark."

"Don't be ridiculous," Mrs. Bear said. "Get on my back."

"Are you sure?" asked Mrs. Sloth.

"We're absolutely sure," Mr. Bear said. "Now get on and let's go."

"Okay, but if we become too much for you, please let us know," Mrs. Sloth said. "I would hate to burden you and you not tell us."

"It's no burden," Mrs. Bear answered.

As Mr. and Mrs. Sloth got on the backs of Mr. and Mrs. Bear, Mr. Lion gathered the animals to pray before they continued their journey to the Ark.

CHAPTER 15

The Elephants (Reason)

The group was now twenty-five animals as they continued their journey to the Ark. This time they came across some elephants who were listening to another elephant speak.

"I see elephants up ahead through the tall brush," Mr. Giraffe announced. "It looks like an elephant is teaching a class."

"Who would be teaching a class out here?" Mrs. Mongoose asked.

"Let's just keep moving before we get trapped into another heated debate," declared Mr. Hyena.

"Hold up, I'm curious," Mr. Giraffe said. "Let's just listen for a moment without disturbing them."

All twenty-five animals gathered a short distance away from the elephants to hear what the elephant teacher was saying to his students. As the animals listened they heard the elephant teacher say, "Don't let anybody tell you that you are a bad animal just because you question the existence of God. If someone believes in God, try to persuade them with reason. Question everything, and don't accept nonsense with silence. It's okay to mock and ridicule an idea that deserves ridicule."[1]

Mr. Pig whispered to the group, "Uh-oh, they're going to mock us as soon as we mention God."

"You got that right," Mrs. Mongoose said. "And they're going to ridicule us even more once we mention God's coming judgment."

"I told you we should have kept moving," Mr. Hyena said. "Maybe we should just get out of here while we have a chance."

"I agree," Mrs. Mongoose said, "I don't think God wants us to get mocked and ridiculed for believing in Him. Let's get out of here."

"Shhhhhhh, keep it down or they'll hear us," whispered Mrs. Monkey.

"Come on, let's go," whispered Mr. Bear.

Slowly they turned and began to walk away. After just a few steps, Mr. Giraffe tripped on a rock and bumped his head on a high tree branch.

Thump!

"Ouch!" exclaimed Mr. Giraffe.

"Shhhhhhh!" Mr. Kangaroo ordered. "Let's go before they hear us."

All the elephants heard the noise and turned to see all the animals freeze in place, hoping they were invisible.

"Too late," Mr. Sheep said.

"Uh-oh," Mrs. Sheep muttered.

"Hey, what are you animals doing over there?" an elephant asked.

"Hello," said a reluctant Mr. Bull.

"Hello to you," the professor elephant said. "What are you all doing over there?"

"Um…uh…we were just passing through, and we stopped for a moment because we heard you speaking," answered Mr. Sloth. "Please excuse us, and we'll be on our way. Sorry for disturbing you."

"Don't be sorry," answered the professor elephant. "You didn't disturb us. I was just teaching my students how to refute religion with reason."

"Refute religion with reason?" asked Mr. Beaver. "Why?"

"Because reason soundly refutes the claims of religion,"[2] answered professor elephant.

A student elephant chimed in, "Yeah, and unlike the oppressive superstition of religion, we are the brights and freethinkers[3] leading the world through reason, science, and logic."

"Well said, student," answered professor elephant. "You're already on your way to making this a better world."

"What is a bright and a freethinker?" asked Mrs. Mongoose.

"My students will answer that," professor elephant replied. Then he pointed to one of his students and asked, "What is a bright?"[4]

The student answered, "A bright is one who has a sharp and intelligent mind that bases everything on reason and science unlike the dim and unintelligent mind of the religious who base everything on superstition and blind faith."

"Well said, student," answered the professor elephant. Then he turned to another student and asked, "What is a freethinker?"[5]

"A freethinker forms their opinion about religion on the basis of reason, independent of tradition, authority, or established belief," the student answered.

"Outstanding answers!" exclaimed the professor elephant. "Both of you are on your way to making the world better by refuting any belief in a nonexistent god."

"Nonexistent God?" asked Mr. Kangaroo realizing that he had just set himself up for a barrage of ridicule. "How do you know that God doesn't exist?"

Professor elephant looked at Mr. Kangaroo and said, "Your question implies that you believe in God. Do I have that right?"

"Yes, we believe in God, let's reason together,"[6] answered Mr. Kangaroo as he thought to himself, *Why did I just say that?*

"You believe in God, do you?" asked the professor elephant. "We would love to reason with you." He turned to his student elephants and said, "Students, we have some religious animals who want to reason with us. This will be good training for you."

Then professor elephant turned back to Mr. Kangaroo and said, "This is going to be fun. Since you mentioned that you want to reason with us, I'll let you go first. Say something reasonable."

"God sees all the evil, unbelief, and violence in the world, especially the humans, and He knows that it will never end, so He is going to flood the whole earth and destroy all flesh," Mr. Kangaroo said as he prepared himself for ridicule. "The only way to escape God's coming judgment is to go the Ark before the flood comes."

"Bwaaaaa ha ha ha ha," the professor elephant and the students could not control themselves, and they burst into laughter. After the professor elephant finally stopped laughing, he turned to his students and said, "Do you see how belief in God makes you totally unreasonable and wacky?"

"Professor, they're totally unreasonable just like you said," a student said.

"Indeed, they are," professor elephant said.

Then professor elephant looked back at the group of animals and said, "How am I supposed to seriously reason with you guys when you talk about this God of yours flooding the whole earth and destroying everything?"

"It's not unreasonable when you know how holy God is and how evil the world is," answered Mr. Mongoose. "The humans are especially evil and violent, and they get worse every day. Even the animals cannot stop fighting."

"There is no chance for peace with all your end-of-the-world fear mongering," professor elephant replied. "It only creates more hostility. When reason, science, and logic govern a society, then each animal is allowed to nurture their own existence and achieve their full potential to think, feel, love, and question."[7]

"Think, feel, love, and question?" Mr. Lion asked. "None of those can be explained by science. Those are immaterial realities."

"Material or immaterial makes no difference," a student answered. "We must allow science to discover the truths about the world we live in."

"We all know intuitively that there is a reality external to our mind that includes immaterial things,"[8] Mrs. Lion answered. "Where does the ability to reason come from? Where do the laws of logic come from? Where do all our natural laws come from?"

"The laws of reason and logic are grounded in our mind,"[9] professor elephant answered.

"You are right that these laws are rooted in a mind, but it's not our mind," answered Mr. Hyena. "The truth is that these laws are timeless, spaceless, immaterial, and unchangeable because these laws come from the mind of God."[10]

"How can you say that they come from God when you can't even prove God exists?" a student elephant asked.

"All laws come from a lawgiver,"[11] answered Mrs. Pig. "Why would we think that the laws of nature and the laws of logic are any different? God is the Lawgiver of these immaterial laws. It's a reasonable and logical conclusion."

"We can figure everything out through science and mathematics," the professor elephant replied. "We do not need an imaginary God."

"How come the physical world can be described so well through mathematics?" asked Mr. Rabbit. "Where do mathematics come from?"

"Um....er..." the professor elephant stumbled for an answer. "Science just needs more time, and we will learn the answers.[12] That's what's so great about science...it's always advancing."

"Science, logic, and reason can only be done because we live in an orderly world created by an orderly Mind,"[13] answered Mr. Mongoose.

"There you go again reverting to an immaterial make-believe god," professor elephant said.

"Are the laws of logic and the laws of nature immaterial?" asked Mr. Bear.

"Yes, they are," answered professor elephant. "But they are just a part of our nature."

"Nature's laws are immaterial because they come from an immaterial God with an infinite mind," Mr. Bear answered.

"These laws are just a natural part of our minds, which science will one day explain," answered a student elephant.

"The universe and everything in it was created by God,"[14] Mr. Lion answered. "The natural laws, our thinking mind, and the orderly universe are evidence of a Great Mind apart from the material world around us. Our minds were designed by God to know God and His creation."[15]

"It's so intellectually lazy to just say that God created everything," another student elephant said.

"Outstanding come back!" exclaimed professor elephant. "Your grasp of reason brings hope to this world."

"How is that intellectually lazy?" asked Mr. Sheep.

"When you say that God created everything, you take the lazy answer rather than do the extra work to discover all that life has to offer," professor elephant answered. "How is it reasonable to suppress a mind thirsty for knowledge by telling them God did it? That's not reasonable!"[16]

"God created the mind," Mr. Giraffe answered. "All of creation reveals the mind of God. Everything we discover, everything we study, everything we learn reveals the mind of God. Science cannot discover the mind. The mind discovers science.[17] To exclude God only results in wrong conclusions about everything, and that's not logical or reasonable."

"Reason is a storehouse of truths independent of any religion,"[18] declared the professor elephant.

"Wrong," answered Mr. Bear. "Reason is the God-given ability to think rationally and to know God and discover His truths."

The professor elephant answered sarcastically, "On one side of your mouth, you tell us to think rationally, while the other side of your mouth, you tell us God is going to flood the world." Then professor elephant looked at his students and said, "Do you see how impossible it is to reason with religious animals? There is no getting through to their stubborn heads."

"It's like they have a mental disorder," another elephant student said.

Then a certain Mr. and Mrs. Elephant came forward and joined the other animals, and Mr. Elephant said, "They do not have a mental disorder. We also believe in God, and He told us about the coming judgment too."

Mrs. Elephant joined in, "And we do not have a mental disorder either. We are perfectly reasonable."

"I had a feeling there was something wrong with you two," professor elephant replied. "You were always asking questions as if you doubted sound reason. I should have known you were bad students."

"We are not bad students," Mrs. Elephant said. "You are an unreasonable professor for separating God from sound reason."

"Wow, we had some religious wackos in our class the whole time," an elephant student declared.

"Yes, they can be difficult to detect sometimes, but they always make themselves known eventually," the professor elephant said.

"We are going to the Ark to escape God's coming judgment," Mr. Lion announced. "Do any of you elephants want to come with us?"

"Mrs. Elephant and I will go with you," Mr. Elephant answered.

"You can have those two unreasonable students," professor elephant replied. "Go your way and take your religious friends with you. The rest of us will continue discovering all there is to learn about life and continue teaching others so we can make a better society without religion dividing us."

"Yeah, take your wacko beliefs and go," another elephant student said.

"Okay, but you won't be able to reason your way out of God's judgment," Mr. Kangaroo said.

"We've heard all this judgment talk before, and life continues as usual," another elephant student replied. "You are just another group of religious wackos with another false prophecy to prove you are unreasonable fools.

"I think religion should be treated with ridicule, hatred, and contempt,"[19] the professor elephant stated with contempt.

"Come on, guys, let's go before things get worse," Mr. Elephant insisted.

"Yes, yes, let's go," Mr. Lion agreed.

As they left the elephants behind, Mr. Elephant said, "It's too bad they try to separate reason from faith. Without good reasons our faith would be blind and irrational."

"That's for sure," added Mr. Bear. "We have good and logical reasons for what we believe."

"Amen!" all the animals said in agreement.

They all paused to pray before continuing their journey to the Ark.

CHAPTER 16

The Snakes (Evil)

As the group of twenty-seven animals continued their journey to the Ark, Mr. Kangaroo was now very troubled that he was the only one without a female.

"Why am I the only one without a female?" he asked as they walked.

All the animals knew it seemed odd that he was the only one without a female, but they didn't know what to say to encourage him, so they didn't mention it. But now that Mr. Kangaroo was very troubled by it, they were all moved with compassion for him, and they all stopped and gathered around him.

Mr. Pig spoke first, "I noticed that you didn't have a female, but I didn't want to mention it because I didn't know what to say. It was like the elephant in the room."

"The elephant in the room?" asked a confused Mr. Elephant. "What does that mean?"

"Yeah, what's that supposed to mean?" Mrs. Elephant asked.

"It means there's an obvious problem that no one wants to discuss," answered Mr. Pig.

"I don't get it," Mr. Elephant said.

"That's dumb," Mrs. Elephant replied.

"Never mind," Mr. Pig said. "Sorry I said it."

"Whatever," Mr. Beaver said. "Anyway, I don't understand why you don't have a female either. God is in control, which means there must be a reason why you don't have a female."

All the animals agreed.

"I know that God is in control, and I trust Him, but sometimes not knowing is very troubling," Mr. Kangaroo said.

"I know what you're saying," Mrs. Mongoose replied. "I wish I had the answer. I understand why it troubles you. All we can do is pray and continue trusting the Lord as we wait on Him."

"Let's pray right now," Mr. Lion said.

They all gathered around Mr. Kangaroo and closed their eyes and prayed to God that He would bring Mr. Kangaroo a female and give him the strength to continue especially when they don't understand.

After they prayed Mr. Kangaroo said, "I trust God, but it is very difficult to be with all of you couples while being the only one without a female. I'm lonely even though I'm not alone."

"Maybe your female is already at the Ark," Mrs. Sloth suggested.

"Yeah, I guess I never thought of that," Mr. Kangaroo replied. "I suppose I am worrying about nothing."

"We all love you, Mr. Kangaroo," Mrs. Sheep announced. All the animals nodded in agreement and gathered around Mr. Kangaroo to give him a hug.

"Thank you, guys. I love you too," he answered. "I'm thankful that God brought us together. I can't imagine what it would be like to have to travel to the Ark on my own."

With all the prayer and uplifting words, Mr. Kangaroo was very encouraged.

The animals continued traveling.

After a while of traveling, they suddenly heard rattling sounds coming from somewhere up ahead beyond some trees and brush…

Shicka shicka shicka shicka shicka.

All the animals stopped immediately in their tracks as several more rattle sounds joined in…

Shicka shicka shicka shicka shicka.

Shicka shicka shicka shicka shicka.
Shicka shicka shicka shicka shicka.

Mrs. Cow whispered to the others, "That sounds like rattlesnakes."

"It sure does," whispered Mrs. Elephant. "I'm afraid of snakes."

"Me too," Mr. and Mrs. Pig said in one voice.

"I'm afraid of snakes too," Mr. Bear said in a panicky tone.

"Me too," Mr. Rabbit said.

"Me too," Mr. and Mrs. Sloth said.

One by one all the animals said they were afraid of snakes until they got to Mr. Mongoose, who said confidently, "I'm not afraid of snakes."

"They're just snakes," Mrs. Mongoose said. "Why are you all so afraid of snakes?"

"They're so creepy the way they slither on the ground," answered Mrs. Hyena.

"They look so different than other animals," added Mr. Sheep. "They're long and skinny with no arms or legs."

"They look like the only thing they can do is bite," Mr. Hyena said with a shiver.

"They have a tiny creepy tongue that always sticks out like they're tasting the air or something," added Mr. Monkey.

"They always do that scary hissing sound," added Mrs. Elephant.

"That rattle sound freaks me out," added Mr. Beaver.

"And they have beady eyes with no eyelids," added Mr. Pig.

"You can't tell what they are looking at," added Mrs. Giraffe.

"And they always see you before you see them," stated Mrs. Bear.

"Do they ever sleep?" asked Mr. Monkey.

"I don't want to move until we know where they are," Mrs. Rabbit insisted.

Mr. Lion looked up at Mr. Giraffe and motioned for him to bend down. When Mr. Giraffe was close to Mr. Lion, he whispered to Mr. Giraffe, "Are you able to see over the trees? Tell us what you see."

Mr. Giraffe was about to take a step...

"Wait," Mrs. Giraffe whispered kind of loud. "You've already stepped in a rabbit hole, and then you also stumbled and bumped your head on a tree and gave us all away to the elephants. I'll take a look this time."

Mrs. Giraffe slowly stretched her neck over the top of the trees and stood motionless as she looked. Then she turned and bent her neck back down to Mr. Lion.

"What do you see?" Mr. Lion asked.

"I see several rattlesnakes surrounding a kangaroo," she answered.

"A kangaroo?" asked Mr. Kangaroo with an excited whisper.

"Yep, a kangaroo," Mrs. Giraffe replied.

"Shhhhhhhh, let's get closer and listen," whispered Mr. Kangaroo.

The animals inched closer until they could hear some voices. From beyond the brush, a female voice was crying and pleading, "Please leave me alone. I just want to get to the Ark before God's judgment comes."

The animals slowly peered through the brush to see a female kangaroo crying and pleading with several rattlesnakes that were taunting her as they surrounded her.

"Did God really say He's going to kill everyone?"[1] a crafty snake asked. "Surely God would not kill everyone."

"God sees all the evil, especially the humans," answered the sobbing female kangaroo. "And He is going to flood the earth and destroy all flesh. Now please let me go."

"God has common sense,"[2] another snake stated. "Surely He would not kill all the animals because of humans. That does not sound like a God who is fair."

"Yeah, think about what you're saying," another snake said. "You say God is going to kill everyone... Really?... Everyone?"

"I know it sounds strange, but God told me that judgment is coming," the female kangaroo replied.

"I can tell by your words that deep down even you don't believe what you're saying," the crafty snake said.

From behind the bushes, Mr. Kangaroo saw the female kangaroo and whispered to the other animals, "It's a female kangaroo, and she is talking about the coming judgment. That's Mrs. Kangaroo! That's Mrs. Kangaroo! And they're trying to deceive her!"

Suddenly, from behind the animals, came the sound of two more rattlesnakes, except their rattling was slower and quieter ...

Shicka...shicka...shicka...shicka...shicka.

All the animals turned around and saw two more rattlesnakes behind them.

"Oh no," whispered a scared Mrs. Hyena. "They found us, and now we're surrounded."

"See what I mean," Mrs. Bear confirmed. "I told you they always see us before we see them."

It was Mr. and Mrs. Snake.

"Shhhhhhhhh," whispered Mr. Snake. "We heard you whispering about the coming judgment. Don't be afraid. We are going to the Ark too. We were kicked out of our rhumba for preaching about the coming flood. We were about to leave when Mrs. Kangaroo came hopping by, and they stopped her and asked where she was going. She told them she was going to the Ark, they have been trying to change her mind ever since. They have been twisting her words."

"Yeah, we heard," answered Mr. Lion. "They are very crafty."

"We tried to save her, but we're outnumbered," Mr. Snake said. "We need to rescue her before they completely deceive her with their crafty words."

"What can we do to save her?" a frustrated Mrs. Bear asked. "We're all afraid of snakes."

"We're not afraid of snakes," answered a confident Mr. Mongoose.

"Boo!" shouted the deceiver snake as he came through the bushes and surprised the animals.

All the animals jumped back out of fear, except Mr. and Mrs. Mongoose.

The deceiver snake was followed by several other snakes who were forcing Mrs. Kangaroo along with them. The deceiver snake began rattling his tail...

Shicka shicka shicka shicka.

Then all the other snakes began rattling at once…

Shicka shicka shicka shicka shicka.

Shicka shicka shicka shicka shicka.

"Stop rattling, you're scaring me!" shouted Mrs. Kangaroo.

"Let Mrs. Kangaroo go," proclaimed Mr. Snake. "I told you, she's going to the Ark with us."

"*Sssssssss*….well, look at that," answered the deceiver snake. "Mr. and Mrs. Snake have returned to try and rescue Mrs. Kangaroo again."

"W-w-why won't you let her go?" Mr. Kangaroo asked while trembling.

"She's been deceived by her religion," a snake answered. "We're just helping her see the truth about religion. We're going to undeceive her."

"But she's not deceived, God is going to flood—" Mr. Kangaroo tried to respond, but the crafty snake quickly lunged forward until his face was just inches from Mr. Kangaroo's face, and he snapped his jaws shut.

Snap!

All the other animals screamed and jumped back, except Mr. and Mrs. Mongoose.

While rattling his tail and face-to-face with a visibly scared Mr. Kangaroo, the crafty snake said, "Stop with the religious nonsense, we've heard it all before. Keep it up, and I'll sink my fangs into you!"

"Give it up, snake," announced Mr. Mongoose. "You don't scare me at all. You're not going to sink your fangs into anybody."

"Leave Mrs. Kangaroo alone," Mrs. Mongoose said. "She's coming with us to the Ark before the flood comes."

"She's not going anywhere," the deceiver snake replied. "We've already convinced her that God never said anything about a flood or judgment. She clearly imagined it all just like you all did."

"They're lying!" a trembling Mrs. Kangaroo shouted. "God really did speak to me, and I did not misunderstand Him. Please help me, they won't let me go."

"We won't let you go until you forsake your religion," answered deceiver snake. "Religion poisons everything."[3]

"Why do you say that religion poisons everything?" asked Mr. Rabbit.

"Just listen to her!" answered deceiver snake. "She claims her God is going to flood the world in judgment and kill all living flesh. That sounds more like an evil God of an evil religion."

"Religion has poisoned her mind with this judgment nonsense," another snake said.

"Religion is evil,"[4] another snake proclaimed.

"This is why we need to rid the world of religion and any belief in God," another snake said. "So we can rid the world of evil."[5]

"So you think getting rid of religion will get rid of evil?" Mr. Mongoose asked.

"Yes, religion poisons everything because religion is evil," declared deceiver snake. "All kinds of fighting, violence, and death occur in the name of religion. The world would be so much more peaceful without religion."

"Believing in God makes everyone crazy," added another snake.

"Evil is happening all over the world, and it isn't coming from religion alone," Mr. Hyena replied. "Atheists are committing evil as well."

"If an atheist commits evil it's because they've been influenced in some way by religion," the deceiver snake said. "Once we get rid of religion, its effects will diminish and evil will finally be abolished."

"You have it backward," Mr. Mongoose answered. "Religion doesn't poison everything, everything poisons religion."

"Oh, okay, you're right," the deceiver snake replied sarcastically. "God killing everyone in a flood is normal. Happens all time. Dumb of me to think that God killing everyone is evil and poisonous."

"Evil comes from the heart because the heart is deceitful and wicked,"[6] answered Mrs. Hyena. "Our hearts will deceive us into believing we are good and that sin is no big deal.[7] Our hearts will deceive us into believing that we are right with God when we're not.[8] Our hearts will deceive us into believing that God wants us to do evil in His name.[9] Our hearts will deceive us so we don't take God's judgment seriously.[10] Our hearts will even deceive us into believing that there is no God[11] when in fact, unbelief is evil."[12]

Mr. Bear joined in, "It's obvious that evil poisons everything when you look at the world and see all the evil. If we just obeyed God, we would have peace on earth. Unfortunately, sin has corrupted our hearts to the point that the whole world has become violent and evil. God sees it all, and He is going to destroy all living flesh except those who trust Him and go to the Ark."

"You insist God is going to kill everyone. Do you animals even hear what you're saying?" asked another snake. "What kind of a God kills everyone just because of a little sin?"

"Sin is not a little problem," Mr. Lion answered. "Sin is serious.[13] Take a look around at all the evil that is continually happening. God sees it, and His judgment is coming."

"Your god is evil," answered a snake. "There is never a good reason to kill everyone."

"God is good, and we are all accountable to Him," Mrs. Bear said. "But there is no longer good in this world because sin has affected everyone so bad that God's judgment is coming,"[14]

"If your God is so good, then why does He allow so much evil?" another snake asked.

"God allows evil because He respects our free choices," Mr. Elephant replied.

"That's nonsense," another snake replied. "All this evil proves there is no God. Evil is just pain in a world of pain."[15]

"Even if there were a god, and there isn't, all this evil just proves he isn't good," the deceiver snake said.

"Evil can't exist unless good exists," answered Mr. Bear. "But good can't exist unless God exists. Therefore, if evil is real, and we all know it is, then God exists."[16]

"Evil is just an illusion,"[17] answered another snake.

"Evil is real, and everyone knows it," stated Mr. Sloth. "Evil is evidence that there is something wrong with this world."

"Without God there is no argument against evil because evil is just a matter of preference,"[18] Mr. Elephant said. "For example, you snakes say religion is evil. Others say atheism is evil. Others say evil is an illusion. And some even say that God is evil. No matter how we define evil, we all know evil exists."

"Apart from God, no one is good,"[19] added Mr. Pig. "Only God is good."[20]

"We don't need God to be good," replied deceiver snake.

"Agreed, you don't need God to be good," answered Mr. Lion. "But without God, *good* is a relative term just like *evil* is. Good is defined by whatever we think it is."

"Only God is good because He is righteous and holy," answered Mr. Mongoose. "God Himself is the standard that we use to measure goodness. Apart from God, nobody is good because of sin."

"Wow. You say that only God is good while at the same time you claim that God is going to murder all living flesh because He's mad at us," deceiver snake exclaimed. "Thanks for proving that religion is evil. Your God sounds like the most unpleasant character in all fiction."[21]

Another snake chimed in, "You believe that God created everything, that means God created evil, which means that God is responsible for evil."

"God did not create evil, nor is He responsible for it," Mr. Giraffe answered. "Evil came about through the exercise of free will, and we used our free will to rebel against God.[22] God is responsible for the fact of freedom, we creatures are responsible for our acts of freedom."[23]

"Doesn't your God care enough to stop evil?" deceiver snake asked.

"Yes," answered Mrs. Rabbit. "God does care enough to stop evil, that is why His judgment is coming."

"Everything is always about God's judgment!" exclaimed deceiver snake. "I've had enough of this poison. Take your poison and get out of here. Go to your Ark!"

"Okay, but we're bringing Mrs. Kangaroo and Mr. and Mrs. Snake with us," Mr. Mongoose declared.

"Don't be silly," deceiver snake replied. "I enjoy tormenting Mrs. Kangaroo. She's staying with us. Just a little while longer and she will know for sure that she imagined God and that all this religious stuff is poison. And as a matter of fact, Mr. and Mrs. Snake are staying with us also. We'll make sure they forsake your religious poison too."

Several other snakes slithered in position and surrounded Mrs. Kangaroo and Mr. and Mrs. Snake.

With a very stern voice, Mr. Mongoose replied, "We are bringing them with us, now back off!"

The deceiver snake looked to the other snakes and said, "Don't let them leave."

Then the deceiver snake turned back toward all the animals and said, "All of you need to leave now, or we will sink our fangs into all of you and watch each of you die from our deadly venom."

"All of you dying from our poison will mean less religious poison in this world," another snake said.

"You can't fight evil with evil,"[24] Mr. Mongoose said.

"Quiet, Mr. Mongoose!" the deceiver snake shouted. "You're annoying me. How about I drop you first?"

All the animals except Mr. and Mrs. Mongoose shrank back in fear.

"I am not afraid of you, snake!" a defiant Mr. Mongoose declared. "Let them go!"

The deceiver snake looked at Mr. Mongoose with his beady eyes and said, "I tell you what. Since you think you're so tough, I challenge you to a duel. If I bite you, I obviously win, because my poisonous venom will kill you, and then we'll sink our fangs into all your friends and watch them die too. If you win, I will release the three of them to go with you to your pretend Ark thing. The fate of all your friends is in this duel, and you don't have a chance. The only antidote to your poisonous religion is our poisonous fangs."

"The fate of my friends is in God's hands," answered a confident Mr. Mongoose. "I accept your challenge, this is going to be easy."

The deceiver snake coiled up to prepare to strike and hissed as he rattled his tail.

Shicka, shicka, shicka, shicka, shicka.

All the other snakes joined in the rattling.

Shicka, shicka, shicka, shicka, shicka.

Shicka, shicka, shicka, shicka, shicka.

Shicka, shicka, shicka, shicka, shicka.

All the animals feared for their lives except Mr. and Mrs. Mongoose.

Mrs. Mongoose chuckled as she watched the battle begin. "Ooooo, they're all rattling their tails. Oooo, I'm so scared. Ha ha ha ha ha."

The deceiver snake hissed again as he stared at Mr. Mongoose and prepared for a strike.

Mr. Mongoose danced around the deceiver snake as he planned his own attack.

Deceiver snake struck first; his body quickly lunged for Mr. Mongoose with a *whoosh*, only to snap his jaws shut around nothing as Mr. Mongoose dodged the oncoming fangs.

"Missed me, snake," taunted Mr. Mongoose. "I'm over here."

Whoosh. Snap.

Mr. Mongoose taunted again, "Missed again, snake. You're too slow."

Whoosh. Snap.

"Missed again."

Whoosh. Snap.

"Missed again."

Whoosh. Snap.

"Missed again."

Little did the deceiver snake know that Mr. Mongoose was strategically moving and weaving around and through the deceiver snake until he was tied in a knot, unable to move. The more he tried to move, the tighter he knotted himself.

"Look what you did to me!" shouted the panicked deceiver snake. "I'm tied in a knot, and I can't move."

"It's over, snake," declared Mr. Mongoose. "You lose. Tell your snake friends to let them go."

The deceiver snake looked to the other snakes and said, "Don't listen to him. Get over here and untie me."

One of the other snakes moved to help the deceiver snake, but Mrs. Mongoose step in front of him, "Don't even think about untying him, or I will tie you in a knot too."

The snake knew she meant it, and he turned around and slithered back to the other snakes.

Mr. Mongoose spoke with determination, "Tell your snake friends to let them go, or we will stay here and make sure nobody unties you."

"*Sssssssssssssssssss!*" the deceiver snake hissed from a knot. "Fine, you can have them. But just remember, your poisonous religion is worse than our fangs. Just look around the world at what your religion is doing—poisoning everyone's mind with this nonsense that God is going to murder all of creation just because of sin."

Then the deceiver snake turned to the other snakes and said, "Let them go."

The snakes backed away and let Mrs. Kangaroo and Mr. and Mrs. Snake join the other animals.

The snakes rattled in frustrated fear.

Shicka, shicka, shicka, shicka.

Then Mr. Mongoose looked at the other snakes and said, "Don't you dare untie him until we are far out of your sight."

The snakes were trembling and just nodded in agreement without saying a word.

"Let's go to the Ark," Mrs. Mongoose announced.

"Amen!" shouted Mrs. Monkey.

As they turned and began walking, Mr. Kangaroo looked at Mrs. Kangaroo with joy and happiness. She smiled with joy as she looked at Mr. Kangaroo. It was obvious to both of them that they would go to the Ark together with the rest of the animals.

"Welcome to our group, Mrs. Kangaroo," he said.

"Thank you, Mr. Kangaroo," she said. "It's a joy to be headed to the Ark with you."

Mr. Lion announced happily, "Well, Mr. Kangaroo, it looks like God answered our prayer for you."

"Indeed," Mr. Kangaroo agreed.

Mr. Hyena asked Mrs. Kangaroo, "How did you get trapped by those snakes?"

"One day God spoke to me about His coming judgment," Mrs. Kangaroo explained. "He said He would lead me to the Ark and that

He would never leave me nor forsake me. I told the other kangaroos how God spoke to me, but they just mocked and ridiculed me. None of them took God's judgment seriously. So I decided to head for the Ark on my own, even though I didn't know which way to go. I traveled for a while, and I would come across other animals and mention God's judgment to them. Each time they rejected God's judgment and laughed at the Ark. But they always mentioned that there were other animals going to the Ark, and I asked them each time which way they went. I just kept going where they pointed and trusting God that I would eventually meet your group or get to the Ark. Then I crossed that rhumba of rattlesnakes, and they stopped me and started trying to deceive me. They were pretty crafty how they twisted God's words. They wouldn't stop tormenting me, and I started crying and pleading with them, and that's when you guys showed up."

"Wow!" exclaimed Mr. Bear. "God had you on our trail the whole time."

"Yeah, and I want to thank Mr. Mongoose for saving my life from those snakes," a grateful Mrs. Kangaroo said. "Thank you, Mr. Mongoose, you really did save me."

"My pleasure," he answered. "Glory to God for our ability to take on snakes."

"I find it amazing that those snakes were using torment and deception to try and rid Mrs. Kangaroo of her so-called evil religion," Mrs. Mongoose said. "They were using evil to get rid of evil. Do you think they were aware of their own hypocrisy?"

"The ends justify the means in their world," answered Mr. Elephant.

"Hey, let's pray before we continue," Mrs. Lion said. "This has been a wild journey, and I don't want to go any farther without praying."

All the animals agreed and bowed their heads and prayed.

CHAPTER 17

The Horses
(Love)

The group of thirty animals continued on their way to the Ark, but now they were very happy and confident after seeing how God answered their prayers to bring Mr. Kangaroo a female. As they traveled, they marveled at how God was in control the whole time.

"God is so amazing!" Mr. Kangaroo exclaimed. "He was totally working things out the whole time!"

"God's timing was perfect," Mrs. Kangaroo added. "Right when I was trapped by those crafty deceiving snakes, God brings your group of animals across our path, and wouldn't you know it, Mr. Mongoose was in your group. Thank you again for saving me, Mr. Mongoose."

"My pleasure. All praise to God," he answered.

"From our perspective, nothing made sense," Mr. Lion said. "But God knew how and when Mr. and Mrs. Kangaroo would meet."

"It was all worth it," Mrs. Kangaroo said as she smiled at Mr. Kangaroo. "I would go through it all again to meet Mr. Kangaroo."

Mr. Kangaroo smiled.

"Thank You, God!" the whole group shouted as they praised God together. "We love You, and we praise You!"

Then the sound of rumbling interrupted their praise.

All the animals looked over to see an approaching herd of horses running toward their group.

"Those horses are running toward us," Mrs. Monkey said.

"Let's get out of their way," Mr. Snake said. "I don't want to be stepped on by a horse."

"Not yet," announced Mrs. Cow. "It looks like they see us."

The group of animals stood still as the horses came to a stop near the group. The leader horse spoke first, "Greetings, animals. We saw you in the distance smiling and laughing, so we came running to meet you."

Mr. Kangaroo tried to answer, "We were just expressing our love for—"

"Ah yes," leader horse interrupted. "I knew I saw love in the air when I saw all of you smiling and full of joy."

"Love always makes us happy," another horse declared.

"Love is all we need," added another horse.

"Love makes the world go round," another horse said.

"God is love,"[1] Mrs. Beaver said spontaneously. "And He is the source of love."

"Love is love regardless of what someone believes," another horse said.

A certain Mr. Horse stepped forward from within the group of horses and said, "Thank you, Mrs. Beaver, for telling my fellow horses that God is love. I've been trying to get them to understand that true love is rooted in God, but they reject it."

"We don't reject love," answered a horse. "We reject your God."

Then Mrs. Horse also stepped forward and said, "We have been trying to get our fellow horses to come to the Ark with us to escape God's judgment, but they won't come. They don't think such judgment would come from a loving God. What about you, animals, do you know about God's coming judgment?"

"Yes, we know about it!" Mr. Hyena answered with excitement. "In fact, we're on our way to the Ark, do you want to go with us?"

"Yes! We would love to," Mrs. Horse answered excitedly.

"How can we accept that your God is love when you keep saying that God told you He's going to destroy all flesh?" the leader horse asked. "What kind of love is that?"

"The whole world has become violent, evil, and unlovable, but God still loves us," Mrs. Sheep answered. "And He is providing an Ark to escape His judgment before the flood comes."[2]

"All this judgment talk is why we reject your twisted view of God's love," answered leader horse.

"Twisted view of love?" asked Mr. Elephant. "God commands us to love Him and our neighbor as ourselves. How is that twisted?"

"God commands us to love?" the leader horse asked with sarcasm. "That's seriously twisted. What good is love that comes from a command?"

"The reason God commanded us to love Him and others is because our hearts are corrupted by sin and we won't do it otherwise," Mrs. Bear answered.

"Speak for yourself, Mr. Holier Than Thou, my heart is fine," answered leader horse. "True love is from the heart. I would rather be loved by someone who means it from their heart than by someone who is doing it to please an angry God or to avoid His judgment. Being compelled to love is not true love. True love happens when we are free to do it."

"Yes, we are free to love, but because of our sinful nature, we use our freedom to reject the ultimate source of love, which is God," Mr. Lion answered. "This is why God commands us to love Him."

"Why would we love a God Who wants to kill everyone for not loving Him?" another horse asked.

"God does not want to kill everyone,"[3] answered Mrs. Sheep. "He wants to save everyone,[4] and that's why He told us to trust Him and go to the Ark before the flood comes."

"If God is truly loving, wouldn't He make certain that everyone goes to heaven?" asked leader horse.

"You can't have it both ways," Mr. Kangaroo replied. "You want the freedom to love who you want while at the same time deny God's love, then you want God to deny your freedom by forcing you into heaven even though you reject His love.[5] Do you hear the contradiction?"

"How is that a contradiction?" leader horse asked. "If your God is truly all-loving, then He would allow everyone into heaven regardless of what we do here on earth."

"God won't force anyone into heaven, just like He won't force anyone to go to the Ark,"[6] answered Mr. Giraffe. "God treats us with respect by honoring our free-will choices. If we choose to reject His love while we live on earth, then we are choosing to reject His love for all eternity. He will respect our choice and allow us to suffer the consequences in hell away from His love."

"So God sends us to hell because our love isn't perfect," answered leader horse. "That's crazy talk."

"God doesn't send anyone to hell," answered Mr. Pig. "We choose hell by rejecting God's love and denying His way of salvation and embracing our sinful nature instead."

"Oh c'mon," leader horse replied. "If your God is all-loving, then He can overlook a few sins."

"Sin is very serious," Mrs. Rabbit answered. "Heaven is a holy place that is not suited for those who reject God and choose to remain in their sin.[7] By trusting God and going to the Ark, He forgives our sins and we escape His judgment."

"Judgment, judgment, judgment—all I hear is God's judgment," another horse said. "Your love is rooted in a fear of God's judgment. True love is from the heart, not from fear."

"There is no fear in God's love,"[8] declared Mr. Rabbit. "His perfect love casts out fear because we escape His judgment by trusting Him and going to the Ark. The only ones who need to be afraid are those who reject God's love and do not go to the Ark."

"All this judgment talk is making it complicated," leader horse said. "True love is from the heart."

"True love is from God, and His love is not based on feelings," Mrs. Elephant said. "God's love is a responsibility, and He calls us to love everyone even our enemies."[9]

"Love our enemies?" asked leader horse. "That totally goes against our animal instincts. My enemies don't deserve my love. What good is loving my enemy if I don't feel it in my heart?"

"We need God's love to love our enemies," declared Mrs. Pig. "When we love God, He gives us the ability to love our enemies even if we don't feel it in our heart."

"We don't deserve God's love, yet He loves us," Mr. Sheep declared. "We were dead in our sins,[10] and we were His enemy,[11] and yet He is providing the Ark to save us."

"Dead in our sins?" another horse said. "We're not dead, yet you say we're dead in our sins. Then you say God is going to kill everybody for their sins. You're not even making sense."

"*Dead in our sins* means we are spiritually dead," Mr. Elephant answered. "And *spiritually dead* means we are separated from God because of our sin."

"Your view of love creates division because it puts God between you and those who disagree with you," another horse responded.

"Actually, the division comes from the conditions we put on love," answered Mrs. Beaver. "We tend to love only those who we think deserve it, but God wants us to love everyone, even those who hate us."

"What if we hate ourselves?" another horse asked. "If you don't love yourself, it's impossible for you to love anyone else. It's just not possible. You can't give away what you don't have."[12]

"It's sinful to hate yourself because you ultimately hate your Creator when you hate yourself,"[13] Mr. Horse answered.

"The way to overcome self-hatred is to love yourself," another horse declared.

"When you're trying to love yourself, you end up loving God less because you cannot love God and others while trying to elevate yourself," Mrs. Kangaroo answered. "This kind of self-love is sinful."

"I'm not talking about a sinful self-love," the horse answered. "I'm talking about proper self-love. If someone hates themselves or has low self-esteem, the solution is to love yourself and elevate your self-esteem so you can properly love others."[14]

"If hating ourselves is the problem, then thinking more about ourselves would not set us free but instead only further enslave us," Mrs. Horse answered. "One of the deceptions of self-esteem is to spend more time thinking about ourselves when thoughts of ourselves already consume us."[15]

"So how do you help someone who hates themselves?" leader horse asked.

"If your thoughts about yourself consume you, your problem is not low self-esteem, it's high self-esteem," Mrs. Bear answered. "A low estimation of yourself implies thinking of yourself less. Self-forgetfulness is the perfect mental attitude for serving others. [16] Instead of loving ourselves we need to deny ourselves."

"Why would a God of love not want His creatures to love themselves and have high self-esteem?" another horse asked.

"Our efforts must be always directed externally, toward God and others, because that is the nature of love,"[17] Mr. Pig answered. "The one who has high self-esteem is more controlled by what others think of them than what God thinks of them.[18] Fear of others or insecurity elevates the opinion of others above the opinion of God."

"How are we supposed to live life confidently if we don't have high self-esteem?" another horse asked.

"The answer is not high self-esteem or high self-confidence," Mr. Sheep answered. "The answer is to place our confidence in God. We need to look outside of ourselves to rest in the reality of someone far superior from ourselves.[19] The answer is to take our mind off ourselves and keep our mind fixed on God because He loves us."

Mr. Lion continued, "God is the answer for inner contentment and outer significance.[20] To be devoted to God is to be all we can be, which is the best we can be."

"Good mental health comes when we decrease and God increases,"[21] Mrs. Elephant added.

"None of this makes sense," the leader horse said as he was getting irritated. "Your God commands us to love even if it's not in our heart. Your God doesn't want us to love ourselves, your God rejects self-esteem. He rejects self-confidence, and to top it off, your God wants to destroy everybody in a flood. In the real world, your love is twisted and impossible, and it will fail."

"Yes, true love is impossible without God," answered Mrs. Snake. "The love we describe is the love of God, and God's love never fails. That's why we need God's love to truly love one another."

"This world is full of evil and violence," leader horse answered. "If your God is so loving, then why does He allow all this evil and violence?"

"God hates evil, and that is why He is going to judge it," answered Mr. Bull. "The command to love God and our enemy applies to everyone. The reason there's so much evil and violence is because everybody's love is rooted in themselves and those who love them back. This conditional love only results in constant evil, violence, and revenge against those we don't love. Without God, we will never truly love one another."

"God sees all the evil and violence, and He sees that it will never end, so He is going to destroy all flesh," Mr. Snake said.

"Your God is so loving that He is going to destroy all flesh," leader horse answered sarcastically. "You would think that a loving God would come up with a better idea than to just kill everyone."

"God has been very patient, and things are still getting worse,[22] Mr. Kangaroo answered. "God's ways are not our ways.[23] If loving ourselves or high self-esteem were the answer, God would not be destroying the world in a flood. God loves us so much that He is giving us a way to escape His judgment. All we have to do to escape His judgment is go to the Ark and enter it before the flood comes."

"Would any of you like to come with us to the Ark and escape the coming judgment?" Mrs. Lion asked.

"Definitely not!" answered leader horse. "You describe a bizarre God Who commands everybody to love Him but then He destroys them when they don't love Him. Sounds more like one of those evil dictators who demands to be worshipped only to kill those who don't."

"God is the Creator, and He is worthy of our love and worship," Mr. Bear declared. "Without God's love, evil will just continue spiraling out of control."

"It's no use," answered Mrs. Horse. "We've been trying for days to convince them that God is love and He is worthy of our love. They just keep rejecting it."

"We know what love is," leader horse replied. "We don't need a command from your God to love."

"Well then, we might as well get going to the Ark," Mr. Horse said.

All the animals agreed.

"Before we go, we would like to ask you all one last time, do you want to come with us to the Ark and escape God's coming judgment?" Mr. Lion asked.

"Same answer as before," leader horse replied. "Absolutely not. Why would we want to follow a God Who demonstrates His love by destroying all flesh?"

"God is demonstrating His love by providing an escape from His judgment,"[24] answered Mr. Hyena. "We love because He first loved us."[25]

"Whatever," leader horse replied.

"As you wish," answered Mrs. Kangaroo.

Mr. and Mrs. Horse joined the group, and the thirty-two animals left the horses and continued their journey to the Ark.

"Isn't it amazing how they think that a loving God is required to tolerate all sin?" Mr. Elephant asked.

"Yeah, they don't tolerate sins from their own family and friends but then claim that God is unloving because He doesn't tolerate their sin," Mr. Bear said.

"They seem to filter the uncomfortable truth about God's judgment but then apply these same truths in judging others and God," Mrs. Sheep said.

"I am thankful that God loves us enough to provide a way to escape His judgment," Mrs. Hyena said.

"Amen!" all the animals shouted in agreement.

"Let's pray before we continue," Mrs. Giraffe insisted.

They all agreed and paused to pray before continuing their journey to the Ark.

CHAPTER 18

The Hippopotamuses (Sexual Identity)

The group of thirty-two animals didn't travel long before they ran into some hippopotamuses.

"There's a group of hippos up ahead," Mr. Giraffe said.

"Let's make this quick," Mr. Lion insisted. "We'll just ask if any of them want to go with us to the Ark and then continue on."

"Exactly," Mr. Bear agreed. "I don't want to get caught up in another long fruitless debate."

As they approached the hippos, one of hippos saw the approaching animals and spoke first, "You animals are entering our territory, but I'm guessing by the diversity of your group that you're a friendly bunch."

"Yes, we are friendly, sir, and we're—"Mr. Beaver tried to answer but was quickly interrupted.

"Why did you just call me *sir*?" the male hippo asked angrily.

"What? I just thought since you're a male, that you—" Mr. Beaver tried to continue, but the hippo interrupted him again.

"Do you always judge others by their appearance?" asked the angry male hippo. "I identify as a female. You may call me *ma'am*."[1]

"Okaaaaaay...*ma'am*," answered a confused Mr. Beaver.

"But you're clearly a male," Mrs. Sheep said.

"My physical appearance does not define who I am,"[2] answered the transgender hippo. "I feel like a female, so that is what I choose to be."[3]

"And I feel like a male, so I identify as a male," another transgender hippo said. "You can call me *sir*."

"What?" asked a confused Mr. Giraffe.

"I'm gay," another hippo declared.

"So you choose to be gay?" Mr. Bear asked.

"I did not choose to be gay!" the gay hippo answered angrily. "I was born this way.[4] It's who I am."

"I'm a pansexual," another hippo declared. "I'm sexually attracted to every kind of animal, male or female, transgender, gay, lesbian, whatever."

Mr. Giraffe needed clarity, so he asked, "So each of you has chosen your own sexual identity based on how you feel regardless of your physical bodies?"[5]

"Not all of us," another hippo answered. "There are a couple of hippos who are still questioning their identity."

"I'm gender fluid," another hippo declared.

"Gender fluid?" asked Mr. Hyena. "What is that?"

"Gender fluid means I'm both male and female, depending on how I feel at any given moment," the gender fluid hippo answered. "Right now I am a male. But this morning I was a female."

A thoroughly puzzled Mrs. Mongoose looked at the two transgender hippos, and then she looked at the gender fluid hippo and asked, "Let me get this straight, he identifies as a *she*, and she identifies as a *he*, but you identify as *he* and *she*?"

"Yes, that's correct," the gender fluid hippo answered. "How do you all identify yourselves?"

"We all identify with the gender God gave us regardless of how we feel," Mr. Lion answered.

"So you're all cisgender," the gay hippo stated.

"What?" asked a confused Mrs. Lion.

"Cisgender means your feelings align with your physical body," another hippo answered.

Mr. Giraffe was thoroughly confused and asked, "God created each of us with an obvious specific gender.[6] How can you just choose to be whatever you feel like?"

"Thank you!" shouted Mr. Hippo from within the group of hippos. "That's what we've been trying to tell them, but they insist that they can choose any identity they want."

Mrs. Hippo joined Mr. Hippo and said, "Finally someone agrees with us that God created us with a specific gender."

"Wait, I thought the two of you were still questioning your identity," a transgender hippo asked while looking at Mr. and Mrs. Hippo.

"Once we mentioned God's coming judgment, we had to say we were questioning our identity to protect ourselves," Mr. Hippo answered.

"So the two of you were never really questioning but were cisgender the whole time?" the transgender hippo angrily asked.

"Yes," answered Mrs. Hippo. "We had to say we were questioning our identity to avoid all the attacks for being homophobic, bigoted, and judgmental haters."[7]

Mrs. Cow perceived that Mr. and Mrs. Hippo heard from God, and she quickly interrupted, "We're going to the Ark to escape God's judgment. Do you want to come with us?"

"Yes, yes! We want to come with you!" answered Mrs. Hippo. "God spoke to us about the coming flood."

"God spoke to each of us too!" exclaimed Mr. Rabbit.

"We tried and tried to tell the other hippos about the coming judgment, but the more we mentioned it, the angrier they got, so we had to pretend that we were still questioning our sexual identity," Mrs. Hippo said.

"So you went into the closet to hide your true identity?" a lesbian hippo asked.

"We had to," answered Mrs. Hippo. "You started threatening our lives once we mentioned God's coming judgment."

Mr. Beaver wanted to hurry this confusing conversation along, so he spoke next, "It's true. God's judgment is coming. Why don't you hippos come with us to the Ark and escape the flood?"

"Why would we believe in a God Who created us with a diversity of sexual feelings only to kill us for agreeing with the way He created us?" the pansexual hippo asked. "That's like a cruel joke."[8]

"God created you with the body He wanted you to have, and the goal is to live in harmony with the body He gave you,"[9] Mr. Horse answered.

"That's easy for you to say," answered the gay hippo. "You weren't born with same-sex attraction like me."

"I once identified as a lesbian," Mrs. Hippo answered. "But I finally decided to accept my body as God's good gift to me, and over time I became attracted to males, and that's how I met Mr. Hippo."[10]

"If you are no longer lesbian, then you never really were gay," the gay hippo replied. "I prayed for years that God would take away my same-sex attraction, but it never happened.[11] Then I realized that God made me this way, and I embraced my gay identity, and now I'm happy."

"God didn't make you gay," Mr. Hippo answered. "Our sinful desires show how sin has distorted us, they are not a reflection of how God made us.[12] Homosexual behavior is forbidden just like any other sin."

"According to your God, same-sex attraction is a sin, so that means only straight animals have a right to love," the lesbian hippo answered. "That's not fair, and that's not right."

"God wants us to love everybody," Mrs. Bear answered. "God would never forbid anyone to love. What God does not want is a relationship based on sin. We don't choose our feelings, but we do choose our behavior and how we respond to temptation.[13] If we have feelings contrary to the way He created us, then we have to deny ourselves."

"God wants us to choose holiness,"[14] Mrs. Beaver said.

"This is ridiculous," a transgender hippo replied. "How are we supposed to deny who we are? Fate has given us our body, and we can do with it as we choose."[15]

"Refusing to act on our feelings is repression and self-hatred," the pansexual hippo said.

"God has created us to live in harmony with the body He gave us," Mrs. Hippo answered. "True and lasting happiness is when we choose an identity that is in harmony with our entire being, which includes our body."[16]

"I have never been happier than when I openly affirmed my same-sex feelings," the gay hippo insisted.

"Your happiness is rooted in your feelings rather than in God's good design," Mr. Elephant answered. "You cannot be whole when your feelings are at war with the body God gave you."[17]

"My feelings define my true authentic self, not my body,"[18] the pansexual hippo answered. "If I go with my body, I will never be happy."

"Gender identity demeans the body because it alienates us from our God-given body,"[19] Mr. Lion said.

"I am not alienating my body," the lesbian hippo answered. "I'm just not allowing it to define who I am. It's my body, and I can do what I want with it."

"Our body is a good gift from God, and it is integral to our entire being,"[20] Mrs. Bear answered. "You cannot do what you want with it."

"Your God is harsh and judgmental," the transgender hippo declared. "He wants us to reject our natural feelings."

"God's ways are right because they're based on respect for our bodies as an integral part of our entire being," Mrs. Monkey answered. "Our body is an observable fact that does not change, it makes sense to treat it as a reliable marker for sexual identity."[21]

"I'm sick of you, haters!" a fed-up gender fluid hippo shouted. "Now get out of here before we drive you out of here ourselves!"

Mr. Hippo looked at the other animals and said, "Now you know why we went into the closet with our true identity."

"Who wants a God who won't let us be who we are?" the gay hippo answered. "Take your judgmental bigotry and your mean, backward thinking God and go to your Ark."

"And take your hate with you too!" shouted the lesbian hippo.

"Fine, we will go," answered Mr. Lion. "But let me ask you all one more time. Do any of you want to go with us to the Ark to escape God's coming judgment?"

"No!" shouted all the hippos in one loud voice,

"You heard them," answered Mr. Lion. "Let's go."

Mr. and Mrs. Hippo joined the animals, and they left the rest of the hippos behind to continue their journey to the Ark.

"Atheists believe that only what they see defines reality, but these hippos reject what they see in their body and believe that their feelings define reality," Mr. Elephant said as they traveled.

"And they only tolerate those who affirm their feelings," Mr. Hippo said.

"If they continue to dishonor their body, God will give them over to their sinful desires,"[22] Mrs. Cow said.

"It looks like God already gave them over to their sin since they reject salvation in the Ark," Mr. Hyena said.

"I think we've come across every argument against God that exists," Mr. Mongoose answered.

"I wonder what's next?" asked Mr. Hyena.

"I didn't say a word during that discussion, but just listening to it wore me out," Mr. Bull answered. "Let's pray before we continue."

All the animals enthusiastically agreed, and they all stopped to pray.

CHAPTER 19

The Camels
(Socialism/Communism)

Much time had passed since the encounter with the hippos, and the group of thirty-four animals had traveled far. It was unusually peaceful after all they had been through.

"It's nice and calm for a change. Do you think we are close to the Ark?" Mr. Kangaroo asked.

"I hope so, but only God knows for sure," Mr. Mongoose answered.

"I hope so too," Mrs. Hyena said. "We need to trust God all the way to the Ark."

"Indeed," Mr. Monkey agreed.

"Hold on," Mr. Lion said as he looked ahead in the distance. "I see animals way over there."

"There are animals over there too," Mr. Hippo said as he looked in another direction.

"I see dinosaurs too!" Mrs. Pig said with a quiver.

"The animals don't seem to be afraid of the dinosaurs," Mr. Hyena noticed.

"Maybe they're getting along because they're going to the Ark too!" Mrs. Horse said with excitement. "Maybe we're close to the Ark."

All the animals in the group began to get excited over the possibility that the journey to the Ark might be over.

"I don't know, hold your excitement," Mr. Elephant cautioned. "Something doesn't seem right."

As the group slowly walked with caution, they began to notice that there were many different animals and dinosaurs coming into view. There didn't seem to be any hostility, and some animals were working to gather food or something. None of the dinosaurs were working, but instead they seemed to be watching and even policing the animals. There didn't seem to be any socializing among the animals. The animals were working, but not very enthusiastically even though everything seemed very orderly.[1]

"Wow, it looks like the animals are living peacefully with the dinosaurs," Mr. Hippo said.

"But the dinosaurs seem to be policing the community," Mr. Lion stated.

As the group got closer, they saw what seemed to be every kind of animal in the community, including the same kind of animals in their own group.

"Hold up," insisted Mrs. Cow. "Let's wait here and watch for a while until we figure out what's going on."

The group paused to watch the animals work. Some horses, camels, and other animals were arriving with various kinds of food such as hay, fruits, vegetables, and other plant foods. Other animals were gathering the delivered food and taking it to a holding area that was being guarded by several utahraptors. Other utahraptors were watching closely as a couple of monkeys passed out food to animals waiting in line to eat. As each animal received their food, they took it to a large community type of eating area to eat. While they ate, they were all listening to a triceratops give a lecture.

There were several T-Rexes walking around keeping order. Everything seemed orderly and controlled.

Then a few stegosauruses came walking through the community announcing to the working animals, "Shift change!"

As soon as the stegosauruses announced this shift change, the working animals stopped and went to stand in line for food while other animals immediately began working in their place, gathering food.

"It's like the dinosaurs are in charge and all the animals take turns doing the work," Mr. Sheep said.

"And the animals seem to be cooperating without opposing or trying to escape," Mr. Horse added.

"This is weird," Mrs. Bear said.

"Look up there!" declared Mr. Hippo as he looked to the sky.

"It's a pterosaur," Mr. Rabbit said. "It sees us."

The pterosaur circled around the animals from above then flew away.

"It flew away," Mrs. Rabbit said. "What do we do?"

"Something is really strange about all this," Mrs. Sloth said.

"After all we've been through, we need to pray for God's favor before we do anything," Mrs. Mongoose insisted.

"Definitely!" answered Mrs. Monkey.

The entire group overwhelmingly agreed, and they bowed their heads as Mr. Lion prayed, *"Oh, God, we come to You thankful for Your continued guidance as we head to the Ark. We come to You asking for Your favor as we have come across a strange community and—"*

"Praying in public, you're all busted!" shouted a spinosaurus.

The group opened their eyes to see that they were surrounded by several spinosauruses.

"Busted? What?" asked a shocked Mr. Bull.

"Busted for praying in public?" Mr. Giraffe asked.

"That's right," a spinosaurus answered. "We have zero tolerance for public expression of religion."

"Zero tolerance? Why?" asked Mr. Pig.

"Religion is just an opiate for repressed individuals, and it's no longer needed in a perfect society,"[2] the spinosaurus answered. "Now come with us. You're all going to jail."

"Jail...for praying?' asked Mr. Bear.

"You'll have your chance to explain yourself in court," answered spinosaurus. "In the meantime, you need to cooperate. Cooperation is essential in a perfect society."

The group was led off to jail by several spinosauruses.

"A perfect society?" asked Mr. Sloth. "What does that mean?"

"Look around," the spinosaurus said. "All the animals are working together for the good of all.[3] It's the cleanest, neatest, most efficiently operating piece of social machinery you'll ever see.[4] It's a perfect society."

"What about the dinosaurs?" asked Mr. Snake. "How come they're not working?"

"We keep order," the spinosaurus said. "Each of us has specific duties to maintain a perfect society. I'm warning you right now to watch what you say because the T-Rexes police the community, and they stifle any restricted speech patterns the moment they arise."[5]

"Restricted speech patterns?" asked Mr. Mongoose. "Like what?"

"In a perfect society, there is zero tolerance for pointless chatter, gossip, or too much speaking of any kind,"[6] the spinosuarus answered, "That's how factions get started."

Another spinosuarus continued, "The utahraptors keep watch on the food supply and make sure it gets spread out equally to the community eating centers.[7] There are other dinosaurs throughout the community with various responsibilities to maintain our perfect society. Any illegal activity, behavior, or unrest is immediately squashed. Don't even think about escaping because the air is patrolled by pterosaurs, and they will see you. In fact, they spotted your group and reported your location to us. Only us dinosaurs make the laws and maintain order because we know what's best for all."[8]

"What is your responsibility in this perfect society?" asked Mrs. Giraffe.

"We are the religious police," answered spinosuarus. "We squash any activity, behavior, or unrest that we deem to be religious.[9] We caught you animals praying. That is a flagrant and offensive violation of our strict religious laws in our perfect society."

"Who are you accountable to?" asked Mr. Snake.

"We are accountable to ourselves," answered spinosuarus. "We know what's best for all the animals."[10]

"That doesn't seem right," Mrs. Kangaroo said.

"Excuse me?" asked spinosuarus in a disturbed tone. "I just told you that we dinosaurs know what's best for all. If you continue to question right and wrong, then I will call the morality police."[11]

"Morality police?" asked Mr. Bull.

"The triceratopses are the morality police," the spinosaurus answered. "They ensure perfect morality in our perfect society. Trust me, you don't want me to call the triceratops as they are very harsh to those who question right and wrong. You're already being charged with flagrant disregard for public religious laws against the free exercise of religion, you don't want to add a morality violation to your rap sheet before you see the judge."

"I'm sorry," Mrs. Kangaroo answered. "I did not mean to question your authority."

"You are in serious trouble," the spinosuarus responded. "Since you're new here, I will accept your apology. You are in our community now. You will obey our rules."

At this point they had reached the jail, which was a cave in the side of a small mountain. A spinosuarus looked at the animals and said, "Get in the cave."

All the animals went into the cave because escaping seemed impossible with so many dinosaurs everywhere and the dinosaurs were much stronger. The cave was guarded by a couple of ornithopods. The cave had a very small opening, which caused Mr. and Mrs. Hippo to almost get stuck, and Mr. and Mrs. Giraffe had to stoop low and bend their necks to enter. Once inside, the cave was just large enough to fit all the animals. The small opening provided a little light inside the cave.

"Wow, this cave is kinda big," Mr. Snake said.

"That's easy for you to say, you're a snake," Mr. Hippo answered. "The rest of us have barely enough room to move."

Mr. Monkey decided to check for an echo, and he yelled, "Hello!"

The echo immediately followed: Hello! Hello! Hello... Hello... Hello.

Another voice from within the cave responded, "Hello!"

The echo immediately followed: Hello! Hello! Hello... Hello... Hello.

"Who's there?" (Who's there...who's there...who's there...) asked Mr. Monkey.

Clop clop clop came the sound of hooves on the ground as two camels came walking from inside the cave.

"It's me and Mrs. Camel," answered Mr. Camel as they approached the other animals. "Let me guess, you all broke some law and disrupted the perfect society and they arrested you."

"How did you know?" asked Mr. Lion.

"This cave is their jail," answered Mrs. Camel. "The only reason anyone comes in this cave is because the all-powerful, centralized dinosaur government arrested them. What did they get you for?"

"Praying in public," answered Mrs. Beaver. "They said we violated their law against any public expression of religion."

"Yep, zero tolerance for praying in public for sure," Mr. Camel replied.

"What are you and Mrs. Camel in here for?" Mrs. Horse asked.

"We were warning everyone about God's coming judgment," Mr. Camel answered.

"God's coming judgment!" exclaimed Mr. Mongoose. "Did God speak to you and tell you to go to the Ark?"

"Yes, do you know about God's coming flood too?" asked Mrs. Camel.

"We sure do," answered Mr. Hyena. "We were on our way to the Ark when we came upon this community. Everything looked weird with all the animals and dinosaurs together that we decided to pray, and before we opened our eyes, they busted us."

"Oh yeah, that's an easy bust," answered Mrs. Camel. "They have strict laws that do not allow any form of public expression of religion or faith."

"Why do they have laws against religion and faith?" asked Mr. Kangaroo.

"They consider this to be a perfect society," answered Mr. Camel. "They say that religion causes division, so they don't allow any religion, especially in public. The only faith that is allowed is faith in the government. Love of government is the highest virtue."[12]

"Faith in government?" asked Mr. Sheep. "Without God and His righteousness, how does anybody know what's right and wrong?"

"All citizens are required to listen to morality sermons during communal dinners,"[13] Mr. Camel answered.

"Oh yeah, we saw a triceratops speaking to the animals as they ate at one of those dinners," Mr. Bear said.

"Yep, he was lecturing everybody on what's right and wrong in a perfect society," Mrs. Camel answered. "In reality they are telling them what to think because citizens are forbidden to think for themselves."[14]

"This place is crazy!" exclaimed Mr. Pig. "How long have you two been in here?"

"We've been in jail for a couple of days, but we've been in this community for a long time," Mr. Camel answered. "Our parents raised us here."

"What is going on around here?" Mrs. Lion asked. "What's with the animals all working and the dinosaurs in control?"

"It happened gradually over time," answered Mrs. Camel. "This whole entire region used to be very civil and orderly without the dinosaurs in control. There wasn't a big centralized government or anything like it, the animals didn't need one because they all governed themselves according to God's righteousness."[15]

"All the animals used to be free to govern themselves?" asked Mr. Hyena.

"Yes," answered Mrs. Camel. "And it was amazing how the fear of God in everyone's heart kept them accountable to God in their behavior because they hated evil."[16]

"Wow, that must have been a long time ago, because except for us, nobody believes in God anymore," Mrs. Sheep said.

"Actually, it wasn't that long ago at all," Mr. Camel said. "Freedom is a fragile thing and is never more than one generation away from extinction."[17]

"So what happened to the God-fearing community?" asked Mr. Snake.

Mr. Camel continued, "Well, the dinosaurs began making friends with all the animals, and they slowly, little by little, started undermining God's righteousness with opposite values. They began by destroying the position of the family as the basic building block of society."[18]

"How did they do that?" asked Mr. Kangaroo.

"They changed the values of the entire society through entertainment, media, and even the education system,"[19] answered Mrs. Camel. "God's morality was undermined through the promotion of free love and promiscuity.[20] Sexual liberation was used to manipulate and control others.[21] Sexual modesty is now regarded as obscene prudery."[22]

"Wow, how deceptive," Mr. Sheep said.

"They believed that truth is not important if a lie will further the attainment of a worthy goal,"[23] Mrs. Camel answered.

"That's not all," Mr. Camel continued. "They changed the whole society through lying.[24] It used to be that everybody understood that you work for your own food. The poor and weak were provided for through charitable giving, and everyone knew that stealing was wrong. But the dinosaurs pitted the strong against the weak by convincing the weaker animals that they were suffering and being oppressed by the stronger animals. Eventually the weaker animals believed they were entitled to anything the stronger animals had. The dinosaurs forced the strong to help the weak by eliminating the idea of charity and instead calling it justice."[25]

"So they made the weak envy the strong," noted Mr. Sheep.

"Yes," answered Mr. Camel. "The dinosaurs also pitted the males against the females by making the females think they were equal and no different than the males. They made the females believe that they've always been systematically oppressed by males through the enforcement of patronizing gender roles."[26]

"So they took God's good design of male and female with different roles and turned it into an unfair equality issue," Mrs. Elephant said.

"Yep," answered Mr. Camel. "As a result, fatherhood was deemed unnecessary and the females believed they required the aid and protection of the government."

"So these feminists sought the banishment of fathers from family life, making mothers totally dependent on the government?"[27] Mrs. Hippo asked.

"That's right," answered Mrs. Camel. "They made the citizens believe that everything has always been racist, sexist, homophobic, and whatever else. The dinosaurs were just pointing it all out.[28] They pitted every animal kind against each other by making them feel they were being oppressed by another kind of animal. They basically made every animal feel that they were victims of an unfair animal kingdom. There was great division and unrest."

"It sounds like they made all the animals rely on their feelings rather than God's righteousness," Mr. Giraffe said.

"That's exactly what they did," Mrs. Camel answered. "And it escalated into major unrest. Fighting began to increase as every animal felt they were a victim of some kind of abuse."

"Why didn't the animals defend God's righteousness?" Mrs. Bear asked.

"They used to, but the dinosaurs labeled any righteous beliefs with a phobia," Mrs. Camel answered. "And phobia was made to be equal to bigotry."[29]

"They changed the culture by making unrighteousness seem logical and God's righteousness seem illogical,"[30] Mr. Beaver noted.

"Yep," answered Mr. Camel. "Their goal was to destroy social norms and create a state of chaos that allowed radical change."[31]

"It sounds like nobody noticed the melting away of their liberty," Mr. Monkey stated.

"Exactly," answered Mrs. Camel. "The cultural change seemed like a completely organic and natural process."[32]

"Anyway," Mr. Camel continued, "the fighting got out of control. All the animals were fighting about everything because everything offended someone."

"What about the dinosaurs, were they fighting?" asked Mrs. Bear.

"No, not the dinosaurs," answered Mrs. Camel. "They were the ones who planned this all along. After they undermined God's righteousness and turned the society upside down, they promised to restore order if all the animals would trust them. The citizens felt it was necessary to trade in their personal liberties in exchange for their safety."[33]

"Wow, their plan seemed to work perfectly," Mr. Sloth replied.

"Yes, the dinosaurs' plan worked," answered Mr. Camel. "It worked because they were patient as it took years to undermine God's righteousness. Eventually they were able to teach everyone to rely on their feelings and they would pass their feelings-based value system to their children and so on until they had a morally confused society completely ignorant of God's righteousness."

"Speaking of children," Mrs. Beaver said, "I don't see any babies or children, where are they?"

"Pregnant animals are under the care of the Birth Approval Committee,"[34] Mr. Camel answered. "They ensure that only healthy and useful babies are born and raised."

"Healthy and useful?" asked Mr. Beaver. "What does that mean?'

"Babies that appear to have birth defects[35] or a weakness or are deemed to be inconvenient for any reason are eliminated because they have no value in a perfect society,"[36] Mrs. Camel answered.

"That's horrible," announced Mrs. Sheep.

"Indeed it is," Mrs. Camel continued. "Children are raised without parents, no knowledge of God, and no memory of the past. This way they can be molded into selfless, obedient workers, untroubled by any original thoughts or individual differences. This enables the government to foster in them an atmosphere of total dependence on the government."[37]

"No wonder all the animals are working peacefully with the dinosaurs," Mr. Beaver said. "They were raised to depend on the dinosaurs."

"Everything is so twisted," declared Mrs. Lion.

"By changing the values of each animal, the dinosaurs were able to destroy the community from within," Mrs. Pig noted.

"Exactly," answered Mr. Camel. "The undermining of God's righteousness was their method of conquest.[38] Eventually the animals were desperate for peace, so they relented and put their hope in the dinosaurs. The dinosaur government restored the citizens' happiness by removing their freedom"[39]

"Wow, they traded their freedom for a counterfeit happiness," Mrs. Hippo declared.

Mrs. Camel continued, "Once the dinosaurs got the trust of the animals, they took control and formed an all-powerful centralized government of dinosaurs who controlled every aspect of the animal's community. The dinosaurs controlled all the labor assignments, all the food, how the food will be redistributed, and so on."

"Why don't they allow praying or religion?" asked Mr. Bull.

"Because they believe that religion requires faith in a God or something other than the all-powerful government, which is contrary to their perfect society," answered Mr. Camel. "They believe that individuals only turn to religion when they are oppressed by inequality. By outlawing religion, they keep animals believing this society is perfect because of the government."

"So here we are," Mr. Bear replied. "In jail because we disrupted a perfect society by praying."

"I trust God to get us out of here," stated Mr. Mongoose. "Mr. and Mrs. Camel, when God gets us out of here, will you join us on our way to the Ark?"

"Of course," answered Mr. and Mrs. Camel together.

"We need to violate another religious law right now and pray right now," Mr. Lion declared.

"Agreed!" all the animals exclaimed.

They all bowed their heads and prayed in the cave.

Shortly after they prayed, several ankylosauruses showed up at the cave opening. "It's time for all you PSDs to see the judge," declared one of the ankylosauruses. "Follow us, and don't even think about trying to escape. It's our sole responsibility to make sure all PSDs make it to court without any further disruption."

"What's a PSD?" asked Mr. Mongoose.

"PSD is a perfect society disrupter," an ankylosaurus answered. "You are all guilty of disrupting our perfect society with your public religious expression."

"What do you think the judge will do to us?" asked Mrs. Sheep.

"That all depends on your attitude," an ankylosaurus answered. "You can be set free today if you convince the judge that you will obey the rules of our perfect society."

"Has that ever happened?" asked Mr. Hyena. "I mean, has anyone ever been arrested and immediately set free?"

"Yes," the ankylosaurus answered. "A while back an animal unknowingly came into our perfect society and was arrested when a utahraptor caught him eating unauthorized food. The judge immediately set him free when he promised to eat only at the community eating centers and use his labor skills to work for the good of all in our perfect society."

"Unauthorized food?" Mr. Bull asked. "What does that mean?"

"The only food any animal is allowed to eat is food that has been distributed to each of them by the food police at the community eating centers," the ankylosaurus answered.

"Food police?" asked Mr. Monkey.

"The utahraptors," answered and irritated ankylosaur. "The utahraptors are the food police."

"Oh yeah," answered Mrs. Snake. "They were the ones watching the distribution of food at the eating center."

After several minutes of walking, the animals arrived at a large hole that was dug out of the ground that was large enough for all the animals to fit inside. The hole had several logs laid side by side in the form of a ramp to the bottom of the hole.

"Welcome to court," stated an ankylosaurus. "Go down the ramp and wait in the hole. The judge is on his way now."

All the animals went down the ramp, and as soon as they were all in the hole, a brontosaurus removed the ramp logs so the animals could not get out of the hole.

The brontosaurus ordered, "Keep quiet and wait for the judge."

The animals were each whispering a prayer to God.

Within minutes the judge arrived, and he was a diplodocus with a very large and long, whipping tail. The diplodocus judge whipped his tail into the ground—*whack!*

"Order in the court!" the brontosaurus shouted.

All the animals were trembling as they looked up from the hole at the judge.

The judge began, "It is my understanding that you all have been arrested for disrupting our perfect society by violating our strict antireligious laws. Mr. and Mrs. Camel, you are here for preaching your God's judgment. Is this true?"

"Yes, Your Honor," answered Mr. Camel.

The judge continued and said, "The rest of you are here for praying in public. Is this true?"

"Yes, Your Honor," Mr. Lion answered.

The judge continued, "It is my understanding that all of you, except Mr. and Mrs. Camel, are new to our perfect society, is this true?"

"Yes, we're new here," answered Mr. Kangaroo. "We were just passing through and—"

"Silence!" ordered the diplodocus judge. "It doesn't matter how or why you came to our perfect society. The fact is that you are here now and you broke our laws by praying openly in public. Mr. and Mrs. Camel understand the laws of our perfect society, and yet they still broke our laws by preaching their God's judgment. The punishment for them will be continued jail time while they undergo three months of sensitivity training."

"But, Your Honor—" Mr. Kangaroo tried to object.

"Silence!" ordered the diplodocus judge as he swung his tail around and smashed it into the ground with a *whack*!

The brontosaurus shouted, "Do not speak unless the judge orders you to speak."

The diplodocus judge continued, "Us dinosaurs are much stronger, better, and smarter than all other animals, and we know what's best for all animals, which is why we run the prefect society. We have created a society that has no violence, no division, no hatred, and no crime. All capable animals work for the good of all. No animal is without work or food. Our perfect society is based on a very simple philosophy—which is, "From each according to his ability, to each according to his needs."[40] From what I can see, all of you animals look like you are all able to physically work, is this correct?"

"Yes," answered Mr. Elephant.

"Good," the judge continued. "Then we can expunge your violations from your record and make this all go away and set you free under two conditions. One, you agree to never pray, preach, teach, worship, or perform any other activity deemed religious in public or private, and two, you agree to use your labor skills to work for the good of all in our perfect society. This is your best option. Do you agree to the terms of this court?"

All the animals stood silent, not knowing how to respond.

But then Mr. Kangaroo spoke and said, "Your Honor, we do not agree. You have given us the choice between obeying God or obeying you. We choose to obey God.[41] We will never stop praying, preaching, teaching, or worshipping. In fact, we are going to the Ark with Mr. and Mrs. Camel to escape God's coming judgment. We would like to know if you want to come to the Ark with us."

"GRRRRRRRR!" growled the diplodocus judge. *Crack!* came the sound of his tail as he whipped it within inches of Mr. Kangaroo's head.

"You have offended the judge greatly!" shouted brontosaurus. "This is not good!"

The judge whipped his tail around and cracked it at a tree, causing the tree to snap in half, leaving a stump while the top half fell to the ground violently.

"I will have none of this!" demanded the judge. "Put them in darkness tonight, and they too will spend the next three months with the camels going through sensitivity training starting tomorrow morning. They *will* conform to our perfect society. Now take them away!" The diplodocus judge stomped away while snapping more trees with his tail.

The brontosaurus put the ramp logs in place and called the animals to exit the hole.

The animals were trembling as they came out of the hole.

The ankylosauruses led the animals back to the cave.

As they were walking back to the cave, Mrs. Sheep asked, "Why won't the judge let us just leave and continue our journey to the Ark?"

"Let me put it another way," the ankylosaurus answered. "Our society is perfect because we got rid of religion. We know that once you go through sensitivity training, you will come out understanding that you don't need God anymore because all your needs will be provided to you by our dinosaur government. This will motivate you to embrace our perfect society and do your part to contribute to the good of all."

Mr. Mongoose whispered to Mr. Bear, "Sensitivity training sounds more like dinosaur brainwashing."[42]

"Quiet," whispered Mr. Hyena. "You're going to get us in more trouble."

All the animals kept quiet until they got to the cave. As they entered the cave, Mrs. Hippo almost got stuck again, and Mr. and Mrs. Giraffe had to stoop low again and bend their necks to get into the cave.

"What are we gonna do?" Mrs. Mongoose asked in a panicky tone.

"We're going to pray and trust God to get us out of here," answered Mr. Lion.

All the animals prayed a desperate prayer to God to get them out of this perfect society.

After the animals prayed, the ornithopods moved a large rock over the cave opening.

Suddenly all thirty-six animals were in total darkness…more like total blackness.

CHAPTER 20

The Bats
(Worldviews)

There were now thirty-six animals headed to the Ark, but now they were locked inside a cave in total darkness for breaking the antireligious laws of the perfect society. They were locked in total darkness until morning when their sensitivity training would begin.

"It's totally dark in here!" shouted Mr. Beaver.

"I can't see anything," Mrs. Monkey said.

"I can't even see my own trunk between my eyes," Mr. Elephant said.

"Relax," Mr. Lion said. "Everybody just calm down, there's no need to panic."

"How is God going to get us out of this cave?" Mr. Giraffe asked.

"How are we going to get to the Ark before God's judgment if we're stuck taking sensitivity training for three months?" Mr. Bear asked.

"This cave is deep, maybe we can find another way out," Mr. Sloth suggested.

"How are we supposed to find a way out when we can't even see where we're going?" asked Mrs. Horse.

"Mrs. Camel and I have already searched deep inside this cave, and we didn't find any other way out," Mr. Camel answered.

"What are we supposed to do?" Mr. Monkey asked.

"Maybe we can escape during sensitivity training?" Mrs. Hyena suggested.

"How can we escape with all the dinosaurs everywhere and the pterosaurs patrolling the sky?" Mr. Rabbit asked.

From a sad voice, Mrs. Hippo said, "Looks like we're stuck in this darkness with no way out."

"We know the way out," a small voice said.

"What? Who said that?" asked Mr. Pig.

"I said it. I'm a bat," answered Mr. Bat from the darkness. "Me and Mrs. Bat know another way out of here."

"How do you know the way out when it's totally black in here?" asked Mr. Bull.

"We're bats," answered Mrs. Bat. "God equipped us with an awesome sonar system that allows us to navigate in the dark."

Mr. Bat continued, "We were listening to you all talk, and we heard you mention the Ark and God's coming judgment. God spoke to us about His coming judgment and the Ark. We didn't know where to go or what to do, but when I heard you mention God and the Ark, I knew I'd better speak up."

"Do you want to come with us to the Ark?" asked Mr. Lion.

"Yes, of course," answered Mrs. Bat.

"How will we get out of here?" asked Mrs. Beaver.

"I will use my sonar to lead you to the other side of the cave where there is another opening," Mr. Bat answered. "Keep quiet, and follow my voice. I will keep saying 'This way.' It's kind of far to the other side, so just follow my voice."

"Okay," answered Mr. Lion.

"Let's go then," declared Mr. Bat. "This way."

For a very long time the animals followed the sound of Mr. Bat saying "This way" through the mazelike cave.

Enough time had passed that Mr. Bear began to doubt if Mr. Bat knew where he was going and he asked, "Mr. Bat, we've been following your voice for a long time, and there's still no way out. Are you sure your sonar is working?"

"My sonar works perfect," answered Mr. Bat. "Trust me, I know where I'm going."

"This blackness is scaring me!" declared Mrs. Kangaroo.

"I feel like I'm going to go crazy," Mrs. Sheep added.

"It's making me claustrophobic!" Mr. Mongoose exclaimed.

"Relax and stay calm," answered Mr. Bat. "I know the way out. Just keep following my voice."

"Ouch!" shouted Mr. Giraffe. "I just banged my head on the top of the cave."

"Oops, I'm sorry," Mr. Bat apologized. "I should have let you know so you could duck."

"It's so black," Mrs. Giraffe began to get panicky. "I'm afraid to move."

All the animals were getting more and more anxious as they moved deeper into the black cave.

Mrs. Bat decided to get a conversation going to take their minds off the darkness, and she said, "How about that perfect society? Pretty weird, huh?"

"It sure was," answered Mr. Kangaroo. "They managed to change the way everybody thinks by changing their values."

"Not just their values," Mr. Bat said. "In order to get control, the dinosaurs had to change the worldview of the whole culture."

"Change the worldview?" Mrs. Kangaroo asked. "What do you mean?"

"A worldview is an overall view of the world."[1] Mr. Bat answered. "It's not a physical view of the world, but rather a philosophical view, an all-encompassing perspective on everything that exists and matters to us."

"Everyone has a worldview,"[2] Mrs. Bat continued. "A worldview is like a mental map that tells us how to navigate the world effectively.[3] We do not ordinarily see our own worldview, but we see everything else by looking through it."[4]

"That's right," Mr. Elephant joined in. "Rarely do any two individuals have exactly the same worldview, but they may share the same basic type of worldview. Some believe in God, and others do not. Some affirm evolution, and others do not. Some believe there are absolute morals, and others do not. Some worldviews are more refined than others, but everyone has a worldview because everyone has a set of beliefs through which they view the world."[5]

"Well said, Mr. Elephant," answered Mr. Bat. "An individual's worldview represents his most fundamental beliefs and assumptions about the universe and how he answers the fundamental questions about who we are, where we came from, why we're here, where we're headed, the meaning and purpose of life, the nature of the afterlife, and what counts as a good life here and now."[6]

Mr. Camel joined in, "Worldviews also largely determine opinions on matters of ethics and politics."

"Since the dinosaurs control the entire political system, they must have changed everyone's worldview through politics," Mr. Bear said.

"Actually, politics is downstream from culture, not the other way around,"[7] answered Mr. Bat. "Real change starts with the culture.[8] That's why the dinosaurs began by undermining God's values until the entire culture saw the world through a godless worldview."

"Wow," Mr. Camel said. "Now it makes sense that when matters of public policy were debated, nothing religious was allowed in the discussion."[9]

"Once society had a godless worldview, it was much easier to convince society to trust the dinosaur government," Mr. Bat said. "Now the entire culture has a worldview that has no idea how to navigate life on their own apart from the government. If they could escape it, they would be left with no possible way to provide for their existence."[10]

"That's why none of the animals are trying to escape the prefect society," Mr. Mongoose said. "They don't know how to survive without the government."

"That's right," Mr. Camel said. "Nobody guarded their worldview because they never knew it was under attack."

"The most effective way to ensure that we have a correct worldview is to apply the grid of creation, the fall, and redemption,"[11] Mrs.

Bat replied. "Creation tells us where everything came from and how we got here. God created the heavens and the earth, and He created us for His glory. The fall refers to when the first humans sinned against God and brought the curse of sin on all of creation. Sin is the reason why there is something wrong with this world and why there so much evil and violence. Sin is the source of evil and suffering, and it is rooted in the heart. And finally, redemption engages our heart with hope that God will one day reverse the effects of sin and set the world right again."

"That's exactly right," Mr. Bat added. "And developing a godly worldview means submitting our entire selves to God in an act of devotion to Him."[12]

"God's righteousness must guide our perspective on all our thoughts and actions,"[13] Mr. Beaver said.

"A godly worldview is a holistic worldview," Mrs. Bat declared. "A godly worldview is very liberating."[14]

"Amen to that!" all the animals agreed in the black darkness.

"I SEE LIGHT!" shouted Mr. Hyena.

"Yay!" all animals cheered and began to hurry toward to the light.

They finally made it to the opening on the other side of the cave.

As they exited the darkness and walked into the light, they praised the Lord and cheered.[15] But the light was so bright that they could barely keep their eyes open.

"Oh, it's so bright," stated Mr. Monkey as his eyes had trouble adjusting to the light.

"I can hardly keep my eyes open," Mr. Sheep said.

All the animals were trying to adjust to the light.

"Just give it a minute until your eyes adjust," answered Mr. Bear.

After a few minutes all the animals began to adjust to the light until they could see normal again.

"Thank you, Mr. and Mrs. Bat!" Mrs. Mongoose said.

"Yeah, for sure, thank you so much," Mr. Bull agreed. "We would never have found this opening without you."

All the animals agreed and thanked Mr. and Mrs. Bat.

"Glory to God for orchestrating a divine appointment with all of you in that dark cave at the perfect time," Mr. Bat said.

"Amen to that!" shouted Mr. Hyena.

"Unfortunately, we don't know where to go from here," Mrs. Bat said. "Do any of you know where the Ark is?"

"No, we don't," answered Mr. Kangaroo. "God has been supernaturally guiding us to the Ark and picking up all of us animals along the way."

"We need to pray before we go any farther," Mr. Lion declared.

"I see a very large oak tree over there," added Mrs. Hyena. "Let's go rest under it and pray."

"Good call," Mr. Mongoose agreed.

All the animals headed toward the large oak tree to pray and rest.

CHAPTER 21

❧

The Owls (Wisdom)

After escaping the perfect society, the group of thirty-eight animals gathered under the very large oak tree to pray, but before they could pray, a wise old owl from up in the oak tree interrupted them and said, "Well, well, well, what have we here? A large group of animals all gathered under the Debater's Tree."

"Debater's Tree?" asked Mr. Horse as he looked up. "What do you mean by that?"

"All of you have gathered under the largest oak tree in the world known as the Debater's Tree," the wise old owl answered. "This tree is where great philosophers, intellectuals, sages, and great thinkers gather to debate the issues of life.[1] What new truth or philosophy do you bring to the Debater's Tree to debate against the wisdom of owls?"

"I'm glad you asked," Mr. Kangaroo answered. "We have a message from God, He is going to—"

"Judge the world," the wise old owl finished. "This is not new. We've heard all this judgment talk already from Mr. and Mrs. Owl."

"Mr. and Mrs. Owl?" Mr. Lion asked. "Did they mention the coming flood and the Ark?"

"Yes, they did," the wise old owl answered. "In fact, they just left to go to the Ark."

"If they're headed to the Ark, then they must know where it is," Mr. Kangaroo said with excitement. "Can you tell us where the Ark is?"

"No, I can't. I've never seen it," the wise old owl replied. "But Mr. and Mrs. Owl know where it is."

Then the wise old owl motioned to one of the other owls and said, "Quickly, go get Mr. and Mrs. Owl before they get too far and tell them to come back."

The other owl flew off to find Mr. and Mrs. Owl.

"Since you know about God's coming judgment, did God speak to you or your other owl friends about going to the Ark to escape His judgment?" Mr. Lion asked.

"No, God didn't speak to me or the others," the wise old owl answered. "Only to Mr. and Mrs. Owl, they insist that God spoke to them. They have been ranting about God's coming judgment for a couple of weeks. They'll be here shortly. They will be glad to see that they aren't the only ones going to the Ark."

"Why don't you go with them to the Ark?" asked Mr. Giraffe.

"I don't believe in all that judgment stuff," the wise old owl replied.

"God's judgment is coming regardless of what you believe," Mr. Hippo replied.

"To each his own," answered the wise owl. "Everyone has the choice to believe whatever they want to believe. There are literally millions of different beliefs in various gods throughout the world. Over the years I've been warned countless times of judgment by way of fire, famine, disease, and so on, but I must say that this is the first time I've been warned of a judgment by a flood."

"It's true," answered Mrs. Monkey. "And the only way to escape His judgment is by going to the Ark and entering it before the flood comes."

"I'm glad you've found something that works for you,"[2] the wise old owl replied. "I've learned that God helps those who help themselves.[3] The notion that God would judge anybody who helps themselves is preposterous."

"When it comes to God's salvation from judgment, God helps those who can't help themselves," Mr. Hyena answered. "God helps those who humble themselves. You will not be able to save yourself when the flood comes."

"Your hysterical judgment talk is a bit fanatical," the wise old owl responded. "Life has its problems, but God never gives us more than we can handle."[4]

"Actually the opposite is true," answered Mr. Camel. "God sometimes gives us more than we can handle so that we will depend on Him rather than ourselves."

"Everything happens for a reason,"[5] the wise old owl answered. "If we don't think we can handle a difficult thing we're going through, then it's up to us to determine why it's happening and what we can learn from it."

"God's judgment is happening for a reason," answered Mrs. Elephant. "And the reason is that the world is full of violence and nobody believes in Him anymore."

"I believe in God," the wise old owl replied. "There are plenty of believers all over the world. Just because we don't believe in your judgment talk doesn't mean we don't believe in God. All roads lead to heaven, and others just take a different road."[6]

"Do you think you will escape God's judgment by believing in the god of your understanding?"[7] Mr. Sloth asked. "There is only one God, and since you're a wise old owl, you should know that by wisdom the Lord created the heavens and the earth.[8] It is He Whose judgment is coming."

"You are all so negative," the wise old owl responded. "God wants us to be happy."

"Actually, God commands us to be happy in Him," Mrs. Horse replied. "God also commands us to be holy because true happiness and living righteously go together.[9] Apart from Him our happiness won't last beyond this life."

"No, true happiness comes when we are true to ourselves,"[10] the wise old owl answered.

"What good is being true to yourself if what you believe about yourself is false?"[11] answered Mr. Bear. "We have a sinful nature, so being true to ourselves will just mean more sinful behavior."

Mrs. Kangaroo joined in, "Being true to ourselves requires that we first mourn over our sin.[12] This kind of godly sorrow produces repentance leading to salvation from God's judgment."

Mr. Elephant noticed that everything the wise old owl said was typical worldly wisdom. He was curious to know more about the wise old owl, so he asked, "So you're a wise old owl, right?"

"Yes," answered the wise old owl. "I have gained a wealth of wisdom over the years by debating the greatest minds of the world right here, under this tree."

"I have a question for you," Mr. Elephant said.

"Ask me anything," answered the wise old owl.

"What would you say is the most valuable thing in life?" Mr. Elephant asked.

"Now that is a good question," the wise old owl said. "There are many valuable things in life, but I would say that love is the most valuable thing in life because a life without love is no life at all."

"Love is valuable and very important, but it's not the most valuable thing in life," Mrs. Horse answered. "Love can be misplaced, misguided, corrupted, and even counterfeited like the love for idols and false gods."

"The most valuable thing in life is our family," another owl answered. "Our family will always be there for us."

"Our family is very valuable, but they're not the most valuable thing in life," Mr. Kangaroo answered. "My family rejected me when I told them about God's coming judgment."

"Health is the most valuable thing in life," another owl said. "Without our health, life is too difficult."

"Health is very valuable, but it's not the most valuable thing in life," Mr. Beaver answered. "After all, there are those with terrible health, yet they are still happy."

"Happiness," another owl answered. "Being happy is the most valuable thing in life."

"Happiness is valuable, but it's not the most valuable thing in life," Mrs. Giraffe answered.

"Time," answered another owl. "Time is the most valuable because we only have a limited amount before we die."

"Time is valuable, but it's not the most valuable thing in life," Mr. Hyena answered.

"Okay, Mr. Elephant," the wise old owl chimed in, "since you asked the question, what would you say is the most valuable thing in life?"

"The most valuable thing in life is wisdom,"[13] Mr. Elephant replied.

"You got me!" answered the wise old owl. "Of course, wisdom is the most valuable thing in life. Wisdom is the quality of having good insight, knowledge, and judgment. Wisdom is the ability to make right decisions and have good judgment in all situations."[14]

"You just gave the typical worldly definition of wisdom," Mr. Elephant answered. "The true definition of wisdom is to fear the Lord and depart from evil.[15] In fact, the fear of the Lord is the beginning of wisdom."[16]

"Fear of the Lord?" questioned the wise old owl. "Actually, conquering fear is the beginning of wisdom.[17] Wisdom is antithetical to fear. In fact, wisdom enables us to overcome fear."[18]

"God's judgment is a very fearful thing," Mrs. Elephant replied. "Because of all the evil, violence, and unbelief, God's judgment is coming, and it's a terrifying thing to fall into the hands of the living God."[19]

"That sounds like a dreadful God," answered another owl.

"God is dreadful to those who reject Him," answered Mr. Camel. "But we speak of a healthy fear of God that is rooted in love, awe, reverence, and respect for His amazing grace and awesome power."[20]

"Wisdom is not rooted in fear," the wise old owl responded. "Wisdom resides beneath our conscious awareness. Wisdom is belief turned into action. It isn't something we create. It's something we discover in ourselves. It's something we must activate."[21]

"Trusting that wisdom resides in our own mind to discover is foolishness,"[22] Mr. Sheep answered.

"You don't have the only definition of wisdom," another owl chimed in. "Wisdom is acquired through reflection on experience. Wisdom involves considering many different perspectives of a situation rather than just your black-and-white thinking."[23]

"True wisdom comes from God,"[24] Mr. Monkey replied. "What you've described is the wisdom of this world because it's rooted in our sinful nature and does not involve God. This is not the wisdom that comes down from God, but is earthly, unspiritual, and demonic.[25] God freely gives His wisdom to those who ask for it."[26]

Mr. Elephant continued, "The wisdom of this world is not capable of solving spiritual problems, nor can it answer life's most basic spiritual questions like, How did we get here? Where do I go when I die? What is the meaning of life?"[27]

"I have solved plenty of spiritual problems in my life," answered the wise old owl. "By attaining ageless wisdom I have found lasting spiritual peace."

"Ageless wisdom?" asked Mrs. Rabbit. "What is that?"

"Ageless wisdom is a consensus from all cultures about the spiritual reality of all souls," [28] the wise old owl answered.

"So your spirituality is based on a consensus of all beliefs from all cultures?" asked Mr. Rabbit.

"Yes," he answered. "Ageless wisdom gives me spiritual peace."

"You have a counterfeit peace," answered Mrs. Sloth. "It is impossible to know God through worldly wisdom."

"Wisdom is the ability to know when to turn God off," the wise old owl replied. "All you've done is spout your judgment talk since you came to the Debater's Tree."

"We can't turn God off, He spoke to each of us," answered Mrs. Monkey. "There's no time to waste. God's judgment is almost here, and your wisdom will not save you. The wisdom of this world is folly with God."[29]

"INCOMING!" shouted an owl approaching the Debater's Tree accompanied by Mr. and Mrs. Owl.

Mr. and Mrs. Owl landed on a branch, and Mr. Owl spoke first, "Are you the animals headed to the Ark?"

"Yes, do you know where it is?" asked Mrs. Snake.

"Yes, we do," answered Mr. Owl. "It's not far from here, it's gonna take a day maybe two to get there."

"That's awesome!" Mr. Kangaroo answered. "We have been traveling for so many days that we've lost count. Which way do we go?"

"It's that way," Mrs. Owl said as she pointed in the direction of the Ark.

"Let's get going!" declared Mr. Lion. Then he looked at the wise old owl and asked, "Will you or the other owls come with us to the Ark to escape God's coming judgment?"

"No, we won't," the wise old owl answered. "God has a wonderful plan for our life, and it doesn't include terrifying judgment."[30]

"God's wonderful plan for your life is that you repent, believe in Him, and go to the Ark with us," Mrs. Cow answered. "If you don't come to the Ark with us, then God's plan for your life is judgment in the coming flood."

"You're all so heavenly minded that you are of no earthly good,"[31] the wise old owl replied.

"You have it backward, wise old owl," Mr. Lion answered. "You are so earthly minded that you are of no heavenly good. When God's judgment comes, you will seek wisdom, and you will not find it because you did not choose the fear of the Lord."[32]

"It's no use," answered Mr. Owl. "We have been preaching God's judgment for a couple of weeks, and they steadfastly reject it. Let's go to the Ark."

Mr. Lion looked at the wise old owl and asked, "Before we go, I will ask you one last time. Do you want to do the wise thing and come with us to the Ark and escape God's judgment?"

"No, I do not want to come with you," answered the wise old owl. "I prefer to stay here and look out for number 1."

"See, I told you," answered Mr. Owl. "Let's go."

"Okay then, goodbye, wise old owl," Mr. Lion said.

"Goodbye," answered the wise old owl. "In the end you will see that your judgment talk was much ado about nothing because we all worship the same God anyway."[33]

As they left behind the wise old owl and the Debater's Tree, Mr. Hyena said, "For a wise old owl, he sure seemed ignorant of God's truth and righteousness."

"That's because he had the wisdom of the world, not the wisdom of God," Mrs. Owl said. "Notice all his wisdom was based on self rather than God's wisdom."

"Wow," answered Mr. Hyena. "I didn't realize it, but you're right, all his wisdom was based on self."

"What a shame that with all their wisdom, they still wouldn't go to the Ark," Mr. Owl said.

"That's because only God can make one wise for salvation,"[34] Mr. Kangaroo answered.

"It all boils down to this," Mr. Rabbit declared. "Fear God and keep his commandments, for this is our whole duty. God will bring every deed into judgment, with every secret thing, whether good or evil."[35]

"Amen!" all the animals said as they nodded in agreement.

"Which way do we go from here?" Mr. Monkey asked.

"The Ark is not far from here," Mr. Owl answered. "Just keep moving, and we will lead you to it."

"Awesome! Thank You, God!" shouted Mr. Kangaroo. "Let's go!"

"Wait!" shouted Mr. Lion. "Let's pray before we continue on."

They all huddle and prayed.

CHAPTER 22

The Rhinoceroses (Morality)

After leaving the Debater's Tree and adding Mr. and Mrs. Owl, the group had now grown to forty animals. After they prayed, they looked up at Mr. and Mrs. Owl hovering above, and Mr. Kangaroo asked, "Which way to the Ark?"

"It's that way," Mr. Owl said as he pointed in the direction of the Ark.

"Let's get moving!" declared Mr. Lion.

"Yeah, let's go!" all the animals shouted.

All the animals continued their journey full of hope and excitement because the Ark was very close. There was now an unwavering determination to get to the Ark. All the animals sensed God's presence.

Mr. Bear looked up at Mr. and Mrs. Owl and asked, "Hey, Mr. Owl, how close were you to the Ark before you turned around?"

Mr. and Mrs. Owl flew down and landed on Mr. Hippo as he walked and Mr. Owl said, "We were close enough that we could see the Ark way up ahead in the distance, we were about to make our descent when one of the other owls caught up to us and told us that some animals showed up at the Debater's Tree asking for directions to the Ark. The wise old owl sent an owl to bring us back to the

Debater's Tree to help you. That was the wisest thing that that wise old owl has ever done."

"Ha ha ha ha ha ha ha," all the animals shared a laugh.

"We knew that you would need our help, so we came back," Mrs. Owl said.

"Thank you again for coming back," Mr. Elephant replied.

"Yes, thank you," all the animals expressed their gratitude.

"It must have been difficult to turn around when you were so close to the Ark," Mrs. Sloth said.

"No, not really," answered Mrs. Owl. "As soon as we heard that you all didn't know the way to the Ark, we had no problem turning back to come get you. It was the right thing to do."

"Mr. Owl, will you fly ahead and give us an overview and see if there might be any danger or opposition in our path that we can hopefully avoid?" Mr. Lion asked.

"And please let us know exactly how far away the Ark is," Mrs. Hyena said.

"Of course," answered Mr. Owl. "We will go for a fly and check things out and come back with the answer."

They took off in flight toward the Ark and Mr. Owl immediately turned and yelled, "There are some rhinos just up ahead!"

The animals didn't have to travel far before coming across the rhinoceroses.

"I can see the rhinos up ahead," declared Mr. Giraffe. "They're just grazing."

As the animals approached the rhinos, Mr. Bull said, "Let's make this quick and just see if they want to come with us to the Ark and then we can continue on."

"We tried that before, remember?" answered Mr. Lion. "But it turned into a long, drawn-out debate."

As they approached the rhinos, Mrs. Bear spoke first and asked the rhinos, "We're all going to the Ark to escape God's coming judgment, do any of you rhinos want to come with us?"

"We've already heard this judgment garbage before from Mr. and Mrs. Rhino," a rhino replied. Then the rhino turned and looked at Mr. and Mrs. Rhino, nodded his horn at them, and said, "Take

Mr. and Mrs. Rhino with you to the Ark and free us from all their judgment talk."

"We would love to go with them to the Ark and escape this moral wasteland,"[1] Mrs. Rhino answered.

"Moral wasteland?" an irritated rhino replied. "There you two go again. Ever since you—quote—heard from God—unquote—you've been trying to shove your morality down our throat, and now you won't stop with this judgment nonsense."

"We're not trying to shove our morality down your throat," answered Mr. Rhino. "We didn't invent morality.[2] Objective moral rights are self-evident,[3] after all, everyone knows murder and stealing is wrong. We were merely recognizing the unchanging objective morality that is rooted in God's nature."[4]

"We don't need a god to tell us what is right and wrong," a rhino replied.

"You don't need God?" Mr. Monkey asked. "How does objective morality exist if there is no God?"[5]

"The fact that we can know objective morality is the reason why it exists," a rhino answered.

"What?" several animals asked at the same time.

"He means that objective morality exists because we instinctively know it through evolution," another rhino answered. "Through millions of years of mutated genes and natural selection, evolution has given us objective morality to survive. If we don't cooperate with one another, we will not survive."[6]

"If evolution is your guide, then it's impossible for morals to be objective or unchanging,"[7] Mrs. Monkey answered. "Evolution is a process of change, so morals must change."

"Even if evolution was true, how can a mutating genetic code have the moral authority to tell you how you ought to behave?"[8] Mr. Monkey asked.

"Even if your God were real, He is immoral for wanting to kill everyone," a rhino answered. "There is no way we can follow an immoral God Who wants to kill everybody for not being perfect."

"God demands morality,"[9] Mr. Camel replied. "The problem is that we all fall short of God's perfect standard of morality.[10] It has gotten so bad that His judgment is coming, but He is gracious and has given us a way to escape His judgment by going to the Ark."

"There is no God, and there is no judgment," another rhino answered. "Morality is founded on nature itself. Objective morality is determined by the degree it increases our well-being or decreases suffering.[11] That's how objective morality exists without God."

"That's just an opinion about morality," Mr. Giraffe answered. "Everybody has a different understanding of well-being, and suffering isn't always bad. God is able to use suffering to build our character."[12]

"It's not our opinion," a rhino replied. "Objective morality is determined through science and philosophy."

"Wait...what?" asked Mrs. Monkey.

The rhino continued, "Philosophy is needed to complete any system of ethics, but those ethics need to be informed by the latest data that science can give us." [13]

"How can objective morality come from philosophy and science when both are always changing?" Mr. Sloth asked.

"Moral progress is required to achieve a perfect moral code," a rhino answered. "In order to achieve a perfect moral code, we need to have complete knowledge of physics and biology and know the full outcome of every action we make. This knowledge is out of our reach, which means any moral code is always in need of continued progress."[14]

"God knows everything," Mr. Elephant replied. "Which is why His moral commands are perfect and unchanging."

"Moral codes that forbid any progress are defective right from the start,"[15] another rhino replied. "This is why the harm of a society is greatly increased if we follow religious morals. For now there is no perfect moral code, but we are still responsible for our own actions."[16]

"All you have to do is look around at society, and you will see that everybody abuses morality," Mr. Sheep stated. "With all this abuse, whose morality is the standard until this moral progress is made?"

"The fact that everybody abuses morality proves that morality is still in progress," a rhino answered. "If it was objective, you couldn't abuse it."[17]

"No, no, no," Mr. Elephant replied. "You're confusing sociology, which is how we behave, with morality, which is how we ought to behave."[18]

"God's nature is the unchanging objective moral standard that we are accountable to,"[19] Mr. Pig declared.

"We don't need your religion to know morality," a rhino insisted.

"No society has ever been successful in teaching morality without religion,"[20] answered Mr. Beaver.

"There would be no morality unless God exists,"[21] Mr. Elephant added. "Without God there is no basis to declare anything good or bad."

"Moral values must appeal to reason, not religion,"[22] a rhino answered.

"Reason is a tool by which we discover what the moral law is," Mr. Hippo answered. "But it can't account for why the moral law exists in the first place.[23] We know objective morality because God has written His moral law on our heart when He created us."[24]

"Science will answer the missing questions of morality in time," a rhino answered.

"You can't explain God's immaterial moral law through science,"[25] answered Mr. Rhino.

"Yes, it will," another rhino insisted. "Just give it time."

"Every law has a lawgiver,"[26] Mr. Camel stated. "And since there is an objective moral law, there is therefore an objective moral lawgiver."[27]

"If there is a moral lawgiver, then the actual morals themselves mean nothing," a rhino replied. "The only thing that matters is whether God commanded it, even if it deliberately increases suffering."[28]

"God would never allow suffering without a good reason," Mrs. Elephant answered. "All of God's commands are good because they come from His good nature.[29] God sees everything.[30] His decisions are based on infinite knowledge and understanding."[31]

Another rhino chimed in, "If you want to prove that objective morality comes from God, then you have to show how moral values like love, kindness, fairness, and generosity would not have a positive effect in a universe without God."[32]

"Just look around," Mr. Pig replied. "The whole earth is filled with nothing but violence and evil. Moral values like love, kindness, fairness, and generosity are not having a positive effect because the whole world has rejected God. If you want to know what a universe without God is like, then just look around. We are living in a world without God, and His judgment is coming."[33]

"Only an unchanging God can prescribe and enforce an objective standard of morality,"[34] Mr. Lion declared. "And His judgment is coming to execute swift justice, and the only escape is to get on the Ark. Do you want to come with us to the Ark?"

"Don't be silly," answered a rhino. "Since there is no God and no judgment, we will stay here and make the world better through moral progress."

"Fine," answered Mr. Lion. "C'mon, animals, let's get going."

"By the way," a rhino said. "Your God poses a moral dilemma: Is something morally good because God commands it, or does God command it because it is morally good?"[35]

"That is a false dilemma," answered Mr. Elephant. "You ask the question as if there can only be two answers."

"There are no other answers," the rhino answered. "Your God is completely irrelevant as to whether these morals are right and wrong, they are either right or wrong independent of whether God exists or not."[36]

"That is a false dilemma because God doesn't look up to another standard beyond Himself," Mr. Elephant replied. "He wouldn't be God if He did.[37] The third answer is that God's nature is the standard.[38] God is completely relevant because He is the unchanging standard of good."

"The best reason to do what is morally right is for its own sake,"[39] a rhino said. "The result will be a clean conscience."

"God gave us a conscience as our soul's warning system to allow us to make moral evaluations of what is right and wrong,"[40] Mr. Monkey answered.

"Again, no need for a god," the rhino replied. "Conscience is an evolved intellectual attribute that enhances the survival of our species."[41]

"Our conscience is part of God's good design," Mr. Elephant answered. "In order for our conscience to work as God designed it, our conscience must be informed to the highest moral and spiritual level, which is God's righteousness."[42]

Another rhino joined in, "It's no accident that the word *conscience* ends with the word *science*. I'd forget about your God in relation to conscience."

"Stop!" shouted Mr. Kangaroo. "This argument is never going to end. It seems that their conscience is seared.[43] Let's get going!"

All the animals, plus Mr. and Mrs. Rhino, agreed and left the other rhinos to continue their journey to the Ark.

As they left the rhinos, Mrs. Rhino said, "Now you know why we call it a moral wasteland."

"Yeah, we do," answered Mr. Horse. "Objective morality is self-evident. Progressive morality is not self-evident because it's always changing."

"They use intellectual objections to disguise the real issue, which is that they hate God's morals," Mr. Rabbit said.

All the animals nodded in agreement.

"Wow," exclaimed Mrs. Hippo. "I'm glad that's over. My brain feels like it's been tied in a knot."

"No kidding," answered Mrs. Rabbit. "My ears hurt from all that."

"We need to pray," Mr. Mongoose insisted.

All animals huddled and prayed before continuing on.

CHAPTER 23

Dinosaur Danger

There were now forty-two animals in the group on their way to the Ark, although Mr. and Mrs. Owl flew off ahead to survey the land for any potential opposition and to determine how far away the Ark was. It had been a while since the group left the rhinos, and Mr. and Mrs. Owl still hadn't returned with an update. Mr. Lion was growing concerned.

"The owls have been gone for a while," Mr. Lion said. "Hey, Mr. Bat, can you fly above and see if you see them?"

"Sure," answered Mr. Bat as he and Mrs. Bat flew up to take a look around.

"Don't be gone long," Mr. Lion said. "You're our only air support right now."

Mr. and Mrs. Bat were only gone for a few minutes when they came rushing back. Mr. Bat spoke with urgency, "We didn't see the owls, but we did see a squadron of six pterosaurs flying in formation and headed this way![1] It looks like they're from the perfect society air patrol, I think they're looking for us!"

"We need to pray now!" declared Mr. Lion as he paused and prayed a quick and simple prayer to the point, *"Dear God, protect us and help us get to the Ark!"*

Right after Mr. Lion prayed, Mr. and Mrs. Owl showed up and said, "The Ark is only a few miles away, you're almost there!"

"But there's a squadron of pterosaurs coming for us," Mr. Bear said with urgency. "How will we avoid them with so many of us?"

Just then the pterosaurs came swooping down and did a very low flyover just above the group of animals, and one of the pterosaurs shouted, "AHA! We have located you fugitive PSDs! You can turn around and go back to the perfect society on your own, or we will bring you back by force!"

"God's judgment is coming!" Mr. Monkey shouted. "Come with us to the Ark!"

The pterosaurs turned around in perfect formation and did another flyover and shouted again, "God can't help you now, your religion prevents unity and disrupts a perfect society. You will be made an example of what happens to anybody who disrupts a perfect society!"

"We're not going back to the perfect society!" shouted Mr. Giraffe. "We're going to the Ark before the flood comes!"

"Have it your way!" declared the lead pterosaur. Then he motioned to the other pterosaurs and said, "Arrest the smaller and weaker ones first, then we will come back with more help."

Immediately all six pterosaurs swooped down and began trying to snatch the smaller and weaker animals.

"Go after their legs!" shouted Mr. Bat "Their legs are connected to their wings just like us bats.[2] It's too difficult for them to fly if you mess with their legs. Go after their legs!"

One pterosaur snatched Mrs. Sheep and began to fly, but Mr. Lion was able to leap up just in time to claw the pterosaur's leg, which disrupted his flight, and it dropped Mrs. Sheep. It flapped its wings and regained control of itself and flew above and out of Mr. Lion's reach.

Meanwhile, the other five pterosaurs were trying to snatch Mrs. Beaver, Mrs. Rabbit, Mrs. Pig, Mr. Mongoose, and Mr. Sloth.

Mrs. Beaver used her tail to slap the pterosaur repeatedly: *Slap! Slap! Slap! Slap!*

"*Ouch! Ouch! Ouch! Ouch!*" the pterosaur shouted as it started to wobble and lose control. It immediately let go of Mrs. Beaver.

Mr. and Mrs. Hyena jumped up and bit the legs of the pterosaur that snatched Mrs. Rabbit, causing it to drop Mrs. Rabbit immediately.

Mrs. Lion jumped up in time to claw the pterosaur holding Mrs. Pig. The pterosaur dropped her before she was barely off the ground.

Mr. Elephant grabbed the back leg of the pterosaur just in time as it was trying to snatch Mr. Mongoose. The pterosaur immediately let go of Mr. Mongoose then spun his beak around and smacked Mr. Elephant's trunk, causing Mr. Elephant to let go of the pterosaur. The pterosaur immediately flew up above, not sure what to do.

The pterosaur holding Mr. Sloth was flapping its wings above and about to clear the animals, but a quick thinking Mr. Monkey jumped onto Mr. Giraffe and quickly climbed his neck to the top of his head and leaped from the very top of his head as high as he could just enough to get his hands on the leg of the pterosaur as it was flying away. All three of them came crashing back to the ground.

The pterosaur let go of Mr. Sloth and quickly regained control and took off. From above looking down, the pterosaur shouted, "Resisting arrest will not be tolerated! Your punishment will be severe! We know where you are, and we will be back!"

The pterosaurs flew off in formation in the direction of the perfect society.

"What in the world was that all about?" Mr. Rhino asked.

"They are the air patrol from the perfect society," Mr. Lion answered. "We unknowingly passed through their perfect society and got arrested for praying and preaching God's coming judgment. It's a long story, but we managed to escape with the help of Mr. and Mrs. Bat. The bottom line is that we have to get to the Ark before those pterosaurs return with help."

"He called us fugitive PSDs, what is a PSD?" asked Mrs. Rhino.

"A PSD is a perfect society disrupter. Their society is run by an all-powerful, centralized dinosaur government that has zero tolerance for any religious activity," answered Mrs. Camel.

"There's no time to explain now," declared a scared Mr. Sheep. "The pterosaurs said they're coming back! We need to get moving."

"We'd better hurry," Mrs. Horse said. "We need to run."

All the animals took off running in the direction of the Ark. It was a thirty-eight-animal stampede with Mr. and Mrs. Bat and Mr. and Mrs. Owl flying above.

But before long, Mr. Owl announced from above, "There is a large patch of trees up ahead."

The animals came to the trees and stopped to catch their breath. It was a thick patch of eucalyptus trees.

Mr. Sloth was riding on Mr. Bear's back and said, "Now would be a good time to pray. I'll pray while you all catch your breath."

Mr. Sloth finished praying, and all the animals said, "Amen."

Then they looked at the patch of trees like an unwanted obstacle.

CHAPTER 24

The Koala Bears (Truth)

The animals stared at the patch of eucalyptus trees as if it were a huge mountain blocking them from the Ark. They knew they were very close to the Ark, yet it was still not visible through the large patch of trees.

"You're almost to the Ark," Mr. Owl shouted from above. "It's not far beyond these trees."

The animals approached the trees and began to make their way through them.

"This sure is a large patch of trees," Mr. Mongoose said.

"Yeah, it's pretty dense too," added Mr. Bear.

"It's like a forest," Mrs. Sheep said. "I don't like forests, it's too easy to get lost."

"If only we could see the Ark through these trees," Mr. Beaver stated.

"I can't see the forest through the trees," Mrs. Cow said.

"Huh?" muttered several confused animals.

"Never mind," answered Mrs. Cow. "I heard someone say it once, not sure what it meant, but it sounded cool."

"It means you can't see the big picture because you're too focused on the details," answered a koala bear from up in a tree.

"What?" asked several animals at once as they looked toward the voice.

"It's an expression," answered the koala bear. "*You can't see the forest through the trees* is an expression that means you can't see the big picture because you're too focused on the details."

"Oh, okay, I guess that makes sense," Mrs. Cow said.

The koala bear was about to speak again, but Mr. Kangaroo quickly interrupted and got straight to the point and asked, "We're going to the Ark to—"

"No, we don't want to go to the Ark," the koala answered. "Just keep moving on through."

"We want to go!" shouted Mr. Koala from a tree. "God spoke to me and Mrs. Koala about the coming judgment."

"We would love for you two to join us on our way to the Ark," answered Mr. Lion.

"How come you're still here?" asked Mrs. Rabbit. "If the Ark is so close, why haven't you gone to it yet?"

"We've been waiting for it to be finished," answered Mr. Koala. "The humans were still building it the last time we checked."

"It's not finished?" asked Mr. Rabbit.

"We have been watching them build it for many years, and the last time I checked, it looked like it was almost done," Mr. Koala answered. "We came back to try and convince the other koalas to come with us before it's finished."

"We've been speaking the truth about God's coming judgment, but the other koalas reject it because they say it's not true for them," Mrs. Koala said.

"Not true for them?" Mr. Mongoose asked. "God's coming judgment is true for every living creature."

"Oh great, more truth-claimers," announced another koala.

"What's wrong with proclaiming God's truth?" asked Mr. Bull

"How can you be so arrogant to say that this so-called judgment is true?" a koala asked from another tree.

"We know it's true because God spoke to each of us," answered Mrs. Beaver.

"God speaks to many animals in different ways," another koala answered. "There is no way you can say that only what God said to you is true."

"We know that all the evil and violence is true because we see it everywhere and every day," Mr. Rabbit answered. "God sees it all, and He knows it will never end, so His judgment is coming. It's a hard truth, but it's definitely true."

"There is no truth,"[1] a koala declared.

"Is that true?"[2] Mr. Kangaroo asked sarcastically.

"What he means is, you can't know the truth,"[3] another koala answered.

"Are you saying it's true that you can't know the truth?" Mr. Elephant asked. "Do you see how your statement is self-refuting?"

The koala tried to explain further, "What I'm saying is that truth is relative because it's always changing."

"Is what you just said relative, or is it always true?" asked Mrs. Snake.

The koala tried to explain even further, "What's true for you is not true for me."[4]

"Is that true for everybody?" asked Mr. Sloth.

"This is amusing," Mr. Pig said.

"Are you koalas hearing yourselves?" Mrs. Giraffe asked. "You keep making a truth claim that nothing is true, but then you want us to believe that it's true that there is no truth."

"You're twisting my words and making it complicated," the koala answered.

"We didn't twist anything," answered Mrs. Lion. "We just applied your truth claim to itself and showed how it's self-refuting."

"No wonder we got confused!" exclaimed Mr. Koala. "They made their own version of truth seem true when in reality, it was impossible to be true, which is why we got confused. We didn't know how to refute them because it was our claims versus theirs. But it's easy to see the fallacy of their arguments when you simply apply their truth claims to themselves."

"You are all so arrogant and judgmental toward the truth claims of others," another koala declared.

"Hey, you just judged us!" Mr. Sloth exclaimed.

"Since you all seem to think you know everything," another koala said. "Let me ask you, what is truth?"[5]

"Truth is the way God sees things," [6] answered Mrs. Elephant. "God sees and knows everything as it truly is."

Mr. Mongoose declared, "Truth is true—even if no one knows it. Truth is true—even if no one admits it. Truth is true—even if no one agrees with what it is. Truth is true—even if no one follows it. Truth is true—even if no one but God grasps it fully."[7]

"Truth is God's perspective on reality," Mr. Snake added.

"God's perspective on reality?" asked a koala. "How are we supposed to know God's perspective on reality?"

"How are we supposed to know God's perspective on anything?" another koala asked.

"God has revealed the basic truth about Himself in nature,"[8] Mr. Hippo answered. "His knowledge, beauty, and wisdom are seen in nature."[9]

"That's true for you, but others see nature in different ways," the koala answered.

"The world is the creation of God,"[10] answered Mrs. Bear. "All creation must be interpreted in light of its relationship to God."[11]

"Your words are just another truth just like everybody else," another koala said. "Your reality is different from everybody else's reality."

"God's Word is truth, which makes it a trustworthy basis for reality,"[12] answered Mr. Snake. "And God gave us His Word that His judgment is coming."

"Please stop with the judgment talk," another koala said.

Mr. Kangaroo joined in and said, "Truth is that which is consistent with the mind, will, character, glory, and being of God. Truth is the self-expression of God."[13]

"You make it sound so easy," a koala answered. "It's impossible to know God's perspective on reality. The way to find truth is to strip the mind of everything that can possibly be doubted until we finally reach a bedrock of truths that cannot possibly be doubted."[14]

"Any overall system of thought constructed apart from God will be false,"[15] answered Mr. Giraffe.

"You animals are so arrogant to claim that only your truth is true and valid," a koala replied.

"All truth is God's truth,"[16] answered Mr. Giraffe.

"All the truth in the world adds up to one big lie,"[17] another koala said.

"God is truth,"[18] declared Mrs. Hyena. "Therefore, it is impossible for God to lie."[19]

"I have heard many truth claims, and they are all valid to those who make them," a koala answered. "I will not judge others by denying their truth."

"That means you're denying our truth, which is based on God's truth," answered Mr. Mongoose.

"This conversation is going nowhere," Mrs. Lion stated. "We are very close to the Ark, and we need to get there before the flood comes."

"We don't have much time, and we must get going," Mr. Lion said. "Let me ask you koalas one last time. Do any of you want to come with us to the Ark and escape God's coming judgment?"

"No, we don't want to come," answered a koala. "You have found your truth, and I hope it makes you happy. We will stay here and enjoy our truth."

"You all are so fixated on your own version of truth that you can't see the forest through the trees," a koala said.

"Ha ha ha ha," all the koalas laughed.

"Whatever," Mr. Giraffe said.

"Let's go," Mr. Lion announced.

With that all the animals turned in the direction of the Ark and continued on through the trees.

After the koalas were out of sight, Mr. Koala asked, "Isn't it amazing how different definitions of truth can bring so much confusion."

"Ain't that the truth!" exclaimed Mr. Sloth.

"It seems everybody is eager to believe anything except the truth about God," Mrs. Pig stated.

"Yep," Mr. Horse agreed. "In our sinful nature, we suppress the truth in unrighteousness."[20]

"How much further till we're out of these trees?" Mrs. Horse asked.

"I don't know," Mr. Bear answered. "Let's pray now before we continue on."

All the animals paused in the trees to pray.

CHAPTER 25

The Ark!

With the addition of Mr. and Mrs. Koala, the group had grown to forty-four animals. After they all finished praying, Mr. and Mrs. Owl, along with Mr. and Mrs. Bat, flew above, encouraging the animals to hurry because they could see the end of the trees and the Ark only a couple of miles away.

The animals were hurrying through the trees. Slowly but surely, the trees began to thin out until they reached the edge of the trees. Finally, off in the distance, they could see the Ark.

There was nothing but flatland between the animals and where the Ark was resting.

"There it is!" shouted Mr. Giraffe.

Without realizing it, the animals stopped moving to stare at the Ark.

"Wow!" exclaimed all the animals as they fixed their eyes on the Ark off in the distance.

Mrs. Koala looked up at Mr. and Mrs. Owl and asked, "Can you tell if the door is open on the Ark?"

"Yes, the door is open!" announced Mr. Owl.

"The door is finally open!" shouted Mrs. Koala.

"The Ark is finally finished!" shouted Mr. Koala.

"We finally made it!" declared Mr. Beaver.

"Hooray!" All the animals began to cheer with excitement.

"Don't celebrate yet!" shouted Mr. Owl. "I see another fleet of pterosaurs flying this way!"

"Hurry! Get going!" shouted Mrs. Owl from above.

"Let's go!" shouted Mr. Lion.

All the animals took off running toward the Ark. While they were running as fast as they could, Mr. Owl noticed that the fleet of pterosaurs was actually two squadrons of six this time. Each squadron of six was flying in formation headed toward the animals. There were twice as many air patrols coming for the animals this time. But Mr. Owl noticed something else about the pterosaurs; they were each carrying an ankylosaurus. The ankylosauruses were the ones responsible for escorting PSDs to their court appearance. The consequences for failing to escort the PSDs were unthinkable in a perfect society. The ankylosauruses were coming to fulfill their duty and escort the fugitive animals back to the perfect society.

Mr. Owl shouted from above, "There are twelve pterosaurs this time, and each one is carrying an ankylosaurus!"

The animals were running as fast as they could, but the pterosaurs were flying much faster than the animals could run.

"Hurry, the pterosaurs are gaining on you!" Mrs. Owl shouted.

"What do we do?" Mrs. Sheep asked in a panicky tone.

"O God, help us!" Mr. Rabbit shouted.

Before the animals could figure out what to do, the two squadrons of pterosaurs flew ahead of the animals and each pterosaur set an ankylosaurus on the ground up ahead in front of the animals. Then the pterosaurs all took off flying back toward the perfect society, and one of the pterosaurs looked back at the ankylosauruses and shouted, "We're going to get more help, don't let them escape!"

The animals now had twelve ankylosauruses blocking their path to the Ark.

The leading ankylosaurus spoke, "You animals thought you could escape from our perfect society, but you underestimated us ankylosauruses. It's our responsibility to make sure you PSDs make it to your court-ordered destination, and we always fulfill our responsibility."

"God's judgment is almost here," Mr. Elephant shouted. "Come with us to the Ark before it's too late!"

"You're still preaching religious stuff even after we caught you running away and resisting arrest," the ankylosaurus replied. "Your punishment will be severe, and you will surely be spending an extended amount of time in sensitivity training until you get your minds right. Now turn around and go back!"

"We're not going back!" Mr. Kangaroo shouted. "We're going to the Ark!"

The ankylosaurus whipped his hammer tail at a rock on the ground and launched the rock within an inch right passed Mr. Kangaroo's head.

"The next rock will be right between your eyes," the ankylosaurus declared. "Now turn around and go back!"

"What should we do?" asked Mr. Hyena.

"How is God going to save us?" asked a terrified Mrs. Cow.

The ankylosauruses began moving closer to the animals with their hammer tails up high and ready to force the animals to turn around. The animals had traveled far and had been through so much, and now the ankylosauruses were in the way of the Ark.

As the animals looked on in fear, Mr. Lion shouted, "Our only hope is for God to save us!"

"Lord, save us!" All the animals were shouting to God.

The ankylosauruses continued their approach; they were closing in on the animals.

"Your God can't help you!" an ankylosaurus shouted. "You are all under arrest, and you will be made an example of what happens to those who disrupt our perfect society. Turn around now, or we will turn you around by force."

All the animals began to tremble with fear as there seemed to be no escape.

Then Mr. Lion turned to the animals and declared, "Fear not, stand firm, and see the salvation of the LORD, which He will work for you today. For the ankylosauruses whom you see today, you shall never see again."[1]

There was a moment of silence as the animals looked at the approaching ankylosauruses.

Suddenly the ground began to shake violently. The shaking caused all the animals and the ankylosauruses to stop moving and stare at the ground. As the ground shook, the earth split apart right beneath the ankylosauruses, causing them to fall into the crack one by one. It was as if the earth opened its mouth and swallowed them up.[2]

After the last ankylosaurus fell into the earth, the crack in the earth closed up, and the shaking began to settle down until it completely stopped.

Just like that the ankylosauruses were gone. All that remained was a calm silence as all the animals looked on in stunned amazement. The calm silence seemed to last forever as each animal wondered if what just happened had really happened.

Finally, Mr. Bat broke the silence and shouted from above, "The earth has opened up and swallowed all the ankylosauruses! They're gone! It's safe to keep going!"

"Behold the salvation of the Lord!"[3] Mr. Bear shouted as loud as he could.

"Thank You, God!" Mrs. Giraffe shouted.

"God's judgment is coming!" Mr. Lion shouted. "Come on, let's go to the Ark!"

All the animals took off running toward the Ark as fast as they could, and none of the animals dared to slow down until they got to the Ark.

When they finally got to the Ark, they stopped to look at it. The size of the Ark was breathtaking.

"Wow!" exclaimed Mrs. Hyena.

"Whoa!" expressed Mr. Elephant. "It's huge!"[4]

"Look how tall it is!" shouted Mr. Monkey.

"It's long too!" Mrs. Snake announced.

"It's beautiful!" declared Mr. Bull.

"It's awesome!" shouted Mr. Beaver.

The door to the Ark was on the side about halfway up. There was a long ramp along the side of the Ark that went from the side door down to the rear of the Ark.

Mr. and Mrs. Owl landed on the ramp rail at the top of the ramp and looked down at the animals staring at the Ark.

Mr. Owl asked, "Are you all just going to stare at the Ark all day, or are you going to climb aboard?"

"The ramp begins over there at the rear," Mr. Bear said. "C'mon, let's board this thing."

The animals began walking to the rear of the Ark toward the ramp opening. As they approached the ramp opening, they saw a human inspecting the hull of the Ark. The human was checking for any damage that the earthquake might have caused. Suddenly the human turned to see the animals approaching. The animals slowed to see what the human would do. Was the human going to be another problem? The animals all stopped to look at the human. The human looked at the animals. The animals stared in silence for what seemed like forever.

Then the human lifted his arm and waved the animals onto the ramp and said, "Welcome aboard, I've been expecting all of you!"

All the animals gasped a sigh of relief and boarded the ramp. The human turned back around to continue inspecting the hull of the Ark.

Mr. Lion was leading the group up the ramp. As they walked up the ramp, the animals were speechless as the reality that they were actually boarding the Ark was surreal. Just before they got to the top of the ramp, Mr. Lion paused and looked out into the world. All the other animals also paused and looked out into the world as well.

"Take a look out there," Mr. Lion said. "This is the last time we will see this world before God brings His judgment."

As they looked out, they could see other animals gathering outside the Ark looking on as if it was just another form of entertainment. None of the onlookers even considered climbing aboard the Ark because none of them took God's coming judgment seriously. They just looked at the Ark in amusement. Some mocked and others cracked jokes. There were even animals out there plotting on how they might destroy the Ark.[5]

"Look at all the animals out there," Mr. Lion said. "They're completely oblivious to what's about to happen to all of them."[6]

"We tried to warn them," answered Mrs. Mongoose. "They rejected our warnings."

"They all rejected God's only plan for salvation,"[7] declared Mr. Hyena.

"They chose instead to continue doing what's right in their own eyes,"[8] answered Mr. Kangaroo.

Mrs. Lion prayed out loud, *"Lord, have mercy on all of them. They don't know what they're doing."*[9]

"Come on, let's get inside," Mr. Lion said.

All the animals went into the Ark.

CHAPTER 26

Cᴏꜱꜱ̊ꜱ̊ᴋꜱ̊ꜱ̊ᴏ

Inside the Ark

The animals entered the Ark two by two, male and female. As they entered, there was a human guiding each pair of animals to their living quarters. Their living quarters were nest cages that were set up to accommodate each animal kind. Each nest was equipped with food and water. Each nest had a clay water container that kept a water bowl continuously full.[1] Each nest also had a similar clay feeder bowl or just a trough. The food, depending on the animal kind, consisted of grains, grasses, seeds, nuts, fruits, and vegetables including dried fruits and vegetables.[2]

There were two passageways that ran parallel the entire length of the Ark. On each side of each passageway were nests for every kind of land creature on the earth.

The Ark had three decks: a lower, middle, and upper deck.[3] There was plenty of room for all God's land creatures and just enough room to store food and water as well as supplies for the humans.[4]

The human was guiding the animals to their nests when suddenly he was called away by one of the other humans to help repair some damage caused by the previous earthquake that swallowed the ankylosauruses.

The Ark was built with a system to collect rainwater from the roof that would distribute the water to various parts of the Ark through bamboo piping.[5] The earthquake caused the bamboo piping to come loose in some places, and some of the Ark's wood joints also came loose. The earthquake also caused several clay vessels storing food and water to fall over and spill.[6] The humans were very busy repairing the damage and cleaning up the various messes caused by the earthquake. Since the humans were busy repairing the Ark, they were unable to shut all the gates to each nest, and the animals were able to roam around freely.

The animals walked down the passageways, marveling at everything inside the Ark.

"The Ark seems bigger on the inside," Mr. Beaver said.

"Yes, it does. How amazing since it looked so huge on the outside," answered Mrs. Beaver.

"Look at all the nests!" exclaimed Mrs. Kangaroo. "There're so many of them."

"And this is only the middle deck," Mr. Bull added. "There are two more decks."

"There must be thousands of animals in here," Mrs. Elephant said.

"It must have taken a long time to build this Ark," Mr. Rabbit said.

"The humans were already building the Ark before I was born," answered Mr. Koala. "And others have been watching them build it for at least seventy-five years."[7]

"That's a long time!" exclaimed Mr. Kangaroo.

"Yeah, that's why unbelievers continue to mock and never take God's coming judgment seriously," answered Mrs. Koala. "They mistake God's patience as proof that His judgment is never coming."[8]

"Just by looking around in here, I can see why it took so long to build," answered Mr. Mongoose. "It must have taken a lot of time to gather the wood and all the supplies and everything else needed to build this thing."

"They also had to plan it out," added Mrs. Pig. "And let's not forget that they had to gather all the food and water that we see."

"This Ark is incredible, and there's plenty to look at," declared Mr. Horse. "However, we can look around later. I'm starving, and all the nests have food and water. Mrs. Horse and I are going to our nest to eat."

"Me too!" shouted several animals at once.

All the animals immediately began eating and drinking water as soon as they entered their nests. The animals were so hungry that they all ate and drank without talking much until they were full. After how far they traveled, and all that they had been through, they were overcome by drowsiness. After they ate, they all fell asleep in their nests. They were so tired that they were sound asleep for two days.

Mr. Hyena was the first to wake up as the daylight shone through the opened door of the Ark into his nest. Mr. Hyena yawned so big that he squealed a little bit. Mrs. Hyena and all the other animals woke up to the squeal, and each followed with their own yawn. There was so much yawning that Mr. Hyena couldn't help it, and he yawned again, which triggered another round of yawns from all the other animals.

"Wow. I've never yawned so much in all my life," announced Mr. Hyena.

"I feel like I've been asleep for a year," Mrs. Sheep said.

"It hasn't been that long because the door of the Ark is still open," Mr. Camel replied.

Mr. Owl was perched on a beam above and said, "Actually, you've all been asleep for two days."

"Wow, really?" exclaimed Mrs. Mongoose.

"I feel like I could sleep some more," Mr. Bear said.

"Shouldn't the door be shut if God is going to flood the earth?" asked Mrs. Beaver.

"You would think so," answered Mr. Elephant.

"The humans are still running around, fixing and cleaning things," Mr. Bat said.

"I need some fresh air," announced Mr. Hippo. "Do you think we can go out on the ramp?"

"I don't know," answered Mr. Owl. "The humans have been going out there from time to time."

"I'm going out on the ramp for some fresh air," declared Mr. Hippo. "Hopefully it won't be a problem."

Mr. Hippo went out on the ramp, and to his surprise, there were a lot of animals down on the ground gathered around the Ark. As soon as they saw Mr. Hippo, they started shouting and mocking him.

"Hey, Mr. Hippo, is this hunk of wood supposed to save you from God's judgment?" shouted an animal from the crowd.

"Bwaaaaa ha ha ha ha," came the laughter from the crowd.

"You left the freedom of the outdoors to go live in a box built by humans!" shouted another mocker.

"Ahhhhh ha ha ha ha ha." The crowd laughed even more.

The other animals inside the Ark heard all the shouting and came over to the door to see what was going on. Several of the animals joined Mr. Hippo out on the ramp.

"Wow, they're still out there mocking us," Mrs. Mongoose said.

Mr. Hippo shouted back at the mockers, "Judgment is coming, climb aboard before it's too late!"

"No way!" shouted another mocker. "We've already heard all your judgment nonsense! Why would we come aboard and listen to it even more?"

"This Ark is the only thing that can save you from God's judgment!" shouted Mr. Lion.

"What? Are you blind?" shouted another mocker. "Look around...you're the laughing stock of the whole world!"

"Ha ha ha ha ha ha," came the roar of more laughter.

"The whole world is about to experience the wrath of God," shouted Mr. Rhino. "Come aboard and escape God's judgment before it's too late!"

"You're all suffering from a God delusion!"[9] shouted another mocker. "When one animal suffers from a delusion, it's called insanity. When many animals suffer from a delusion, it's called religion."[10]

"Ahhhhh ha ha ha ha ha," the crowd burst into thunderous laughter.

"Your religion is so bad that you would rather live in a box made by humans!" shouted another mocker.

"Ha ha ha ha ha," came even more laughter.

"It's no use," declared Mrs. Kangaroo. "The devil has blinded their minds, so they don't want to be saved."[11]

"We do!" shouted a voice from the bottom of the ramp. "We want to be saved! We want to come aboard and escape God's judgment!"

The animals looked toward the bottom of the ramp and saw Mr. and Mrs. Turtle walking slowly up the ramp. Mr. and Mrs. Monkey quickly ran down the ramp and picked up the turtles and brought them to the top.

"Welcome aboard," Mr. Monkey said.

"Thank you," answered Mr. Turtle. "We didn't think we would ever get here."

"What do you mean?" asked Mrs. Mongoose.

"Every time we got close to the ramp, somebody would pick us up and set us far away and laugh at us as we began walking toward the ramp again," answered Mrs. Turtle.

"How did you make it this time?" asked Mr. Hippo.

"With all the yelling going on back and forth between you and them, they all became distracted and forgot about us, and we were able to make it to the ramp," Mr. Turtle answered.

"Thank you for distracting them," Mrs. Turtle said.

"Don't thank us, thank God!" answered Mr. Hyena. "It was God who used their mocking to distract them so you could make it to the ramp."

"Amen to that, and thank You, God!" exclaimed Mr. Turtle. "I'm always amazed at how God works all things for good to those who love Him.[12] He even used their mocking for our good."

"No sense in staying out here and listening to all their ridicule," declared Mrs. Cow. "C'mon, let's all go back inside."

"Hold on before we go back in," Mr. Lion said as he turned to the crowd of mockers and shouted, "This is your last chance! Do any of you want to come aboard and escape God's coming judgment?"

"What, and live in a large wooden box full of phobic, religious, judgmental, insane bigots?" shouted another mocker from the crowd. "No, thank you!"

"Ah ha ha ha," came more laughter.

"You heard them," Mr. Lion said. "It's just like Mrs. Kangaroo said, they don't want to be saved."

All the animals turned and went back into the Ark.

By this time the humans had finished repairing the Ark and cleaning up all the messes. Now they were going down the passageways and assisting the animals to their nests and shutting all the gates behind them. As each pair of animals entered their nest, the humans would pet them, shut the gate, and say, "Don't be afraid, God is with us."

The inside of the Ark was a sight to see. Every nest was occupied with every beast according to its kind, and all the livestock according to their kinds, and every creeping thing that creeps on the earth according to its kind, and every bird according to its kind, every winged creature. They all went into the Ark with Noah and seven other humans, two and two of all flesh in which there was the breath of life.[13] All the animals were secure in their nests and talking amongst each other.

Three more days passed, and the Ark door was still open.

"It sure is a weird feeling being inside of this Ark waiting for God's judgment to come," Mr. Sloth said.

"I wonder if all those animals are still outside mocking and joking at us in here," Mrs. Rabbit asked.

All the animals began to wonder if the judgment would ever come.

Mr. Kangaroo looked across the passageway at Mr. Lion's nest and asked, "Why is the Ark door still open?"

"I don't know," answered Mr. Lion.

"I wonder how much longer until God's judgment comes?" Mrs. Sheep asked from a nearby nest.

"Only God knows," answered Mrs. Lion.

After six days inside the Ark, there was still no sign of God's judgment.

Occasionally the mockers could be heard yelling from outside the Ark door, but other than the mockers, the sixth day in the Ark was uneventful. All the animals went to sleep.

It would be their last calm night of sleep for a very long time.

CHAPTER 27

The Flood

All the animals, including the humans, slept sound on the sixth night inside the Ark. Then on the seventh day,[1] early in the morning, Mr. Giraffe was the first to wake up and noticed that the Ark door was shut.

"Everybody wake up!" shouted Mr. Giraffe. "Look...the door is shut!"

"Who shut it?" asked Mrs. Snake. "I didn't see anybody shut it."

"The humans were asleep too," answered Mr. Koala. "So they couldn't have shut it."

"I didn't hear anything all night long," Mr. Rabbit said. "How could a door that large get shut without me hearing it?"

"God must have shut the door,"[2] declared Mr. Lion.

All the animals began to get fearful as they realized that they were now locked in the Ark. Suddenly God's judgment seemed eerily close.

"Is this it?" asked Mrs. Sloth. "Is the flood happening now?"

"How do we know what's happening outside?" asked Mr. Rhino. "Is the flood happening outside?"

All the animals began to get nervous with apprehension.

"If the door is shut, then it must mean that God's judgment is happening...right?" asked Mrs. Bear.

"Everybody just calm down!" ordered Mr. Lion. "Let's not panic—"

Suddenly the earth began to shake violently, causing the entire Ark to shake. Several animals screamed, "Aaaarrrrgghhhh!"

The earthquake was so severe that all the animals lost their footing and all throughout the Ark every animal was doing everything they could to withstand the shaking and rocking. Some animals were holding on to the rails. Some were trying to stand fast through the bumping and swaying. Others were lying down. The earthquake was causing a great panic, and every animal sound could be heard throughout the Ark: squealing, clucking, oinking, howling, roaring, screeching, hissing, chirping, cooing, mooing, snorting, cawing, bellowing, barking, baaing, hee-hawing, quacking, trumpeting, bleating, cloaking, tweeting, gobbling, neighing, groaning, whining, and every other sound could be heard.

Then the sound of very heavy rain began pounding on the roof as the earth began to flood.

Outside the Ark, colossal fissures opened up all over the earth as the fountains of the great deep burst forth and the windows of heaven were opened,[3] releasing massive columns of water that geysered upward into the earth's atmosphere.[4] The water was coming back down to earth in a very heavy rainfall.

The earthquakes were global as the earth's preflood single continental landmass began to break apart and separate into multiple continents. This catastrophic reshaping the earth's surface was rapidly changing the earth's crust from a uniform surface to multiple separate tectonic plates.[5]

"God's judgment is here!" shouted a terrified Mrs. Sheep.

"I'm scared!" shouted Mrs. Elephant.

"It's really happening!" shouted a frightened Mr. Beaver.

"God is doing exactly what He said He would do," announced a trembling Mr. Bull.

"The whole world is really going to die!"[6] shouted Mr. Mongoose.

The animals were terrified and full of fear, yet they were safe. The God they trusted was now demonstrating His absolute intolerance of sin and His power and authority over all creation. The reality of God's judgment was upon them. They were safe in the Ark while God's wrath was being poured out on a sinful world.[7]

Volcanoes of molten lava and geysers of scalding water spewed into the air and came down in a continuous heavy downpour of global rain. All those who rejected God's salvation were now running for higher ground as the water continued to rise on the earth.

The floodwaters combined with volcanic ash and sediment resulting in global tsunamis of mud and soot that buried every living thing that was in its path.

The dinosaur government left the perfect society behind and fled for higher ground. As the dinosaurs ran, they left footprints in the mud that were quickly covered by a tsunami of muddy sediment, preserving their footprints underneath.[8]

All over the earth, animals were now fleeing to higher ground in order to escape God's judgment, but the great day of their wrath has come, and no one will survive.[9]

The muddy, sooty, sedimentary floodwaters overcame every land-dwelling creature and buried them alive instantly wherever they were. The rising flood water also carried with it marine life, which mixed with plants and land-dwelling creatures and buried everything together in many places all over the earth.[10]

The earth became a global graveyard as billions creatures were rapidly buried by the flood.[11]

The terrified animals inside the Ark just stayed in their nests as the relentless shaking and pounding rain continued nonstop; they did not know how to handle this kind of terrifying reality. The animals were gripped with fear as they thought of the death and destruction happening outside the Ark.

Thanks to the previous repairs by the humans, the Ark was holding up well under the constant punishment of the earthquakes and pouring rain.

The waters continued to rise until the Ark was suddenly lifted off the earth by the flood waters[12] and the ramp was torn away from the Ark.

"Do you feel that?" asked Mr. Camel. "I think we're floating."

"Yes, I feel it," answered Mrs. Camel. "The floodwaters have lifted the Ark, and now we're floating."

As the floodwaters continue to rise, the Ark began to rock and sway as the wind and rain caused large waves to pound against the Ark.

The rocking and swaying on the water was much different from the shaking from the earthquakes. The Ark would rise and fall from front to rear and side to side as the waves moved the Ark over the water. The animals were unable to keep their balance as the high angle of the Ark on the large waves would cause the animals to slide along the deck and crash into the opposite side of their nests. It would take some time for the animals to figure out how to stay balanced enough to stop crashing from side to side in their nests.

Eventually the animals figured out how to maintain their balance through all the rocking and swaying. After the animals got used to the swaying and were able to keep their balance, Mr. Lion took this opportunity to encourage everyone to stay strong.

"Everybody listen up!" shouted Mr. Lion from his nest. "It's a terrible thing what's happening out there. But remember our journey to get here and how we warned everyone we saw that God's judgment was coming. We invited them to come with us, but they rejected our invitations. They did not want to be saved. Instead, they mocked and ridiculed us right up until the end. We all saw how evil and violent the world was. God called each of us to go to this Ark, and He led us here. We are here because of His mercy and grace. So even though what's happening out there is a terrible thing, remember that God's judgment is righteous and true, and we can be thankful that He saved us!"

"Amen to that!" shouted Mrs. Giraffe. "We are sinners just like those outside, but God saved us!"

"Halleluiah!" shouted Mrs. Hippo.

"Let's pray right now!" shouted Mr. Bear.

"Yes, yes," all the animals agreed.

Mr. Bear began the prayer, *"O God, thank You for saving us from Your wrath. Thank You for opening our eyes so that we can see the truth of our own sin and our need for Your salvation. We thank You for for-*

giving our sins and saving us in this Ark. O Lord, we don't know what the future holds, but we know that You hold the future because You have shown us that You are in control of all creation, and we trust You with our lives. We pray for Your continued mercy and grace in our lives. Amen."

"Amen," answered all the animals in agreement.

One by one all the other animals took turns praying out loud while the Ark continued to rock and sway.

Little did they know, the rain would continue to fall on the earth for forty days and forty nights.[13]

The animals and the humans soon learned how to cope with rocking and swaying. Soon after that, the humans began going through each nest and cleaning them up. They would also let out certain animals in small groups to let them exercise. Mr. Elephant was one of the first animals to be led out of his nest by a human to get some exercise. But the humans did not return Mr. Elephant to his nest for a few hours.

Finally, when they brought Mr. Elephant back to his nest, Mrs. Elephant immediately asked, "Where have you been all day?"

Mr. Elephant answered, "I was walking on a treadmill thing that operated some kind of conveyor pump thing. The humans would bring all the waste they collected on a cart and then dump it in a large container. From there, the treadmill I was on would operate a pump that would scoop up the waste and transfer it to a larger tank full of water or something."

"That sounds like a lot of work," Mr. Camel said.

"The work wasn't so bad, but the smell was horrible," answered Mr. Elephant. "It made my eyes water. Thankfully they washed me off before they brought me back to our nest, otherwise this whole place would stink."

"Gross!" exclaimed Mrs. Elephant.

Mr. Horse chimed in, "They had me pulling one of those carts full of waste down the passageways. The humans cleaned each nest and put the waste in the cart. I would follow along pulling the cart."

"It seems we all have to do our part while we are on this Ark," Mr. Rhino said from across the passageway.

The humans developed a system that used several animals to help them accomplish various chores. The humans and the animals got used to their daily routines. The daily routines would continue even with the swaying and pounding rain.

The animals began sleeping more and more as the days went by. Mr. and Mrs. Bear were sound asleep for many days.

The Ark floated on the waters as the flood continued to rise until the waters were twenty-two and a half feet above the highest mountains.[14]

Then God made a strong wind blow over the whole earth,[15] and the catastrophic reshaping of the earth's crust began to settle as the fountains of the deep and the windows of heaven were closed and the rain from the heavens were restrained.[16]

The waters began to slowly recede from the earth.

Then, after 150 days of floating on the flood waters, the Ark rested on the mountains of Ararat.[17]

"Hey!" shouted Mr. Beaver. "I think we stopped floating."

"Yes, it's true!" shouted Mrs. Hippo. "We stopped floating!"

All the animals that were asleep were now wide awake, including Mr. and Mrs. Bear.

"Hoooray!" all the animals were cheering all throughout the Ark on all three decks.

"Is the door open yet?" asked Mr. Hippo as he looked over at the door. "I need some fresh air really bad."

All the other animals looked over at the door, but it was still shut.

"I wonder what it's like outside the Ark?" asked Mrs. Rabbit.

"If we're no longer floating, I would love to go outside and walk on solid ground," declared Mrs. Beaver.

"Let's not get excited," Mr. Lion said. "We have no idea what's going on out there. We may have to stay inside until the earth dries out."

"How long will that take?" asked a troubled Mr. Sloth.

"We will just have to wait," answered Mr. Lion.

Days went by as the animals wondered when the door would be opened. With the Ark resting on the mountains of Ararat and the waters slowly receding, the animals and humans continued with their daily routines.

The Ark rested on the mountains of Ararat for another seventy-four days before the waters receded enough so the tops of the mountains were visible.[18] By this time the animals were sleeping a lot again. Every so often they would wake up and look to see if the Ark door was open. Then they would eat, get some exercise, and go back to sleep.

Things remained fairly calm inside the Ark. There were still earthquakes but not as severe. The waters continued to subside while the earth's surface was still making changes. Mountain ranges continued to slowly rise while valleys sank.[19] The earth's surface was still settling down. As the ocean floors sank and deep trenches slowly formed, the flood waters drained into the oceans.

For the next forty days, life in the Ark continued with the normal daily routines and sleeping.

It has now been 264 days since the flood began. Right about this time, Mr. Elephant was returning to his nest after a day working on the treadmill, but this time he had some interesting news. As Mr. Elephant entered his nest, he looked at Mrs. Elephant and said, "I heard something interesting today."

"Like what?" asked Mrs. Elephant.

Interesting news was not uncommon in the Ark. There were stories of animals getting stir-crazy and biting the humans or chewing up their nests. One time Mr. Monkey threw poop at one of the bird nests because they were driving him crazy with their chirping. So Mrs. Elephant was expecting to hear some typical interesting Ark news.

"I just got word that the humans opened a small door on the roof and sent out a raven to survey the land and the raven never returned,"[20] answered Mr. Elephant.

"Why didn't the raven come back?" asked Mrs. Elephant.

"I don't know," answered Mr. Elephant.

Mrs. Elephant called out to all the other animals in the nests and shouted, "Hey, everybody, Mr. Elephant said that the humans sent out a raven to survey the land, but the raven never came back."

"Do you think the raven died out there?" asked Mrs. Snake.

"No, not the raven," answered Mr. Turtle. "If anybody can survive out there, a raven can. A raven is a hardy and intelligent bird who can survive in harsh environments. Plus, they will eat just about anything."[21]

"If the raven is surviving out there, then that would mean that the world outside is slowly but surely becoming livable," Mr. Bull said.

All the animals agreed, and they were all filled with a new hope that they would be getting out of the Ark soon.

"We just need to continue to wait until the earth is ready for us," answered Mr. Lion.

"We've trusted God through this whole ordeal," answered Mrs. Beaver. "We just need to continue to trust God, He will let us know when the earth is ready for us."

"Indeed," answered Mrs. Rhino.

All the animals nodded in agreement.

The animals were excited but tempered this time, and they all went back to their daily routines.

Seven days after the raven story, Mr. Elephant returned from his chores with more interesting news.

"I have more interesting news," declared Mr. Elephant as he entered his nest.

"What is it this time?" asked Mrs. Elephant. "Did the raven finally come back?"

"No, no, the raven never came back," answered Mr. Elephant. "This time the humans sent out a dove, and the dove flew around for a while, and then she came back because the flood waters were still too high."[22]

Mrs. Elephant spoke to the other animals, "Hey, everybody, the human sent out a dove, but unlike the raven, she came back."

"Why didn't she stay out there like the raven?" asked Mrs. Sloth

"Doves eat seeds,"[23] answered Mrs. Mongoose. "Since the dove came back, there must not be sufficient plant life yet."

"I sure wish I could take a peek outside," Mr. Rabbit said.

"I guess we just have to go back to waiting," answered Mrs. Rabbit.

The hope of the animals increased a bit more as they went back to their daily routines.

Another seven days passed since the dove incident, but this time the interesting news was exciting.

Mr. Elephant came back from his chores and declared to Mrs. Elephant, "I have some exciting news this time!"

"Well, what is it?" asked Mrs. Elephant. "What is your exciting news?"

"The dove was sent out again." answered Mr. Elephant.

"Did she come back again?" asked Mrs. Elephant.

"Yes, she did," answered Mr. Elephant. "But this time she brought back a freshly plucked olive leaf."[24]

"An olive leaf!" shouted Mrs. Elephant. "That means plants have begun to grow!"

The other animals overheard Mrs. Elephant, and excitement spread throughout the Ark. The animals began to sing...

The dove plucked an olive leaf
We are glad and rejoicing
The earth is finally drying
We are happy, happy, happy
There is plant life outside and growing
Our God is awesome, awesome, awesome
Pretty soon we will be leaving
We praise the God of our salvation.

The animals celebrated the rest of the day because the olive leaf meant that the earth was almost ready.

Now every time Mr. Elephant returned from his chores, Mrs. Elephant would eagerly ask him if he heard any more news.

Seven more days passed, and Mr. Elephant returned from his chores, and Mrs. Elephant eagerly asked him, "Any news today?"

"Yes," answered Mr. Elephant. "They sent the dove out again, but this time she never returned."[25]

"That means there is sufficient plant life for her to survive out there!" declared Mrs. Elephant.

"That's exactly what it means!" answered Mr. Elephant.

Mr. and Mrs. Elephant told the other animals, and the news rapidly spread throughout the Ark. All the animals were full of hope because they knew the earth was drying and plants were growing outside the Ark. The animals continued to do their routines, but they would often look over at the Ark door, waiting for it to open.

Mrs. Elephant continued to ask Mr. Elephant if he heard any news, but he had nothing to report each day.

One week went by—still no news.

Two weeks went by—still no news.

Three weeks went by—still no news.

Four weeks went by—still now news.

Mr. Elephant returned from his chores, and Mrs. Elephant was waiting eagerly and asked, "Any news today?"

"No, honey," answered Mr. Elephant. "I'm sorry, there's nothing to report."

"It's been four weeks since the dove left the Ark," Mrs. Elephant said. "I thought for sure we would able to go outside by now."

All the animals began to get discouraged. Some even started complaining.

"Are we ever going to get out of here?" asked Mr. Pig.

"Don't get discouraged," declared Mr. Lion from his nest. "We know that the raven and the dove are out there, and we know that plants are growing out there. The Lord will open the door when the time is right. Let's not forget that God promised to never leave us nor forsake us. So don't be discouraged. Instead, let's pray."

Mr. Lion prayed, and all the animals said, "Amen,"

"Thank you for praying, Mr. Lion," announced Mrs. Giraffe. "Turning to God and remembering His promise is the best way to fight discouragement."

All the animals went back to their routines while they waited on the Lord to open the Ark door.

Then, on the following day, which was the twenty-ninth day since the dove left the Ark, there was a commotion stirring on the top deck. The news from the top deck traveled to all three decks in just a matter of minutes. From one nest to the next, the news was being reported that the humans opened up a covering in the roof and looked outside to see that the land was dry as far as they could see.[26]

"The land is finally dry!" shouted Mr. Kangaroo.

"The flood is over, and the earth is ready for us!" shouted Mr. Mongoose.

All through the Ark the animals were celebrating. There was joy upon joy in every heart.

The animals stared at the Ark door, expecting it to open at any second.

"I can hardly wait to see daylight," announced Mr. Rhino as he and all the other animals stared at the door.

A few hours went by, and the excitement began to fizzle out as the door remained closed. The animals finally fell asleep.

The next day the humans continued with the chores just like always.

"I guess we're still not leaving this Ark," Mrs. Beaver said in frustration.

"I don't know how much longer I can take it in here," announced Mr. Hippo. "If I don't get some fresh air soon, I will probably go crazy. I'm tired of the humans throwing buckets of water on me. I'm dying to go jump in a real lake!"

"I wish we could at least look outside and see what it looks like," Mrs. Sheep said.

All the animals began wishing they could go outside so much that they were becoming filled with discontentment. Mr. Lion again had to remind the animals that God was in control and He had a reason why He wasn't allowing them to go outside yet. Mr. Lion gave them a pep talk and prayed again. Mr. Lion would have to encourage the animals a few more times over the coming weeks as the Ark door remained closed.

The animals continued their daily routines waiting eagerly for the Ark door to be opened.

It was now fifty-five days since the humans opened the covering on the roof and looked outside. As usual, the animals went to sleep that night hoping that they would wake up and see the Ark door open.

This night was different. Each animal had the same dream. In their dream God appeared to each of them in a light and said, "The earth has dried out. Go out from the Ark and swarm the earth and be fruitful and multiply on the earth."[27]

The same God Who called each of them to the Ark was now calling each of them to be fruitful and multiply on the earth.

CHAPTER 28

✦

The New World

M r. Kangaroo woke up first and immediately remembered the dream.

Did God speak to me in my dream? he thought to himself. *He sure did.*

While he was thinking about his dream Mrs. Kangaroo woke up and immediately looked at Mr. Kangaroo and said, "I dreamed that God spoke to me."

"Me too," he replied. "In my dream God said the earth is dried out and to go out from the Ark and swarm the earth and be fruitful and multiply."

"That's exactly the same dream I had!" she said, trying not to shout. Unfortunately, her voice was just loud enough to wake Mr. Bear.

"Why are you shouting so early in the morning?" asked Mr. Bear. "You woke me up from a dream I was having about God."

"We had a dream about God too!" shouted Mrs. Kangaroo. This time her voice was loud enough to wake many other animals.

"We both dreamed that God said the earth is dried out and to go out from the Ark and swarm the earth and be fruitful and multiply," Mr. Kangaroo said.

"That's the same dream I had!" shouted Mr. Bear.

"That's the same dream I had too!" shouted Mrs. Beaver.

"Me too!" shouted several other animals at once.

"We all had the same dream!" shouted Mr. Kangaroo. "God has spoken to each of us through a dream!"

The realization that all the animals had the same dream caused a great commotion of excitement all throughout the Ark.

"God told each of us that the earth is dried out and to leave the Ark!" announced Mrs. Bear.

"We've been in this Ark for 371 days, and we're finally going to leave!"[1] announced Mr. Hippo.

"Hooray!" Cheering could be heard throughout the Ark.

"God said to be fruitful and multiply," Mr. Rhino said. "What do you think He meant by that?"

"Well, let's think it through," answered Mr. Elephant. "We have been in this ark for over a year while God was wiping out a sinful world where everybody's thoughts were continually evil, being fruitful obviously means we must reject evil."

"We are to multiply, which means to have a lot of children," answered Mrs. Cow. "But not just any children, in order to be fruitful, we must have godly children.[2] And having godly children requires that we teach them the way of the Lord."[3]

"We must raise them up to walk in God's truth and fear the Lord," Mr. Hyena declared.

"We must continually tell them about the flood and God's terrifying judgment on a sinful world," Mr. Kangaroo stated. "Future generations must remember and never forget how a violent, evil, and unbelieving world provoked the Lord to wrath."[4]

"Let me put it another way," answered Mr. Lion. "To be fruitful and multiply is a cultural mandate from God.[5] We must work diligently to create cultures and build civilizations that fear the Lord."

"Otherwise society will rebel against the Lord and forsake Him again," added Mrs. Lion. "And we have seen how God will consume those who forsake Him."[6]

Mr. Mongoose joined in, "By obeying the cultural mandate, we are participating in God's work in maintaining and caring for His creation."[7]

"God saved us because of our faith, and now we must pass it on to our children and future generations," declared Mr. Pig.

"When you take the time to understand, there's a lot of meaning packed in God's Word when He says to be fruitful and multiply," Mr. Hippo said.

Right about this time, four humans came to the Ark door and began working on the door. It was actually two doors that swung inwardly and latched in the middle.

"It looks like they're going to open the door!" announced Mrs. Mongoose.

The entire Ark was sealed with pitch inside and outside, and the humans were chiseling and scraping the pitch to expose the edges and hinges of the doors.[8]

The word spread throughout the Ark that the humans were opening the door. The animals looked on with excitement as the humans were scraping the pitch off the doors. It would take some time to get the doors open because they were sealed thoroughly during the flood.

Finally, after much effort, the humans opened the doors, and immediately bright sunlight shone into the Ark, exposing the first signs of the new world. It was the first time the animals had seen daylight in over a year.

"Daylight!" shouted Mr. Hippo.

"Oh, it's bright and beautiful!" exclaimed Mrs. Giraffe.

"Glory to God!" shouted Mr. Bear.

All the animals were praising the Lord as the daylight brought with it the realization of a new beginning. The animals were so excited that they had to resist the temptation rip open their gates rather than wait for the humans to let them out.

After opening the door, the humans looked out the door as if they were figuring out what to do. The Ark rested on a fairly flat section of a mountain range. The flood sediment had created a sand dune that was built up against the side of the Ark just a few feet below the bottom of the door opening. The dune gradually sloped down to the surrounding land.

The humans removed both of the doors from their hinges and laid them down side by side as a makeshift ramp from the Ark doorway to the top of the dune, and the dune sloped to the surrounding land to make exiting the Ark very easy.

All the animals were restless and eager to go outside.

The humans began opening the nests and releasing the animals. As the humans opened each nest, they blessed the animals and said, "Be fruitful and multiply and fill the earth."

Mr. and Mrs. Kangaroo were the first ones to be let out of their nest, and they stood at the top of the ramp and looked out at the world outside.

"Wow!" declared Mr. and Mrs. Kangaroo in one voice.

"It's like a whole new world!" exclaimed Mr. Kangaroo.

"It's beautiful!" exclaimed Mrs. Kangaroo.

There were snow-covered mountains, grassy fields, streams, lakes, plants, clouds, and blue sky. Even though the sun was shining on the Ark and it was a beautiful day, there were active volcanoes and lightning-filled storm cells visible in the distance. Earthquakes will still be quite common as the earth goes through postflood instability. For many years to come, there will be continuing isolated catastrophes until the earth's climate along with plate tectonics stabilize around the world.[9]

Mr. and Mrs. Kangaroo marveled at the new world as they walked down the ramp together while the other animals were right behind them.

Many animals left the Ark and immediately took off running in different directions until they were out of sight. It took the entire day for the humans to finally release the thousands of animal kinds on all three decks. The birds were released out of the opening in the roof; they could be seen flying away from the Ark out into the new world.

The forty-four animals that journeyed to the Ark together all gathered in a group at the base of the dune.

"Look at how beautiful everything is!" exclaimed Mr. Rabbit.

"We are looking at a world that has been cleansed of all sin," Mr. Rhino said.

"It's a new world," declared Mr. Camel.

There was an awkward moment of silence as all the animals knew that this was the end of their journey together.

"Well, this is it, my friends," announced Mr. Kangaroo. "We have been through so much together, and we have finally reached the end of our journey when we each have to go our own way." Mr. Kangaroo's eyes began to well up with tears. "I love you all!"

"We love you too, Mr. Kangaroo!" Mrs. Bear replied. Then she looked around through her tears at all the animals and said, "I will always remember every one of you!"

"Just think about all we've been through together," Mrs. Mongoose said with a weepy voice. "We journeyed to the Ark together with all its trials. Then we spent over a year inside the Ark together with all its trials. But I never thought saying goodbye would be the most difficult of all."

All the animals were crying and hugging each other.

Mr. Lion spoke up and said, "Please allow me to say one last prayer before we leave each other and go our own way."

"That is a great idea!" Mrs. Giraffe exclaimed.

"Please do," Mr. Hyena said.

All the animals bowed their heads in prayer as Mr. Lion prayed, *"O Heavenly Father, we thank You for saving us from Your wrath against a sinful world. We thank You for demonstrating Your love toward us in that even though we are sinners You provided the Ark to escape Your judgment. Lord, You have cleansed Your creation of all unrighteousness and chosen those of us on the Ark to repopulate the world. O righteous Father, we are excited about the future, but we are fearful because we are sinful and we need Your help to carry out Your will. O Lord, help us to carry out Your cultural mandate and be fruitful and multiply. Lord, we trust You because You said You will never leave us nor forsake us. Lord, bless each of us as we go our own way. We love You, Lord. Amen."*

"Amen!" all the animals agreed in one voice.

The animals paused in silence for a moment as no one wanted to be the first to say goodbye.

Finally, Mr. Lion said, "Goodbye, my friends."

"Goodbye, we will always remember you," Mrs. Lion said.

All the animals said goodbye to Mr. and Mrs. Lion and to each other.

Then Mr. and Mrs. Lion took off running out into the new world. Each of the animals also took off running as well.

CHAPTER 29

The Rainbow Covenant

Mr. and Mrs. Kangaroo left the Ark headed out into the new world, unsure of where they were going. They just knew that God was with them, and they believed He would lead them to wherever He wanted them to start a family. As they traveled further and further from the Ark, the realization that there were no other animals around began to settle in.

"This is surreal," Mrs. Kangaroo said. "There are no other animals—no bullies, no atheists, no evil, no violence, no mockers, no one at all to contend with anywhere."

"The world has been completely cleansed of sin," Mrs. Kangaroo said.

"God spared nobody," Mr. Kangaroo said. "Sin had corrupted the entire earth, and now they're all gone."

"They all died because they rejected God," Mrs. Kangaroo said as she began to cry. "Why wouldn't they listen?"

Mr. Kangaroo hugged her to comfort her, but he couldn't control his grief, and he, too, broke down in tears. The thought of all those who perished in the flood was overwhelming. The empty world around them was going to take some time to get used to.

"Even without all the evil, violence, mocking, and unbelief, I never thought I would feel so lonely," Mrs. Kangaroo said through her tears.

"I know," Mr. Kangaroo agreed. "I definitely don't want to go back to the way things were, but I didn't know starting over would feel this way. We must remember that God is with us and these feelings will pass."

"Amen to that," Mrs. Kangaroo agreed. "Let's also not forget that there were thousands of animals on that Ark, and they are out there somewhere. God is with us all."

"I am glad God brought us together," Mr. Kangaroo said. "There is no one else I would want to start the new world with."

"I love you, Mr. Kangaroo."

"I love you too, Mrs. Kangaroo."

"You're my favorite kangaroo in the whole world," Mrs. Kangaroo said with a smile.

"Ha ha ha ha," they both laughed together.

"Shall we pray," asked Mr. Kangaroo.

"Yes, we shall," she answered.

Mr. and Mrs. Kangaroo prayed together for the first time in the new world, *"O Lord, we are thankful that You saved us from Your judgment. We are thankful that You chose us to start the new world. We need You to watch over us and guide us as we are very excited yet very fearful and lonely. Strengthen us so that we can fulfill Your calling to be fruitful and multiply. Amen."*

After they prayed, they soon came across a pasture with nearby woodlands. The sun was going down, and they decided to make this their home. After much traveling, they had no problem falling asleep for the night.

The following morning, Mr. and Mrs. Kangaroo were awakened by rainfall. The rain began to taper off, and a beautiful rainbow appeared in the clouds. Mr. and Mrs. Kangaroo both saw the rainbow at the same time. Before they could speak, the voice of God said, "Behold, I establish My covenant with you and your offspring after you: never again shall all flesh be cut off by the waters of a flood, and never again shall there be a flood to destroy the earth. I have set My rainbow in the cloud, and it shall be a sign of the covenant between Me and the earth. When the rainbow is in the clouds, I will see it and remember the everlasting covenant between God and every living creature of all flesh that is on the earth."[1]

The voice stopped, and Mr. and Mrs. Kangaroo sat in silence for a few moments looking at the rainbow, marveling at what God just said to them.

"It's a rainbow," Mrs. Kangaroo said.

"It's meant to remind us of the promise of the Lord to never destroy the world again by flood," Mr. Kangaroo said.

"It's beautiful," she said.

"Yes, it is," he agreed.

"Guess what?" Mrs. Kangaroo asked.

"What?" he asked.

"We're going to have a baby," Mrs. Kangaroo answered.

"That's wonderful!" he said.

Mr. and Mrs. Kangaroo looked at each other in love then turned and looked at the rainbow again.

"Praise the Lord," Mr. Kangaroo said.

"God is good," she replied.

One year later...

Dad looked at his son and said, "Son, now you know the meaning behind the rainbow."

Joey just stared at his dad with his mouth dropped open.

Dad continued, "The rainbow reminds us of the promise of the Lord to never destroy the world again by a flood. When you see the rainbow, remember the holiness and righteousness of God as He punished the world because of sin. The rainbow also reminds us of God's goodness and love to save those who trust in Him. The rainbow is also a reminder that God always keeps His promises."

"Wow!" exclaimed Joey. "The rainbow will also remind me of all you and mom went through." Then Joey looked around at the world around them and asked, "Dad, if everything was underwater, how come nothing looks like it was underwater? Shouldn't there be some way to tell that all this was underwater?"

"That is a very good question son," Dad replied. Then Dad pointed at some mountains with some slanted and bent rock layers. "Do you see how those rock layers are slanted and bent?"

"Yes," answered Joey.

"Rock cannot be bent without it breaking, which means the rock layers were rapidly deposited and folded while still wet and pliable during the flood. After the flood they hardened in the shape they are in."[2]

"So that's how those rock layers got bent," Joey said.

"Yep," answered Dad. "They were formed during the flood when they were still soft. Also, the flat and sharp boundaries between rock layers show that each layer was laid one after another with no time for erosion."

"Now every time I see the rock lines, I will think of the flood," Joey said.

"That's good, son," Dad said. "God loves you, but there is evidence of His judgment all around us for those who reject Him."

Dad had his son's full attention and said, "My son, listen to me, and I will teach you to fear the Lord."[3]

"I want to fear the Lord just like you, Dad!" Joey claimed.

"Son, do not be deceived: bad company ruins good morals,"[4] Dad said. "If sinners entice you, turn your back on them!"[5]

Joey was listening intently.

Dad paused and gently held his son's cheeks and looked directly into Joey's eyes and said, "My son, listen to me and do as I say, and you will have a long, good life.[6] The world is still corrupted by sin and death and all of creation is groaning[7] for God to restore all things. Until then, sin will be crouching at the door to destroy you, but you must rule over it."[8]

Mom added, "Above all else, guard your heart, for everything you do flows from it."[9]

"I will!" Joey replied confidently. "But how do I guard my heart?"

"You guard your heart by standing firm in your faith in God,"[10] Mom answered. "Because without faith it is impossible to please God."[11]

"I believe in God!" Joey declared.

"My son, if your heart is wise, my heart will be glad too,"[12] Dad said.

"I will make you glad, Dad!" announced Joey. "Glad, Dad... hey, that rhymes!"

With that they all laughed.

Then Joey noticed a bird flying in the sky above and said, "Mom and Dad, look...a dove!"[13]

The End

Epilogue

Thank you for reading my story on how the animals got to the Ark. This story hopefully caused you to think about what you believe in light of God's judgment. It seems that in today's culture there is not much concern about God's judgment. Should we be concerned about God's Judgment? Why?

More often than not, if you asked someone if they think they are a good, they will say yes. But God says that no one is good. The reason for this conflict is because many people have their own standard of righteousness which is very low compared to God's standard. God's standard of righteousness is perfection and we have all fallen short of God's perfect standard. Falling short of God's standard is called sin. Sin is a moral crime against God. God's standard is so perfect that it even applies to our thoughts and God knows our thoughts. The seriousness of sin is often overlooked because, after all, we're all sinners. If we're all sinners than God has to lower His standard otherwise we're all going to hell, right? Why would a loving God send all sinners to hell?

Sin is not just some mistake that can be overlooked. The truth is that sin is very serious because we have all done evil in the sight of a holy God. God is a loving God but He is also a God of justice and so He must punish sin. The worst possible thing that can happen to any person is for them to die with their sin and face God in judgment.

God loves us so much that He has provided a way to escape His judgment by sending His Son Jesus to suffer a brutal death on the cross in our place. On the third day Jesus rose from the dead affirming that the penalty for sin was paid in full.

Jesus came to die for our sins but He also promised that He will return. The next time He comes He will come to judge the world of sin. If you want to make sure you will escape God's judgment then you must repent of your sins and believe in Jesus Christ.

To repent means "to change your mind regarding sin and Jesus Christ." We change our mind regarding sin by acknowledging that we have committed evil in the sight of a holy God. We are sorry for our sin so much that we turn from our sin and turn toward God.

To believe means "to put all your trust in Jesus Christ alone for the forgiveness of sins and to receive Him as your Lord and Savior." This kind of belief results in a changed heart and a changed life committed to God and His Word.

Jesus said in Mark 1:15, "The time is fulfilled, and the kingdom of God is at hand; repent and believe in the gospel."

Noah's Ark was the only way to escape God's judgment in the Genesis flood. The Ark was a picture and a foreshadow of Jesus Christ who is the only way to escape God's coming final judgment.

Jesus is the Ark of our salvation.

Go to the Ark!

ENDNOTES

Introduction

1. The Genesis flood is often referred to as a myth as shown in this Wikipedia entry, Wikipedia contributors, "Genesis flood narrative," Wikipedia, The Free Encyclopedia, https://en.wikipedia.org/w/index.php?title=Genesis_flood_narrative&oldid=910808203 (accessed August 19, 2019).

2. Jesus referred to the Genesis flood as a historical fact in the days of Noah:

> Just as it was in the days of Noah, so will it be in the days
> of the Son of Man. (Luke 17:26, ESV)

3. The secular world often discovers evidence of a global flood but they never attribute it to the Genesis flood. For example: scientists at the Australian National University (ANU) say the early earth was almost entirely under water 4.4 billion years ago. For full context, see: Australian National University. "Earth was barren, flat and almost entirely under water 4.4 billion years ago." ScienceDaily. www.sciencedaily.com/releases/2017/05/170508112409.htm (accessed August 5, 2019).

4. The fossil record shows that there are billions of dead things buried all over the earth, which is clear evidence of the Genesis flood. For more information on how the fossil records point to the Genesis flood, see Ken Ham, "The Most Horrific Graveyard in the World", https://answersingenesis.org/fossils/fossil-record/the-most-horrific-graveyard-in-the-world/ (accessed August 5, 2019).

5. Before the flood, the earth was full of violence:

> Now the earth was corrupt in God's sight, and the earth
> was filled with violence. (Genesis 6:11, ESV)

6. Before the flood God saw the heart of man and it was continually evil:

> The LORD saw that the wickedness of man was great in
> the earth, and that every intention of the thoughts of his
> heart was only evil continually. (Genesis 6:5, ESV)

7.   Before the flood everybody was unconcerned about God's impending judgment:

> For as in those days before the flood they were eating and drinking, marrying and giving in marriage, until the day when Noah entered the ark, and they were unaware until the flood came and swept them all away, so will be the coming of the Son of Man. (Matthew 24:38–39, ESV)

8.   Noah was a preacher of righteousness to an ungodly world:

> If he did not spare the ancient world, but preserved Noah, a herald of righteousness, with seven others, when he brought a flood upon the world of the ungodly. (2 Peter 2:5, ESV)

9.   God made the animals come to Noah:

> Of the birds after their kind, and of the animals after their kind, of every creeping thing of the ground after its kind, two of every kind will come to you to keep them alive. (Genesis 6:20, ESV)

10. For a commentary on why Jesus was better than the ark, see Brandon D. Smith, "The Better Version of Noah's Ark", https://www.thegospelcoalition.org/article/better-version-noahs-ark/ (accessed August 5, 2019).

Chapter 1—The Rainbow

1.   The rainbow is a sign from God to never flood the earth again:

> And God said, "This is the sign of the covenant that I make between me and you and every living creature that is with you, for all future generations: I have set my bow in the cloud, and it shall be a sign of the covenant between me and the earth. When I bring clouds over the earth and the bow is seen in the clouds, I will remember my covenant that is between me and you and every living creature of all flesh. And the waters shall never again become a flood to destroy all flesh." (Genesis 9:12–14, ESV)

2.   It literally rained for forty days and forty nights:

> And rain fell upon the earth forty days and forty nights. (Genesis 7:12, ESV)

3.   The wickedness on the earth was ripe for God's judgment:

> The LORD saw that the wickedness of man was great in the earth, and that every intention of the thoughts of his heart was only evil continually. (Genesis 6:5, ESV)

Chapter 2—God Speaks to Mr. Kangaroo

1. God spoke to Saul (Paul) through a bright light:

> Now as he went on his way, he approached Damascus, and suddenly a light from heaven shone around him. (Acts 9:3, ESV)

2. God promises all believers that He will never leave us nor forsake us:

> It is the LORD who goes before you. He will be with you; he will not leave you or forsake you. Do not fear or be dismayed. (Deuteronomy 31:8, ESV)

Chapter 3—The Mongooses (Apostasy)

1. God's invisible attributes are clearly seen in His creation:

> For his invisible attributes, namely, his eternal power and divine nature, have been clearly perceived, ever since the creation of the world, in the things that have been made. So they are without excuse. (Romans 1:20, ESV)

2. Satan has blinded the minds of the unbelievers:

> In their case the god of this world has blinded the minds of the unbelievers, to keep them from seeing the light of the gospel of the glory of Christ, who is the image of God. (2 Corinthians 4:4, ESV)

3. Unrepentant sin keeps us hidden from God:

> But your iniquities have made a separation between you and your God, and your sins have hidden his face from you so that he does not hear. (Isaiah 59:2, ESV)

4. Some hear the Word of God and receive it with joy but have no root so they fall away from the faith:

> And the ones on the rock are those who, when they hear the word, receive it with joy. But these have no root; they believe for a while, and in time of testing fall away. (Luke 8:13, ESV)

5. Those who leave the Christian faith were never really Christians to begin with:

> They went out from us, but they were not of us; for if they had been of us, they would have continued with us. But they went out, that it might become plain that they all are not of us. (1 John 2:19, ESV)

6. Apostasy is often the result of being exposed to false teaching. For a short video commentary on apostasy, see "What is apostasy and how can I recognize it?," YouTube video, 4:40, posted by "Got Questions Ministries," September 2, 2019, https://youtu.be/V1Z8COt10wI.

Chapter 4—The Hyenas (Terrorism)

1. Islam regards the Prophet Muhammad as the Messenger of God. For full context, see *Muhammad, the Messenger of God*, http://www.kinghussein.gov.jo/prophet_muhammad.html (accessed August 6, 2019).
2. Islam claims to be a religion of peace. For a monthly report on those who have died or have been injured by Islamic terrorist attacks around the world, see *List of Killings in the Name of Islam: Last 30 Days*, https://thereligionofpeace.com/attacks/attacks.aspx?Yr=Last30 (accessed August 6, 2019)
3. The Quran calls for believers to fight unbelievers:

> O you who believe! fight those of the unbelievers who are near to you and let them find in you hardness; and know that Allah is with those who guard [against evil]. (Quran 9:123)

4. Paraphrased from a quote in the hadith by the Prophet Muhammad, "…I have been made victorious with terror":

> Allah's Apostle said, "I have been sent with the shortest expressions bearing the widest meanings, and I have been made victorious with terror [cast in the hearts of the enemy], and while I was sleeping, the keys of the treasures of the world were brought to me and put in my hand." Abu Huraira added: Allah's Apostle has left the world and now you, people, are bringing out those treasures [i.e. the Prophet did not benefit by them]. (Bukhari 4.52.220).

5. You shall not take the LORD's name in vain is God's third commandment:

> You shall not take the name of the LORD your God in vain, for the LORD will not hold him guiltless who takes his name in vain. (Exodus 20:7, ESV)

6. Paraphrased from Shadrach, Meshach, and Abednego when they would not bow down to King Nebuchadnezzar:

> If this be so, our God whom we serve is able to deliver us from the burning fiery furnace, and he will deliver us out of your hand, O king. But if not, be it known to you, O king, that we will not serve your gods or worship the golden image that you have set up. (Daniel 3:17–18 ESV)

Chapter 5—The Lions (Pride)

1. God provides food for the lions:

   > The young lions roar for their prey, seeking their food from God. (Psalm 104:21, ESV)

2. The unafraid lion has a stately stride:

   > Three things are stately in their tread; four are stately in their stride: the lion, which is mightiest among beasts and does not turn back before any. (Proverbs 30:29–30, ESV)

3. God doesn't favor anyone:

   > For God shows no partiality. (Romans 2:11, ESV)

4. There was a lion that would not eat meat. For full context, see David Catchpoole, "The lion that wouldn't eat meat", https://creation.com/the-lion-that-wouldnt-eat-meat (accessed August 7, 2019).

5. Rather than praying for God's mercy, the lions responded just like the self-righteous Pharisees and thanked the Lord that they are not like others:

   > The Pharisee stood and was praying this to himself: "God, I thank You that I am not like other people: swindlers, unjust, adulterers, or even like this tax collector." (Luke 18:11, ESV)

6. God does not favor the proud:

   > Everyone who is arrogant in heart is an abomination to the LORD; be assured, he will not go unpunished. (Proverbs 16:5, ESV)

7. Do not compare yourself to others:

   > Not that we dare to classify or compare ourselves with some of those who are commending themselves. But when they measure themselves by one another and compare themselves with one another, they are without understanding. (2 Corinthians 10:12, ESV)

8. We all fall short of God's righteousness:

   > For all have sinned and fall short of the glory of God. (Romans 3:23, ESV)

9. The proud don't need God:

   > In the pride of his face the wicked does not seek him; all his thoughts are, "There is no God." (Psalm 10:4, ESV)

10. Pride comes before the fall:

> Pride goes before destruction, and a haughty spirit before a fall. (Proverbs 16:18, ESV)

11. Pride is deadly, and it infects all of us. For a commentary on the deadly effects of pride, see Glenn Sunshine, "Pride: The Deadliest Sin", June 14, 2018, http://www.breakpoint.org/2018/06/29936/ (accessed August 11, 2019).

12. Some animals were carnivores before the flood, but the ones on the ark may still have been eating plants and obeying God's directive. For full commentary, see Andrew Lamb, "Feeding carnivores on the Ark, and refuting an accusation of 'closet scientism,'" 15 November 2008, https://creation.com/feeding-carnivores-on-the-ark-and-refuting-an-accusation-of-closet-scientism (accessed August 11, 2019).

Chapter 6—The Monkeys (Evolution)

1. Evolution is being taught as fact. In this article the author attempts to prove evolution is a fact by using theories that are just stories of how the past unfolded. For full context, see Tom Chivers, "7 Things That Show That Evolution Is An Actual Fact," February 26, 2015, https://www.buzzfeed.com/tomchivers/things-that-show-evolution-is-an-actual-fact (accessed August 8, 2019).

2. Skull fossils do not prove evolution and they are often misidentified. For more info, see Joel Tay and Dr Robert Carter, "Do these skulls prove common ancestry between apes and humans?" 6 October 2018, https://creation.com/ape-human-transitional-skull (accessed August 11, 2019).

3. Dinosaur bones do not have the right elements so the age of dinosaur bones are determined by measuring the elements in surrounding sedimentary rock layers. For full context, see Tracy V. Wilson "How Do Scientists Determine the Age of Dinosaur Bones?" 15 January 2008. HowStuffWorks.com, https://science.howstuffworks.com/environmental/earth/geology/dinosaur-bone-age.htm (accessed 8 August 2019).

4. Soft tissue found in T-Rex and other dinosaur fossils have brought serious questions to dinosaur dating methods. For more info, see "Dinosaur soft tissue with Brian Thomas," YouTube video, 16:25, posted by "Evidence Press," Oct 13, 2015, https://www.youtube.com/watch?v=2phFPZfy4S0&feature=youtu.be.

5. Future evolutionary process is impossible to predict because the pace of evolution is impossible to verify. For example, new research suggests a more rapid pace in primates rather than millions of years. For full context, see: Cornell University. "Primate evolution in the fast lane." ScienceDaily. www.sciencedaily.com/releases/2016/04/160407150740.htm (accessed July 29, 2019).

6. The odds of random mutations causing improvement over millions of years are mathematically impossible. For more info, see Dr. Gary Parker, "2.5 Mutations,

Yes; Evolution, No," March 28, 2016, https://answersingenesis.org/genetics/mutations/mutations-yes-evolution-no/ (accessed August 11, 2019).

7. Unbelievers intuitively know that God is the Creator, but they suppress this truth in their unrighteousness, and they will be without an excuse in God's judgment. Read Romans 1:18–21.

8. Creation versus evolution is a battle between worldviews. For more info, see Dan Manthei, "Two worldviews in conflict," https://creation.com/two-world-views-in-conflict (accessed August 8, 2019).

Chapter 7—The Cow and the Bull (Addiction)

1. Some marijuana users insist that it makes them more creative. For full article, see Bob Young, "High thoughts: Does pot make you more creative?" last modified April 25, 2016, https://www.seattletimes.com/seattle-news/marijuana/high-thoughts-does-pot-make-you-more-creative/ (accessed August 11, 2019).

2. Many marijuana users insist that it opens up their mind. For an online discussion, see "Opening up the mind," marijuana.com, https://www.marijuana.com/community/threads/opening-up-the-mind.149122/ (accessed August 8, 2019).

3. Some religions use marijuana to assist them in their spirituality. For online article, see "Cannabis (Marijuana) and Religion." ReligionFacts.com. March 14, 2017, http://www.religionfacts.com/cannabis (accessed August 9, 2019).

4. Former KLOS spiritual guru Michael Benner said that cannabis put him in a reflective state to consider the questions of the universe. For full context, Frank Sontag, *Light the Way Home: My Incredible Ride from New Age to New Life,* (Frank Sontag and Mike Yorkey, September 2, 2014) 99.

5. God wants us to be sober-minded:

> Be sober-minded; be watchful. Your adversary the devil prowls around like a roaring lion, seeking someone to devour. (1 Peter 5:8, ESV)

6. This "herb" scripture is often taken out of context to justify marijuana use. Before the curse of sin, mankind and all creatures were vegetarians:

> And God said, "See, I have given you every herb that yields seed which is on the face of all the earth, and every tree whose fruit yields seed; to you it shall be for food." (Genesis 1:29, NKJV)

7. God does not want us getting high to cope with life. Instead He wants us to trust Him with all our heart:

> Trust in the LORD with all your heart, and do not lean on your own understanding. (Proverbs 3:5, ESV)

8. For a biblical commentary on idolatry and addiction, see "How should a Christian view addiction?" last modified July 26, 2019, https://www.gotquestions.org/addiction-Christian.html (accessed August 18, 2019).

9. Regular marijuana use may cause mental illness and violence. For more info, see Alex Berenson, "Marijuana, Mental Illness, and Violence," Imprimis, Jaunuary 2019, https://imprimis.hillsdale.edu/marijuana-mental-illness-violence/ (accessed August 8, 2019).

Chapter 8—The Bears (Believers in Name Only)

1. Many professing Christians do not appear to be Christians by their lifestyle. For a commentary on how to recognize a Christian, see Bodie Hodge, "So You're a Christian—Really?" August 9, 2013, https://answersingenesis.org/christianity/christian-life/so-youre-a-christian-really/ (accessed August 11, 2019).

2. Swearing is worldly and unbecoming of a Christian. For a short video commentary on why Christians should avoid swearing, see "Can A Christian Swear?," YouTube video, 3:35, posted by "Wretched," August 20, 2019, https://youtu.be/GCcQexYfObg.

3. Religious leaders gloss over wrongdoing by claiming it is necessary "to advance the ministry" or "to reach more people." For more info, see Nancy Pearcey, *Total Truth: Liberating Christianity from Its Cultural Captivity,* (Wheaton, Crossway Books, 2005) 85.

4. Out of the abundance of the heart the mouth speaks:

> The good person out of the good treasure of his heart produces good, and the evil person out of his evil treasure produces evil, for out of the abundance of the heart his mouth speaks. (Luke 6:45, ESV)

5. Jesus expects repentance from His followers:

> I have not come to call the righteous but sinners to repentance. (Luke 5:32, ESV)

6. Blessed are those who hunger for righteousness:

> Blessed are those who hunger and thirst for righteousness, for they shall be satisfied. (Matthew 5:6, ESV)

7. Blessed are those who mourn over their sin:

> Blessed are those who mourn, for they shall be comforted. (Matthew 5:4, ESV)

8. God made the animals (and humans) on day 6 of His creation week:

> And God made the beasts of the earth according to their kinds and the livestock according to their kinds, and every-

thing that creeps on the ground according to its kind. And
God saw that it was good. (Genesis 1:25, ESV)

9. Believers in name only are those who identify as a Christian but it's just a label because their lives remain unchanged. For a commentary on nominal Christianity, see "What is nominal Christianity?" last modified July 26, 2019, https://www.gotquestions.org, https://www.gotquestions.org/nominal-Christianity.html (accessed August 8, 2019).

Chapter 9—The Sheep (The False Prophet)

1. "Sheep without a shepherd" is how Jesus described the spiritual condition of every soul apart from Him:

> When he saw the crowds, he had compassion for them,
> because they were harassed and helpless, like sheep without
> a shepherd. (Matthew 9:36, ESV)

2. Joel Osteen teaches that we can control our future with positive words. For full context, see Joel Osteen, "Change Your Words, Change Your World, Shape Your Future," https://www.joelosteen.com/Pages/Article.aspx?articleid=6505 (accessed August 8, 2019).

3. The dangers of positive confession far outweigh the benefits. For a biblical commentary on positive confession, see "Is there power in positive confession?" last modified July 26, 2019, https://www.gotquestions.org/positive-confession.html (accessed August 8, 2019).

4. Everyone has an appointment with death and judgment:

> And just as it is appointed for man to die once, and after
> that comes judgment. (Hebrews 9:27, ESV)

5. God has a purpose in our suffering:

> Not only that, but we rejoice in our sufferings, knowing
> that suffering produces endurance, and endurance pro-
> duces character, and character produces hope. (Romans
> 5:3–4, ESV)

6. God wants us to be content:

> But godliness with contentment is great gain. (1 Timothy
> 6:6, ESV)

7. "Speaking things into existence" is a verse often taken out of context to declare that we can speak things that don't exist into existence just like God. This verse actually shows that God is able declare believing sinners to be righteous even though they are not because of their faith in Jesus Christ:

> As it is written, "I have made you the father of many
> nations"—in the presence of the God in whom he believed,

who gives life to the dead and calls into existence the things that do not exist. (Romans 4:17, ESV)

8. Contentment must be learned:

Not that I am speaking of being in need, for I have learned in whatever situation I am to be content. (Philippians 4:11, ESV)

9. Leg lengthening is common tactic used by fake healers. For an evaluation of this deceptive practice, see "Fake Healing Videos Evaluated: Todd White, Tom Fischer and more," YouTube video, 57:52, posted by "Mike Winger," February 6, 2018, https://youtu.be/je20XTohCNo.

10. Andrew Wommack teaches that it's up to the believer, not God, to be healed because God has already healed everyone, we just have to receive it by faith. Andrew Wommack, "God Wants You Well," https://www.awmi.net/reading/teaching-articles/wants_well/ (accessed August 10, 2019).

11. Jesus healed a man who didn't know who He was:

Now the man who had been healed did not know who it was, for Jesus had withdrawn, as there was a crowd in the place (John 5:13, ESV).

12. We live in a fallen world in which all creation is corrupted by sin. God has a plan to eventually liberate creation from its bondage to sin. Until that day, God uses sickness and other evils to bring about His sovereign purpose, to glorify Himself, and to exalt His holy name. For more commentary on sickness, see "Is it sometimes God's will for believers to be sick?" last modified July 26, 2019, https://www.gotquestions.org/sickness-will-God.html, (accessed August 20, 2019).

13. "Don't put God in a box" is a statement often used as a way of accusing someone of limiting God. We honor God by staying in the bounds of His revealed Word. For more commentary, see Ben Edwards, "I Don't Put God in a Box Like That." Really?" https://www.biblestudytools.com/blogs/theologically-driven/i-don-t-put-god-in-a-box-like-that-really.html, (accessed August 20, 2019).

14. "Touch not God's anointed" is a phrase commonly taken out of context by false teachers to use against anyone who questions their teaching. For more commentary, see "Touch not my anointed!" http://www.letusreason.org/Pent47.htm (accessed August 8, 2019).

15. Scriptures are commonly taken out of context to teach that God promises health and prosperity. For a commentary on five errors of the prosperity gospel, see David W. Jones, "5 Errors of the Prosperity Gospel," January 15, 2014, https://www.9marks.org/article/journalerrors-prosperity-gospel/ (accessed August 8, 2019).

16. Here is an example of a false prophetess that speaks positive words over a man. After the man rejects her false doctrine, the prophetess pronounces a rebuke over him and calls the man a demon. For video commentary see, "Wretched:

False Prophet Fiasco," YouTube video, 5:23, posted by "Wretched," June 8, 2012, https://youtu.be/q9Ly6ItuDIs.

Chapter 10—The Beavers (Earning God's Grace)

1. Mormons teach that strict obedience to God's law makes one worthy of God's grace and acceptance into the celestial kingdom. For more info, see John B. Wallace, *Starting at the Finish Line: The Gospel of Grace for Mormons,* (Pomona House Publishing, LLC, 2014) 121.

2. God's grace can't be earned; otherwise it's no longer grace:

    > But if it is by grace, it is no longer on the basis of works; otherwise grace would no longer be grace. (Romans 11:6, ESV)

3. We are saved by grace alone through faith in Jesus Christ alone:

    > For by grace you have been saved through faith. And this is not your own doing; it is the gift of God, not a result of works, so that no one may boast. (Ephesians 2:8–9, ESV)

4. Mormons teach that grace requires that we do our part. For a list of Mormon requirements for salvation, see Wallace, *Starting at the Finish Line,* 134–135.

5. If you think you are righteous, take a look at what God says:

    > As it is written, "None is righteous, no, not one." (Romans 3:10, ESV)

6. Our good works are like a filthy rag because they are rooted in our sinful nature:

    > For all of us have become like one who is unclean, and all our righteous deeds are like a filthy garment; and all of us wither like a leaf, and our iniquities, like the wind, take us away. (Isaiah 64:6, NASB)

7. No matter how much we try, we will never live up to God's perfect moral standard:

    > For all have sinned and fall short of the glory of God. (Romans 3:23, ESV)

8. Mormons teach that we are partners with God. For more info, Wallace, *Starting at the Finish Line,* 147–148.

9. The Book of Mormon teaches the doctrine of grace and works:

    > For we know that it is by grace we are saved, after all we can do. (2 Nephi 25:23)

10. Brigham Young quote—"Pray as though everything depended on the Lord, and work as though everything depended on you." For full context, see Wallace, *Starting at the Finish Line,* 147–148.

11. We cannot contribute anything to our salvation. For a biblical commentary, see "Do we contribute anything to our own salvation?" last modified July 26, 2019, https://www.gotquestions.org/contribute-salvation.html (accessed August 9, 2019).

Chapter 11—The Giraffes (Everyone is Born Good)

1. Many people believe humans are born good. There is even "scientific" research that attempts to show that we are born good. For full context, see Adrian F. Ward, "Scientists Probe Human Nature--and Discover We Are Good, After All," November 20, 2012, https://www.scientificamerican.com/article/scientists-probe-human-nature-and-discover-we-are-good-after-all/ (accessed August 8, 2019).

2. A psychological study showed that being exposed to corrupt environments was more likely to corrupt the individual. For full context, see Ed Yong, "Corruption Corrupts," last modified October 10, 2018, https://www.theatlantic.com/science/archive/2016/03/corruption-honesty/472779/ (accessed August 10, 2019). Corrupt environments are more likely to corrupt individuals because our sinful nature makes corruption more difficult to resist when we are surrounded by it:

> Do not be deceived: "Bad company ruins good morals."
> (1 Corinthians 15:33, ESV)

3. For a five-minute video showing how people are not born good, see "Are People Born Good?" YouTube video, 5:12, posted by PragerU, March 31, 2014, https://youtu.be/phwHEE-Zz_A.

4. We are born with a sinful nature:

> Behold, I was brought forth in iniquity, and in sin did my
> mother conceive me. (Psalm 51:5, ESV)

5. "Sin is not learned, it is inherent within us," paraphrased from John MacArthur. For full commentary on the inherent sin of every child, see John MacArthur, "Your Child's Greatest Need," https://www.gty.org/library/Articles/A359 (accessed August 10, 2019).

6. "Don't let a cute little baby fool you…" quoted from John Macarthur. For full commentary, see MacArthur, "Your Child's Greatest Need."

7. We must deny our sinful nature daily:

> And he said to all, "If anyone would come after me, let him
> deny himself and take up his cross daily and follow me."
> (Luke 9:23, ESV)

8. The Bible makes it clear that the human heart is deceitful and sick:

> The heart is deceitful above all things, and desperately sick;
> who can understand it? (Jeremiah 17:9, ESV)

9. Our sinful nature deceives us into doing what's right in our own eyes:

> There is a way that seems right to a man, but its end is the way to death. (Proverbs 14:12, ESV)

10. God must open our eyes for us to see spiritually:

> Open my eyes, that I may behold wondrous things out of your law. (Psalm 119:18, ESV)

Chapter 12—The Rabbits (Spiritual but Not Religious)

1. At birth, a baby giraffe falls up to six feet to the ground and lands headfirst. For more info on giraffes, see Jamie Farber, "Facts About Baby Giraffes," last modified March 13, 2018, https://sciencing.com/baby-giraffes-8632947.html (accessed August 10, 2019).
2. Those who claim to be spiritual but not religious reject organized religion as defined in this Wikipedia entry, Wikipedia contributors, "Spiritual but not religious," Wikipedia, The Free Encyclopedia, https://en.wikipedia.org/w/index. php?title=Spiritual_but_not_religious&oldid=911024856, (accessed August 19, 2019).
3. We are energy beings as described by former KLOS New Age spiritual guru Frank Sontag. For full context, see Frank Sontag, *Light the Way Home: My Incredible Ride from New Age to New Life,* (Frank Sontag and Mike Yorkey, September 2, 2014) 115.
4. "A heightened spiritual consciousness enlightens us to discover the god within us," paraphrased from former KLOS New Age spiritual guru Frank Sontag. For full context, see Sontag, *Light the Way Home,* 129.
5. Former KLOS New Age spiritual guru Michael Benner explains how to create a third mind by bringing together the conscious and unconscious minds through meditation. For full context, see Sontag, *Light the Way Home,* 91.
6. Former KLOS New Age spiritual guru Michael Benner explains how to choose positive thoughts and feelings. For full context, see Sontag, *Light the Way Home,* 91.
7. Former KLOS New Age spiritual guru Michael Benner explains how to release bad memories to be happy. For full context, see Sontag, *Light the Way Home,* 91.
8. Paraphrased from John Macarthur on those who are spiritual but not religious. For full context, see "John MacArthur | The Ben Shapiro Show Sunday Special Ep. 29," YouTube video, 1:09:12, posted by "The Daily Wire," December 2, 2018, https://www.youtube.com/watch?v=F-ofKxfYqGw.
9. Former KLOS New Age spiritual guru Frank Sontag testifies that New Age has always been about self. For full context, see Sontag, *Light the Way Home,* 139.
10. "You don't judge a religion by its abuse," paraphrased from Frank Turek. For full context, see Frank Turek, *Stealing from God: Why Atheists Need God to Make Their Case,* (Colorado Springs, NavPress, 2014) 96.

11. Those who claim to be spiritual but not religious need to understand that they are far worse off than they could imagine because of their true sinful nature. For more info on how to respond to those who are spiritual but not religious, see "When someone says [I'm spiritual but not religious] how should a Christian respond?" online video, 4:27, July 8, 2013, posted by "Christianity.com," https://www.christianity.com/videos/video-features/how-should-a-christian-respond-to-someone-who-says-i-m-spiritual-but-not-religious.html (accessed August 18, 2019).

Chapter 13—The Pigs (Mother Gaia)

1. Grounding and centering is how to prepare for pagan rituals. For full context, see Joyce & River Higginbotham, *Paganism: An Introduction to Earth-Centered Religions,* (Woodbury, Llewellyn Publications, 2002) 31.
2. Feeling the space around you is a common pagan practice. For full context, see Higginbotham, *Paganism,* 144.
3. Feeling connected to the earth is a common pagan practice. For full context, see Higginbotham, *Paganism,* 24.
4. According to paganism, there is consciousness in all things. For full context, see Higginbotham, *Paganism,* 150.
5. Many pagans believe that everything contains a spark of intelligence. For full context, see Higginbotham, *Paganism,* 133.
6. The GAIA hypothesis suggests that the entire range of living matter is a single living entity. For full context, see James Lovelock, *Gaia: A New Look at Life on Earth*, (New York, Oxford University Press, Reprint Edition, 2016) 9.
7. The GAIA hypothesis suggests that there is circumstantial evidence for Gaia's existence. For full context, see Lovelock, *Gaia,* 26.
8. The GAIA hypothesis suggests that Gaia (not God) maintains the conditions favorable for life in all circumstances. For full context, see Lovelock, *Gaia,* 119.
9. The GAIA hypothesis suggests that some living organisms require special permission from the rest of the world to survive. For full context, see Lovelock, *Gaia,* 83.
10. Friedrich Nietzsche suggests that the earth has skin and the skin has a disease called man. For full context, see James Wanliss, *Resisting the Green Dragon: Dominion, Not Death,* (Burke, The Cornwall Alliance, 2010) 29.
11. James Lovelock seems to suggest that the earth's surface is mostly water to control overpopulation and man's excessive farming without impunity. For full context, see Lovelock, *Gaia,* 99.
12. Nazi propaganda pushed the idea that mass casualties came from famines to eliminate useless eaters rather than their own atheistic government policies. For full context, see Wanliss, *Resisting the Green Dragon,* 29–30.

13. God, not Mother Gaia, created everything:

> In the beginning, God created the heavens and the earth. (Genesis 1:1, ESV)

14. God, not Mother Gaia, is in control of all creation:

> Our God is in the heavens; he does all that he pleases. (Psalm 115:3, ESV)

15. James Lovelock implies that the Gaian process, not God, regulates the environment. For full context, see Lovelock, *Gaia*, 120.

16. "A rat is a pig is a dog is a boy," quoted from the founder of People for the Ethical Treatment of Animals. For full context, see Wanliss, *Resisting the Green Dragon*, 42.

17. By exalting the earth above God, they have exchanged the truth of God for a lie:

> Because they exchanged the truth about God for a lie and worshiped and served the creature rather than the Creator, who is blessed forever! Amen. (Romans 1:25, ESV)

18. A 1990s Harvard University project goal was to find common ground with all religions to reharmonize life on earth in an attempt to push environmental justice propaganda. For full context, see Wanliss, *Resisting the Green Dragon*, 69.

Chapter 14—The Sloths (Karma)

1. According to some Eastern religions, this life may be paying off a karmic debt from a previous life. It's up to the individual to work off their karmic debt. For full context, see Heart's Wisdom, "How to clear your Karmic Debt and set your soul free" https://ekatvam.org/clear-karmic-debt/, (accessed August 19, 2019).

2. According to Hinduism, there may be stored-up, accumulated karmic forces from a previous life. For full context, see Swami Bhaskarananda, *The Essentials of Hinduism: A Comprehensive Overview of the World's Oldest Religion*, (Seattle, Viveka Press, 2002), 80–81.

3. According to Buddhism, you can reduce suffering by creating good karma. For full context, see Traleg Kyabgon, *Karma: What It Is, What It Isn't, Why It Matters*, (Boston, Shambhala Publications, Inc., 2015) 42.

4. According to Hinduism, reincarnation is when our physical body dies and our soul is eventually born into another body. For full context, see Bhaskarananda, *Hinduism*, 91–96.

5. According to Hinduism, karma determines birth and how long you will live. For full context, see Bhaskarananda, *Hinduism*, 81.

6. According to Buddhism, karma is said to be a phenomenon. For full context, see Kyabgon, *Karma*, 73.

7. According to Hinduism, God is the giver of the fruits of karma. For full context, see Bhaskarananda, *Hinduism*, 80.

8. According to Hinduism, karma enables all paths to lead to God. For full context, see Bhaskarananda, *Hinduism*, 191.

9. According to Buddhism, karma is about attaining freedom from karmic hindrances and constraints. For full context, see Kyabgon, *Karma*, 9.

10. According to Hinduism, a soul is liberated when we no longer have any desires. For full context, see Bhaskarananda, *Hinduism*, 95.

11. According to Buddhism, karma is continually evolving. For full context, see Kyabgon, *Karma*, 59.

12. "Karmic residue" is a term quoted from Traleg Kyabgon. For full context, see Kyabgon, *Karma*, 26.

13. We are not reincarnated. We only get this one life and then comes judgment:

> And just as it is appointed for man to die once, and after
> that comes judgment. (Hebrews 9:27 ESV)

14. According to Hinduism, reincarnation is considered a fact. For full context, see Bhaskarananda, *Hinduism*, 91.

15. According to Buddhism, there is no way to escape karma. For full context, see Kyabgon, *Karma*, 149.

16. According to Hinduism, a human soul can be reincarnated as a subhuman to work out very bad karma. For "Go to the Ark," it was reversed so that an animal can be reincarnated as a sub-animal or human. For full context, see Bhaskarananda, *Hinduism*, 95.

17. Buddhists reject the idea that we are morally corrupted by sin. Moral corruption has nothing to do with sin. For full context, see Kyabgon, *Karma*, 109.

18. According to Buddhism, each of us does bad and good things because our karma is mixed. For full context, see Kyabgon, *Karma*, 50.

19. According to Hinduism, the mind can become all-knowing through spiritual discipline. For full context, see Bhaskarananda, *Hinduism*, 4.

20. According to Hinduism, sooner or later your true self, or divinity, must manifest itself. For full context, see Bhaskarananda, *Hinduism*, 8.

21. Unlike those who believe in karma, Christians have a personal relationship with God through faith in Jesus Christ:

> My sheep hear my voice, and I know them, and they follow
> me. (John 10:27, ESV)

Chapter 15—The Elephants (Reason)

1. Paraphrased from a speech by Lawrence Krauss at the 2016 Reason Rally. For full context, see "Lawrence Krauss at Reason Rally 2016," YouTube video, 11:29, posted by Reason Rally Coalition, August 16, 2016, https://youtu.be/NPYszs6v-6o.

2. Atheists claim that reason soundly refutes what a religious person believes. For full context, see Turek, *Stealing from God*, 39.

3. Atheists flatter themselves with nicknames like "brights" and "freethinkers." For full context, see Turek, *Stealing from God,* 39.

4. For a summary of the Brights movement and what they believe, see Wikipedia contributors, "Brights movement," Wikipedia, The Free Encyclopedia, https://en.wikipedia.org/w/index.php?title=Brights_movement&oldid=915446913 (accessed September 21, 2019).

5. For full definition of a *freethinker*, see Dan Barker, "What is a Freethinker?" https://ffrf.org/faq/feeds/item/18391-what-is-a-freethinker (accessed August 10, 2019).

6. God wants to reason with all who will listen:

> Come now, let us reason together, says the LORD: though
> your sins are like scarlet, they shall be as white as snow;
> though they are red like crimson, they shall become like
> wool. (Isaiah 1:18, ESV)

7. Paraphrased from a speech by Lawrence Krauss at the 2016 Reason Rally. For full context, see Krauss, "Reason Rally 2016."

8. We are all aware of "a reality external to our minds" paraphrased from Frank Turek. For full context, see Turek, *Stealing from God,* 36.

9. "The laws of reason and logic are grounded in our mind," surmised by a student named Michael in a question-and-answer session with Frank Turek. For full context, see Turek, *Stealing from God,* 35.

10. Immaterial laws come from the immaterial and unchangeable mind of God. For more commentary, see Turek, *Stealing from God*, 35–36.

11. "All laws come from a lawgiver…" paraphrased from Frank Turek. For more commentary, see Turek, *Stealing from God,* 36.

12. "Just give science more time" is a common response from atheists. For full context, see Turek, *Stealing from God,* 3.

13. An orderly world created by an orderly Mind makes science, logic, and reason possible. For more commentary, see Turek, *Stealing from God,* 36.

14. God created everything:

> Ah, Lord GOD! It is You who have made the heavens and
> the earth by Your great power and by Your outstretched
> arm! Nothing is too hard for You. (Jeremiah 32:17, ESV)

15. "Our minds were designed by God to know God and His creation," quoted from Frank Turek. For full context, see Turek, *Stealing from God,* 37.

16. Paraphrased from a speech by Lawrence Krauss at the 2016 Reason Rally. For full context, see Krauss, "Reason Rally 2016."

17. Paraphrased from actual quote by former atheist Antony Flew, "Science cannot discover the self, the self discovers science." For full context, see Turek, *Stealing from God,* 52.

18. From the Enlightenment reason came to be seen as the storehouse of truths independent of any religion or philosophy. For full context, see Pearcey, *Total Truth*, 39.

19. "I think religion should be treated with ridicule, hatred, and contempt," quoted from Christopher Hitchens. For full context, see Turek, *Stealing from God*, 38.

Chapter 16—The Snakes (Evil)

1. The crafty serpent tempted Eve by twisting God's words:

   > Now the serpent was more crafty than any other beast of the field that the LORD God had made. He said to the woman, "Did God actually say, 'You shall not eat of any tree in the garden'?" (Genesis 3:1, ESV)

2. Common sense apart from the wisdom of God is stupid:

   > I am too stupid to be human, and I lack common sense. I have not mastered human wisdom, nor do I know the Holy One. (Proverbs 30:2–3, NLT)

3. Atheist Christopher Hitchens insisted that religion poisons everything. For full context, see Turek, *Stealing from God*, 120–121.

4. Atheist Christopher Hitchens attempts to explain why he thinks religion is evil and that God is some kind of evil dictator. For full context, see "Why Religion is Evil," YouTube video, 10:57, posted by "Bob Bobson," August 16, 2012, https://youtu.be/Q3r33LO7RBQ

5. Atheist Richard Dawkins says the world would be better off without religion or belief in God. For full context, see "Dawkins-2—"the world is better off without religion," YouTube video, 5:50, posted by "quarlo2," May 28, 2011, https://youtu.be/SiW8-IhLBe0.

6. God's diagnosis of the human heart is not good. The heart is deceitful and sick:

   > The heart is deceitful above all things, and desperately sick; who can understand it? (Jeremiah 17:9, ESV)

7. Those who do not take sin seriously are deceived:

   > If we say we have no sin, we deceive ourselves, and the truth is not in us. (1 John 1:8, ESV)

8. Many will think they are right with God when they are not:

   > And then will I declare to them, "I never knew you; depart from me, you workers of lawlessness." (Matthew 7:23, ESV)

9. Some people think they are serving God by doing evil:

> They will put you out of the synagogues. Indeed, the hour is coming when whoever kills you will think he is offering service to God. (John 16:2, ESV)

10. God's judgment is serious, and He will judge everyone:

> And just as it is appointed for man to die once, and after that comes judgment. (Hebrews 9:27, ESV)

11. A fool's heart says there is no God:

> The fool says in his heart, "There is no God." They are corrupt, they do abominable deeds, there is none who does good. (Psalm 14:1, ESV)

12. An unbelieving heart is evil:

> Take care, brothers, lest there be in any of you an evil, unbelieving heart, leading you to fall away from the living God. (Hebrews 3:12, ESV)

13. Sin is very serious. Sin is more than just a mistake or a poor choice. Sin is an act of moral transgression. For more commentary on the seriousness of sin, see R. C. Sproul, "Sin Is Cosmic Treason," March, 8, 2019, https://www.ligonier.org/blog/sin-cosmic-treason/ (accessed August 11, 2019).

14. Sin has affected everyone:

> For all have sinned and fall short of the glory of God. (Romans 3:23, ESV)

15. Before he was a Christian, C. S. Lewis used to think that evil was just pain in a world of pain. For full context, see Art Lindsley, Ph.D., "The Problem of Evil: C.S. Lewis Speaks to Life's Most Difficult Questions," *Knowing & Doing* (Winter 2003): 1, http://www.cslewisinstitute.org/webfm_send/636147, (accessed August 11, 2019).

16. "Evil can't exist unless good exists, and good can't exist unless God exists" paraphrased from Frank Turek. For more commentary, see Turek, *Stealing from God,* 117.

17. Some religions and people believe that evil is an illusion. For full context, see Turek, *Stealing from God,* 116.

18. If there is no God, then evil behavior is just a matter of preference. For full context, see Turek, *Stealing from God,* 116.

19. God makes it clear that no one is good:

> All have turned aside; together they have become worthless; no one does good, not even one. (Romans 3:12, ESV)

20. God is good:

    > Oh, taste and see that the LORD is good! Blessed is the man who takes refuge in him! (Psalm 34:8, ESV)

21. "God is the most unpleasant character in all fiction," paraphrased from Richard Dawkins. For full context, see Turek, *Stealing from God,* 122.

22. Evil came about through the exercise of free will. For more commentary, see Turek, *Stealing from God,* 141.

23. "God is responsible for the fact of freedom; we creatures are responsible for our acts of freedom," paraphrased from Frank Turek. For more commentary, see Turek, *Stealing from God,* 139.

24. We are never to repay evil with evil:

    > Repay no one evil for evil, but give thought to do what is honorable in the sight of all. (Romans 12:17, ESV)

Chapter 17—The Horses (Love)

1. God is love:

    > Anyone who does not love does not know God, because God is love. (1 John 4:8, ESV)

2. God provided Jesus as a way to escape His judgment:

    > Truly, truly, I say to you, whoever hears my word and believes Him who sent me has eternal life. He does not come into judgment, but has passed from death to life. (John 5:24, ESV)

3. God does not take pleasure in anyone's death:

    > Have I any pleasure in the death of the wicked, declares the Lord GOD, and not rather that he should turn from his way and live? (Ezekiel 18:23, ESV)

4. God wants to save everyone through faith in Christ:

    > For God so loved the world, that he gave his only Son, that whoever believes in him should not perish but have eternal life. (John 3:16, ESV)

5. "You want the freedom to love who you want to love while denying God's love," paraphrased from J. Warner Wallace. For full context, see J. Warner, "Wouldn't a Loving God Make Sure Everyone Goes to Heaven?" September 15, 2017, https://coldcasechristianity.com/writings/wouldnt-a-loving-god-make-sure-everyone-gets-to-heaven/ (accessed August 11, 2019).

6. God won't force anyone into heaven because heaven is not compulsory. For more commentary, see Warner, "Wouldn't a Loving God Make Sure Everyone Gets to Heaven?"

7. Heaven is not suited for sinners. For more commentary, see Warner, "Wouldn't a Loving God Make sure Everyone Gets to Heaven?"

8. There is no fear in God's love because we escape His judgment:

> There is no fear in love, but perfect love casts out fear. For fear has to do with punishment, and whoever fears has not been perfected in love. (1 John 4:18, ESV)

9. God calls us to love our enemies:

> But I say to you, Love your enemies and pray for those who persecute you. (Matthew 5:44, ESV)

10. Without Jesus we are dead in our sins:

> And you were dead in the trespasses and sins. (Ephesians 2:1, ESV)

11. We were enemies of God and yet He still saved us:

> For if while we were enemies we were reconciled to God by the death of his Son, much more, now that we are reconciled, shall we be saved by his life. (Romans 5:10, ESV)

12. "If you don't love yourself it is impossible for you to love anyone else. It's just not possible… You can't give away what you don't have." Paraphrased from Joyce Meyer. For full context, see "Relationship with Yourself by Joyce Meyer," YouTube video, 28:32, posted by Juliett Zoya, October 3, 2014, https://youtu.be/ynpu62V06zM.

13. "It's sinful to hate yourself because you are ultimately hating your Creator when you hate yourself." Paraphrased from Rick Thomas. For more commentary, see Rick Thomas, "What Does It Mean to Love Others As You Love Yourself?" https://rickthomas.net/mean-love-god-love/ (accessed August 11, 2019).

14. It's common for Christians to try and justify a proper self-love to overcome low self-esteem or self-hatred. For a biblical commentary on the self-esteem movement, see Rick Thomas, "Loving Me: The Hidden Agenda of Self-Esteem," https://rickthomas.net/loving-me-the-hidden-agenda-of-self-esteem-2/ (accessed August 11, 2019).

15. Thinking more about ourselves is not the answer for someone who hates themselves. For a biblical response to those who hate themselves, see Thomas, "Loving Me."

16. Thinking less about ourselves is the perfect mental attitude for serving others. For a biblical response to the self-esteem movement, see Thomas, "Loving Me."

17. "Our efforts must be always directed externally, toward God and others, because that is the nature of love," paraphrased from Matt Walsh. For full context, see Matt Walsh, "WALSH: Why You Should Stop Trying to Love Yourself," August

9, 2018, https://www.dailywire.com/news/34283/walsh-self-love-matt-walsh (accessed August 11, 2019).

18. Those with high self-esteem are controlled by what others think. For a biblical commentary on the self-esteem movement, see Thomas, "Loving Me."

19. "We need to look outside of ourselves to rest in the reality of someone far superior from ourselves," paraphrased from Rick Thomas. For a biblical commentary on the self-esteem movement, see Thomas, "Loving Me."

20. "God is the answer for inner contentment and outer significance," paraphrased from Rick Thomas. For a biblical commentary on the self-esteem movement, see Thomas, "Loving Me."

21. Jesus must increase, and we must decrease:

> He must increase, but I must decrease. (John 3:30, ESV)

22. God is patient with sinners:

> The Lord is not slow to fulfill his promise as some count slowness, but is patient toward you, not wishing that any should perish, but that all should reach repentance. (2 Peter 3:9, ESV)

23. God's ways are higher than our ways:

> For my thoughts are not your thoughts, neither are your ways my ways, declares the LORD. For as the heavens are higher than the earth, so are my ways higher than your ways and my thoughts than your thoughts. (Isaiah 55:8–9, ESV)

24. God showed His love for us by sending Jesus to die for us:

> But God shows his love for us in that while we were still sinners, Christ died for us (Romans 5:8, ESV)

25. We love God because He first loved us:

> We love because he first loved us. (1 John 4:19, ESV)

Chapter 18—The Hippopotamuses (Sexual Identity)

1. Here is an example of a furious transgender shopper that threatened a store worker after he called her "sir" instead of "ma'am." For full story, see Chris Dyer, "'Take it outside if you want to call me sir again!' Furious transgender woman rages at store clerk after he calls her 'sir' instead of 'ma'am," *Daily Mail*, December 28, 2018, https://www.dailymail.co.uk/news/article-6536045/Furious-transgender-woman-rages-store-clerk-calls-sir-instead-maam.html.

2. Many argue that gender is completely independent of the body and therefore we are not defined by our physical body. For full context, see Nancy Pearcey,

Love Thy Body: Answering Hard Questions about Life and Sexuality, (Grand Rapids, baker Books, 2018) 31.

3. Many argue that the authentic self is not defined by the physical body. All that matters is a person's inner feelings or sense of self. For full context, see Pearcey, *Love Thy Body*, 31.

4. Due to their overwhelming feelings for the same sex, many insist that they were born gay; they insist that God made them gay. For full context, see Pearcey, *Love Thy Body*, 173.

5. For a comprehensive gender-identity list, see Sam Killermann, "Comprehensive* List of LGBTQ+ Vocabulary Definitions," https://itspronouncedmetrosexual. com/2013/01/a-comprehensive-list-of-lgbtq-term-definitions/ (accessed August 11, 2019).

6. God created male and female:

> So God created man in his own image, in the image of God he created him; male and female he created them. (Genesis 1:27, ESV)

7. Those who believe the Bible are being labeled more and more as hateful bigots. For a news report, see John Blake, "When Christians become a 'hated minority'," *CNN*, May 5th, 2013, http://religion.blogs.cnn.com/2013/05/05/when-christians-become-a-hated-minority/.

8. An ex-homosexual used to say, "If God created some people gay, then God has played a cruel joke on them." As if to say that God created their minds and emotions to be attracted to the same sex against their designed body. For full context, see Pearcey, *Love Thy Body*, 173.

9. Instead of escaping from the body, the goal is to live in harmony with it. For more commentary, see Pearcey, *Love Thy Body*, 211.

10. There are testimonies of homosexuals who became heterosexuals after they recognized that God's ways were best for them. For two examples of ex-lesbians, see Pearcey, *Love Thy Body*, 167, 175.

11. Many people who are same-sex attracted prayed that God would take it away only to never have it removed and it became a "thorn in their flesh." For full context, see Pearcey, *Love Thy Body*, 175.

12. "Desires for things that God has forbidden are a reflection of how sin has distorted us, not how God has made us," paraphrased from Nancy Pearcey. For full context, see Pearcey, *Love Thy Body*, 173.

13. We don't choose our feelings, but we do choose our behavior and how we respond to temptation. For more commentary, see Pearcey, *Love Thy Body*, 173.

14. God wants us to choose holiness:

> Since it is written, "You shall be holy, for I am holy." (1 Peter 1:16, ESV)

15. Camille Paglia, a self-described pagan lesbian, defends the homosexual lifestyle by saying, "Fate, not God, has given us this flesh; we have absolute claim to our

bodies and may do with them as we see fit." For full context, see Pearcey, *Love Thy Body*, 166.

16. The body is an integral part of the entire person. For more commentary, see Pearcey, *Love Thy Body*, 21, 32.

17. You cannot be a whole person when your emotions are at war with your physiology. For more commentary, see Pearcey, *Love Thy Body*, 173.

18. A common mind-set in the LGBTQ community is that the authentic self has no connection to the body. The real person resides in the spirit, mind, will, and feelings. For full context, see Pearcey, *Love Thy Body*, 31.

19. Separating our feelings from our body demeans our body because it alienates us from the body God gave us. For more commentary, see Pearcey, *Love Thy Body*, 30.

20. We should accept our body as a good gift from God. For more commentary, see Pearcey, *Love Thy Body*, 211.

21. The body is an observable fact that does not change. For more commentary, see Pearcey, *Love Thy Body*, 223.

22. If we are unrepentant to sinful behavior, God will give us over to that behavior:

> Therefore God gave them up in the lusts of their hearts to impurity, to the dishonoring of their bodies among themselves. (Romans 1:24, ESV)

Chapter 19—The Camels (Socialism/Communism)

1. Socialism produces a state of stagnation by removing the incentive to work and be productive. For full context, see Alasdair Elder, *The Red Trojan Horse: A Concise Analysis of Cultural Marxism*, (Scotts Valley, CreateSpace Independent Publishing Platform, 2017) 29.

2. A Marxist axiom is that religion is an opiate for the peoples repressed under capitalism. For full context, see William J. Murray, *Utopian Road to Hell: Enslaving America and the World with Central Planning* (Washington, DC, WND Books, 2016) 12.

3. In a Marxist society competition is evil, and all are expected to work for the common good with no selfish desires. For full context, see Murray, *Utopian Road to Hell*, 1.

4. "It's the cleanest, neatest, most efficiently operating piece of social machinery you'll ever see," paraphrased from Rexford Tugwell on Mussolini's fascist government. For full context, see Murray, Utopian Road to Hell, 155.

5. Tyrants will always seek to curb freedom of speech because freedom is a moral principle; this keeps the tyrant's lies from being exposed. For more commentary see Elder, *The Red Trojan Horse*, 6.

6. During the Lycurgus's utopia, even their speech patterns were restricted to avoid pointless chatter, gossip, or too much speaking of any kind. For full context, see Murray, *Utopian Road to Hell*, 42–43.

7. During the Lycurgus's utopia, the citizens were not allowed to eat at home; they were required to eat together at mess halls. For full context, see Murray, *Utopian Road to Hell*, 45.

8. French totalitarian Rousseau's general will opined that the interpretation of the law can safely be left to the leaders since they know what's best for all. For full context, see Murray, *Utopian Road to Hell*, 53.

9. A Marxist society must be a godless society. For full context, see Murray, *Utopian Road to Hell*, 2–3.

10. In a utopian society, the populists are brainwashed into believing that the central planners are benevolent and that their goals are actually those of the people. For full context, see Murray, *Utopian Road to Hell*, 116.

11. Morality police are common in Islamic countries. For a news report, see *BBC Monitoring*, "Who are Islamic 'morality police'?" *BBC News*, April 22, 2016, https://www.bbc.com/news/world-middle-east-36101150.

12. During Lycurgus's utopia, love of government was the highest virtue. For full context, see Murray, *Utopian Road to Hell*, 50.

13. During Sir Thomas More's utopia, citizens were required to listen to sermons on morality during communal dinners. For full context, see Murray, *Utopian Road to Hell*, 31.

14. In Lycurgus's utopia, citizens are forbidden to think for themselves. For full context, see Murray, *Utopian Road to Hell*, 48–49.

15. We are supposed to govern ourselves according to God's righteousness:

    > Righteousness guards him whose way is blameless, but sin overthrows the wicked. (Proverbs 13:6, ESV)

16. The fear of the Lord and hating evil keeps us accountable to God:

    > The fear of the LORD is hatred of evil. Pride and arrogance and the way of evil and perverted speech I hate. (Proverbs 8:13, ESV)

17. "Freedom is a fragile thing and is never more than one generation away from extinction," quoted from Ronald Reagan. For full context, see Murray, *Utopian Road to Hell*, 264.

18. Cultural Marxism undermines Christian values by destroying the position of the family as the basic building block of society. For more commentary see Elder, *The Red Trojan Horse*, 55.

19. Cultural Marxism changes a society through the educational system. For more commentary see Elder, *The Red Trojan Horse*, 62.

20. Cultural Marxism undermines God's morality through an education system that promoted free love and promiscuity. For more commentary see Elder, *The Red Trojan Horse*, 55.

21. Sexual liberation is used to manipulate and control others, for more commentary see Elder, *The Red Trojan Horse*, 57.

22. Margaret Sanger of Planned Parenthood regarded sexual modesty as obscene prudery. For full context, see Murray, *Utopian Road to Hell*, 86.

23. John Dewey believed that truth is not important if a lie will further the attainment of some worthy goal. For full context, see Murray, *Utopian Road to Hell*, 92.

24. Lying becomes the standard of utopian governments. For full context, see Murray, *Utopian Road to Hell*, 116.

25. "Eliminating charity and calling it justice," paraphrased from a quote by a fictional character named Philip Dru in the utopian book by Edward Mandell House. For full context, see Murray, *Utopian Road to Hell*, 131.

26. The cultural Marxist victim narrative is that women have always been systemically oppressed by men through the enforcement of gender roles. It's oppressive and patronizing. For more commentary see Elder, *The Red Trojan Horse*, 87.

27. Under the influence of cultural Marxism, women are made to believe that they require the aid and protection of the government. For more commentary see Elder, *The Red Trojan Horse*, 103.

28. Under the influence of Cultural Marxism, everything is racist, everything is sexist, everything is homophobic, and you just have to point it all out. For more commentary, see Elder, *The Red Trojan Horse*, 92.

29. Cultural Marxism makes phobia to be analogous to bigotry. For full context, see Elder, *The Red Trojan Horse*, 60.

30. Paraphrased from Alasdair Elder, "If it undermines Western culture it is logical, if it supports it then it is illogical." For full context, see Elder, *The Red Trojan Horse*, 53.

31. The utopian's goal is to destroy social norms and create a state of chaos that allows radical change. For full context, see Murray, *Utopian Road to Hell*, 94.

32. Under cultural Marxism, to the unsuspecting public this cultural change seems like a completely organic and natural process. For more commentary, see Elder, *The Red Trojan Horse*, 71.

33. In ancient Rome, citizens felt that it was necessary to trade in their personal liberties in exchange for their safety. For more commentary, see Elder, *The Red Trojan Horse*, 24.

34. The Birth Approval Committee is meant to be symbolic of eugenics where abortion is used to eliminate the genetically inferior. Much like the Birth Control League which was founded by Margaret Sanger and was the forerunner to Planned Parenthood. For full context, see Murray, Utopian Road to Hell, 87.

35. Iceland has eliminated Down syndrome by aborting babies with Down syndrome before they're born. For a news report, see Julian Quinones, Arijeta, Lajka, "[What kind of society do you want to live in?]: Inside the country where Down syndrome is disappearing," August 15, 2017, CBSN: On Assignment, https://www.cbsnews.com/news/down-syndrome-iceland/

Day of Judgment. The gospel works for everybody who repents and believes in Jesus. Jesus is the only way to escape God's judgment. For more commentary, see "Is Jesus the only way to Heaven?" last modified July 26, 2019, https://www.gotquestions.org/Jesus-only-way.html, (accessed August, 12, 2019).

3. "God helps those who help themselves" is a common axiom not found in the Bible. God helps those who humble themselves. For a short video commentary on this axiom, see "God Helps Those Who Help Themselves?" YouTube video, 1:33, posted by "WWUTT," April 15, 2014, https://youtu.be/r8krEP5NMVU.

4. "God never gives us more than we can handle" is a common axiom not found in the Bible. God often gives us way more than we can handle so that we will trust in Him alone. For a commentary on this false axiom, see Mitch Chase, "God Will Give You More than You Can Handle," July 17, 2015, https://www.thegospelcoalition.org/article/god-will-give-you-more-than-you-can-handle/, (accessed August 12, 2018).

5. "Everything happens for a reason" is often quoted for comfort and reassurance in difficult circumstances. But it's actually a true statement because God is sovereign and in control of everything. For a biblical commentary, see "Is it true that everything happens for a reason?" last modified July 26, 2019, https://www.gotquestions.org/everything-happens-for-reason.html, (accessed August 12, 2019).

6. "All roads lead to heaven" is a common saying that is completely unbiblical. Jesus made it clear that He is the only way to heaven:

> Jesus said to him, "I am the way, and the truth, and the life. No one comes to the Father except through me." (John 14:6, ESV)

For a biblical commentary, see Albert Mohler, "All Roads Lead to Heaven?" May 14, 2010, https://www.thegospelcoalition.org/article/all-roads-lead-to-heaven/, (accessed August 12, 2019).

7. "The god of your understanding" is a dangerous belief unless the God of your understanding is the God who is revealed in the Bible. All other gods are false gods:

> Remember the former things of old; for I am God, and there is no other; I am God, and there is none like me. (Isaiah 46:9, ESV)

8. God created everything by His wisdom and understanding:

> The LORD by wisdom founded the earth; by understanding he established the heavens. (Proverbs 3:19, ESV)

9. "God wants us to be happy" is a common misapplied saying. God commands us to be happy in Him, which comes through being holy. For a biblical commentary, see Interview with John Piper, "Does God Want Me to Be Happy or Holy?" Ask Pastor John, Episode 557, March 20, 2015, https://www.desiring-

god.org/interviews/does-god-want-me-to-be-happy-or-holy, (accessed August 12, 2019).

10. "Be true to yourself" is not in the Bible. It comes from a Shakespeare play called *Hamlet* in which the character Polonius says, "To thine own self be true." For full context, see "To thine own self be true," Shakespeare quotes, https://www.enotes.com/shakespeare-quotes/thine-own-self-true, (accessed August 12, 2019).

11. It is possible for us to be true to ourselves and be wrong at the same time. That kind of truth won't set us free. For a biblical commentary on being true to yourself, see Jon Bloom, "Be True to Yourself," January 5th, 2018, https://www.desiringgod.org/articles/be-true-to-yourself, (accessed August 12, 2019).

12. If we understand our true selves, we will mourn over our sin:

> Blessed are those who mourn, for they shall be comforted. (Matthew 5:4, ESV)

13. Wisdom is the most valuable thing in life:

> Blessed is the one who finds wisdom, and the one who gets understanding, for the gain from her is better than gain from silver and her profit better than gold. She is more precious than jewels, and nothing you desire can compare with her. (Proverbs 3:13–16, ESV)

14. The definition of *wisdom* in the dictionary is typical worldly wisdom that does not involve God. See Merriam-Webster, "wisdom," https://www.merriam-webster.com/dictionary/wisdom, (accessed August 13, 2019).

15. The biblical definition of *wisdom*:

> And he said to man, "Behold, the fear of the Lord, that is wisdom, and to turn away from evil is understanding." (Job 28:28, ESV)

16. Wisdom begins with the fear of the Lord:

> The fear of the LORD is the beginning of wisdom, and the knowledge of the Holy One is insight. (Proverbs 9:10, ESV)

17. Worldly wisdom quoted from Bertrand Russell, "To conquer fear is the beginning of wisdom." For full context, see Leon F Seltzer Ph.D., "The Wisest Quotes on Wisdom," Psychology Today, April 3, 2012, https://www.psychologytoday.com/us/blog/evolution-the-self/201204/the-wisest-quotes-wisdom, (accessed August 13, 2019).

18. Worldly wisdom quoted from an article in *Psychology Today*, "Wisdom is antithetical to fear. In fact, it's what enables a person to overcome fear." For full context, see Seltzer, "The Wisest Quotes on Wisdom."

19. It's an unhealthy fear of the Lord to be under His judgment:

    > It is a fearful thing to fall into the hands of the living God. (Romans 3:23, ESV)

20. A healthy fear of the Lord puts us in awe and reverence to Him:

    > Let all the earth fear the LORD; let all the inhabitants of the world stand in awe of him! (Psalm 33:8, ESV)

21. Worldly wisdom quoted from Alex Lickerman M.D., "Wisdom lives in the same place all ideas do—beneath our conscious awareness." For full context, see Alex Lickerman M.D., "Where Does Wisdom Come From?" Psychology Today, October 20, 2013, https://www.psychologytoday.com/us/blog/happiness-in-world/201310/where-does-wisdom-come, (accessed August 13, 2019).

22. Don't trust in your own wisdom apart from God:

    > Whoever trusts in his own mind is a fool, but he who walks in wisdom will be delivered. (Proverbs 28:26, ESV)

23. Worldly wisdom paraphrased from an article in *Psychology Today*: "Wisdom is acquired only through reflection on experience. Wisdom involves nuanced thinking, considering many different perspectives of a situation rather than employing black-and-white thinking." For full context, see "Wisdom," Psychology Today, https://www.psychologytoday.com/us/basics/wisdom, (accessed August 13, 2019).

24. True wisdom comes from God:

    > For the LORD gives wisdom; from his mouth come knowledge and understanding. (Proverbs 2:6, ESV)

25. Wisdom apart from God is demonic:

    > This is not the wisdom that comes down from above, but is earthly, unspiritual, demonic. (James 3:15, ESV)

26. God freely gives wisdom to those who ask for it:

    > If any of you lacks wisdom, let him ask God, who gives generously to all without reproach, and it will be given him. (James 1:5, ESV)

27. "The wisdom of this world is incapable of solving spiritual problems," paraphrased from John MacArthur. For full commentary, see "The Only Source of Wisdom," Grace to You, https://www.gty.org/library/Articles/A299/The-Only-Source-of-Wisdom, (accessed August 13, 2019).

28. Ageless wisdom is the New Age notion that there is a consensus from all cultures about the spiritual reality of all souls. For full context, see Frank Sontag, *Light the Way Home: My Incredible Ride from New Age to New Life,* (Frank Sontag and Mike Yorkey, September 2, 2014) 19.

29. Worldly wisdom is folly to God:

> For the wisdom of this world is folly with God. For it is written, "He catches the wise in their craftiness." (1 Corinthians 3:19, ESV)

30. Instead of preaching the good news that sinners can be made righteous in Christ and escape the wrath to come, many Christians have settled for a "gospel" that implies that God's primary purpose in saving us is to unfold a "wonderful plan" for our lives: to solve all our problems, make us happy, and rescue us from the hassles of life. For more commentary on the myth of this modern message, see Ray Comfort, *God Has a Wonderful Plan for Your Life: The Myth of the Modern Message,* (Bellflower, Living Waters Publications, 2010) 21.

31. "You are so heavenly minded that you are of no earthly good," is an unbiblical lie. The Bible makes it clear that we are to be completely heavenly minded. For a short video commentary, see "So Heavenly Minded You're No Earthly Good?" YouTube video, 1:30, posted by "WWUTT," June 29, 2018, https://youtu.be/pdlFgYEov2Y.

32. Those who do not fear God will not find God's wisdom in time of need:

> Then they will call upon me, but I will not answer; they will seek me diligently but will not find me. Because they hated knowledge and did not choose the fear of the LORD. (Proverbs 1:28–29, ESV)

33. "We all worship the same God" is a common belief that is false. By studying other religions, it becomes clear that none of them believe in the same God. For more commentary, see Simon Turpin, "Do All Religions Lead to God?" September 6, 2017, https://answersingenesis.org/world-religions/do-all-religions-lead-to-god/, (accessed August 13, 2019).

34. Only God's Word can make one wise for salvation:

> And how from childhood you have been acquainted with the sacred writings, which are able to make you wise for salvation through faith in Christ Jesus. (2 Timothy 3:15, ESV)

35. Life is meaningless without God. For life to be meaningful, it all boils down to this—fear God and keep His commandments:

> The end of the matter; all has been heard. Fear God and keep his commandments, for this is the whole duty of man. For God will bring every deed into judgment, with every secret thing, whether good or evil. (Ecclesiastes 12:13–14, ESV)

Chapter 22—The Rhinoceroses (Morality)

1. "We live in a moral wasteland" paraphrased from Nancy Pearcey. For full context, see Pearcey, *Love Thy Body*, 15.
2. Christians are not seeking to legislate their morality. They didn't invent these self-evident facts. They are merely recognizing them. It's the atheists that want to impose their morality. For more commentary, see Turek, *Stealing From God*, 107.
3. Objective moral rights are self-evident. Atheism is not. For more commentary, see Turek, *Stealing From God*, 114.
4. "Since objective morality is grounded in the object known as God's nature, it is unchangeable and authoritative. It is unaffected by our opinions about it," paraphrased from Frank Turek. For full context, see Turek, *Stealing From God*, 98.
5. When deciding what makes something moral, the question to ask is, "Why does a moral law exist at all, and why does it have authority over us?" For more commentary, see Turek, *Stealing From God*, 100.
6. Some atheists persist that evolution gives us objective morality to help us survive and cooperate with one another. For full context, see Turek, *Stealing From God*, 101.
7. The argument for evolutionary objective morals is self-refuting. Evolution is a process of change, so morals must change. For more commentary, see Turek, *Stealing From God*, 102.
8. A simple question for those who believe in evolution, "How could a mutating genetic code have the moral authority to tell you how you ought to behave?" For more commentary, see Turek, *Stealing From God*, 101.
9. God demands morality:

    > Since it is written, "You shall be holy, for I am holy." (1 Peter 1:16, ESV)

10. We all for short of God's demand for morality:

    > For all have sinned and fall short of the glory of God. (Romans 3:23, ESV)

11. An atheist tries to make the case that objective morality is determined by the degree it increases our welfare and well-being or decreases suffering and misery. For full context, see The Thinker, "A Case for Secular Morality," February, 15, 2013, http://www.atheismandthecity.com/2013/02/a-case-for-secular-morality-objective.html, (accessed August 13, 2019).

12. God uses suffering to build character:

    > Not only that, but we rejoice in our sufferings, knowing that suffering produces endurance, and endurance produces character, and character produces hope (Romans 5:3–4, ESV)

13. An atheist tries to make the case that philosophy and science are needed to complete any system of ethics even though philosophy and science are always changing. For full context, see The Thinker, "A Case for Secular Morality."

14. An atheist attempts to make the case that moral progress is required to achieve a perfect moral code even though the knowledge needed for this perfect moral code is out of our reach. For full context, see The Thinker, "A Case for Secular Morality."

15. An atheist posits that moral codes that forbid any progress are defective right from the start. For full context, see The Thinker, "A Case for Secular Morality."

16. "There is no objective moral standard. We are all responsible for our own actions," quoted from the president of American Atheists David Silverman. For full context, see Turek, *Stealing From God*, 94.

17. The American Atheist president asserts that abusing morality shows that morality is relative. If it was objective, you could not abuse it. For full context, see Turek, *Stealing From God*, 96.

18. "You're confusing sociology with morality," parapharased from Frank Turek as he distinguishes sociology from morality in a debate with the president of the American Atheists. For full context, see Turek, *Stealing From God*, 96.

19. God's nature is the standard of morality. For more commentary, see Turek, *Stealing From God*, 104.

20. "No society has yet been successful in teaching morality without religion," paraphrased from non-Christian author Guenter Lewy. For full context, see Pearcey, *Total Truth*, 60.

21. Frank Turek makes the case that if God doesn't exist, then objective moral rights don't exist. For more commentary, see Turek, *Stealing From God*, 107.

22. An atheist attempts to make the case that embracing moral values must appeal to reason or authority. However, he claims that appealing to reason is only for mature people since some people are unreasonable and they must appeal to authority. The implication is that appealing to God's moral authority is immature. For full context, see The Thinker, "A Case For Secular Morality."

23. "Reason is a tool by which we discover what the moral law is, but it can't account for why the moral law exists in the first place," quoted from Frank Turek. For more commentary, see Turek, *Stealing From God*, 103.

24. God's law is written on our heart:

> They show that the work of the law is written on their hearts, while their conscience also bears witness, and their conflicting thoughts accuse or even excuse them. (Romans 2:15, ESV)

25. "You can't explain the immaterial moral law through science," paraphrased from Frank Turek. For full context, see Turek, *Stealing From God*, 101.

26. "Every law has a lawgiver. There is an objective moral law. Therefore, there is an objective moral lawgiver," quoted from Frank Turek. For more commentary, see Turek, *Stealing From God*, 113.

27. God is the only objective moral lawgiver:

> There is only one Lawgiver and Judge, the One who is able to save and to destroy; but who are you who judge your neighbor? (James 4:12, NKJV)

28. An atheist tries to explain how a moral lawgiver makes the moral law meaningless. The only thing that matters is whether God commanded it. For full context, see The Thinker, "A Case for Secular Morality."

29. God's commands are good:

> So the law is holy, and the commandment is holy and righteous and good. (Romans 7:12, ESV)

30. God sees everything:

> The eyes of the LORD are in every place, keeping watch on the evil and the good. (Proverbs 15:3, ESV)

31. God has infinite understanding:

> Great is our Lord and abundant in strength; His understanding is infinite. (Psalm 147:5, NASB)

32. An atheist attempts to make the case that a universe without God would still have the same objective moral values while also claiming that objective morals are always changing through moral progress. For full context, see The Thinker, "A Case For Secular Morality."

33. We can prove what a godless universe would look like by examining the godless societies throughout human history and how they brought about unimaginable human suffering. For more info on the human suffering brought about by godless societies and the positive impact Christianity has had on the human condition, see Jeremiah J. Johnston, *Unimaginable: What Our World Would Be Like without Christianity,* (Bloomington, Bethany House Publishers, 2017).

34. "Only an unchanging God can prescribe and enforce an objective standard of morality," paraphrased from Frank Turek. For full context, see Turek, *Stealing From God,* 100.

35. Atheists commonly try to stump Christians with the Euthyphro Dilemma which asks, "Is something morally good because God commands it, or does God command it because it is morally good?" For full context, see The Thinker, "A Case for Secular Morality."

36. An atheist attempts to make the case that God is completely irrelevant because morals are either right or wrong independently of whether God exists or not. For full context, see The Thinker, "A Case for Secular Morality."

37. "God doesn't look up to another standard beyond Himself. He wouldn't be God if He did," paraphrased from Frank Turek. For more commentary, see Turek, *Stealing From God,* 104.

38. "The third answer (to the Euthyphro Dilemma) is that God's nature is the standard," paraphrased from Frank Turek. For more commentary on this false dilemma, see Turek, *Stealing From God*, 103–104.

39. An atheist attempts to make the case that the best reason to do what is morally right—is for its own sake. For full context, see The Thinker, "A Case for Secular Morality."

40. "The conscience is the soul's warning system," paraphrased from the John MacArthur. For more commentary, see "The Soul's Warning System," Grace to You, https://www.gty.org/library/sermons-library/47-5/the-souls-warning-system, (accessed August 15, 2019).

41. "Conscience is an evolved intellectual attribute that enhances the survival of our species," paraphrased from Rick Thorne in a Quora discussion forum. For full context see: "How Do Atheists Explain The Existence of Conscience in the Absence of God?" answered by Rick Thorne, Nov 18, 2014, https://www.quora.com/How-do-atheists-explain-the-existence-of-conscience-in-the-absence-of-God (accessed August 13, 2019).

42. "In order for our conscience to work as God designed it, the conscience must be informed to the highest moral and spiritual level and best standard," paraphrased from John MacArthur. For more commentary, see MacArthur, "The Soul's Warning System."

43. Beware of a seared conscience:

> Now the Spirit expressly says that in later times some will depart from the faith by devoting themselves to deceitful spirits and teachings of demons, through the insincerity of liars whose consciences are seared. (1 Timothy 4:1–2, ESV)

Chapter 23—Dinosaur Danger

1. Pterosaurs were incredible flying creatures created by God. For more info on pterosaurs, see Brian Thomas, PH.D., "Pterosaur Revolution Confirms Creation," September 06, 2013, https://www.icr.org/article/pterosaur-revolution-confirms-creation/, (accessed August 14, 2019).

2. Pterosaur wings are interconnected with their legs. Their wings were similar to, but not the same as, bat wings—unlike birds which have legs separate from their wings. For more information on pterosaurs, see Mike Habib, "Pterosaur.net Anatomy," https://pterosaur.net/anatomy.php, (accessed August 14, 2019).

Chapter 24—The Koala Bears (Truth)

1. German philosopher Friedrich Nietzsche posited that there is no truth and claimed, "There are no eternal facts, as there are no absolute truths." Nietzsche also rejected Christianity and famously said, "God is dead." For more info,

see "Friedrich Nietzsche," The Basics of Philosophy, Individual Philosopher, https://www.philosophybasics.com/philosophers_nietzsche.html (accessed August, 16, 2019).

2. When confronted with someone who says "There is no truth," always respond by applying their claim to itself by asking, "Is that true?" For more commentary on exposing self-refuting truth claims, see Turek, *Stealing From God*, 34.

3. Can truth be known? For a discussion forum that attempts to explain the axioms of truth, but instead they complicate it and tie your brain in a knot, see Keinosuke Johan Miyanaga, "Is there absolute truth, and how is it determined? If not, how can knowledge exist?" last modifed December 14, 2014, https://www.quora.com/Is-there-absolute-truth-and-how-is-it-determined-If-not-how-can-knowledge-exist, (accessed August 15, 2019).

4. Some people believe everyone's truth is different. For a short video that refutes this claim, see "True for You but Not for Me," YouTube video, 5:24, posted by "PragerU, https://youtu.be/pMzhzqoQh8c.

5. Pontius Pilate asked Jesus, "What is truth?" and then he walked away as if no answer existed:

> Pilate said to him, "What is truth?" After he had said this,
> he went back outside to the Jews and told them, "I find no
> guilt in him." (John 8:38, ESV)

6. An unbelieving college philosophy professor said that truth is "the way God sees things." Unbeknownst to him, that statement was totally true. For full context, see Pearcey, *Total Truth*, 39.

7. "Truth is true" quotes from an article by Paul Copan. For more commentary on refuting relativism, see Paul Copan, "True for you, but not for me?" https://www.bethinking.org/truth/thats-true-for-you-but-not-for-me-relativism, (accessed August 15, 2019).

8. God has revealed the basic truth Himself through nature:

> The heavens declare the glory of God, and the sky above
> proclaims his handiwork. (Psalm 19:1, ESV)

9. God has many invisible attributes revealed through nature. For more commentary on God's truth, see "What Is Truth?" Grace to You, https://www.gty.org/library/Articles/A379/What-Is-Truth, (accessed August 15, 2019).

10. The truth about God and creation is revealed in the very first verse in the Bible:

> In the beginning, God created the heavens and the earth.
> (Genesis 1:1, ESV)

11. In order to know absolute truth, all creation must be interpreted in light of its relationship to God and His Word. For more commentary, see Pearcey, *Total Truth*, 35.

12. God's Word is a trustworthy basis for reality. For more commentary, see Pearcey, *Total Truth*, 395.

13. Truth is the self-expression of God. For more commentary on God's truth, see MacArthur, "What Is Truth?"

14. "The way to find truth is to strip the mind of everything that can possibly be doubted until we finally reach a bedrock of truths that cannot possible be doubted," paraphrased from French philosopher and mathematician, René Descartes. For full context, see Pearcey, *Total Truth*, 39.

15. The overall systems of thought constructed by nonbelievers will be false—for if the system is not built on biblical truth, then it will be built on some other ultimate principle. For full context, see Pearcey, *Total Truth*, 46.

16. St. Augustine posited that all truth was God's truth. For full context and more commentary, see R.C. Sproul, "All Truth Is God's Truth," https://www.ligonier.org/learn/articles/all-truth-gods-truth-sproul/, (accessed August 15, 2019).

17. "All the truth in the world adds up to one big lie," quoted from a Bob Dylan song. For full lyrics, see Bob Dylan, "Things Have Changed," http://www.bob-dylan.com/songs/things-have-changed/, (accessed August 15, 2019).

18. Jesus made it clear that He is the truth:

> Jesus said to him, "I am the way, and the truth, and the life. No one comes to the Father except through me." (John 14:6, ESV)

19. It's impossible for God to lie:

> So that by two unchangeable things, in which it is impossible for God to lie, we who have fled for refuge might have strong encouragement to hold fast to the hope set before us. (Hebrews 6:18, ESV)

20. Our sinful nature suppresses the truth in unrighteousness:

> For the wrath of God is revealed from heaven against all ungodliness and unrighteousness of men, who by their unrighteousness suppress the truth. (Romans 1:18, ESV)

Chapter 25—The Ark!

1. This statement was paraphrased from Moses just before God parted the Red Sea:

> And Moses said to the people, "Fear not, stand firm, and see the salvation of the LORD, which he will work for you today. For the Egyptians whom you see today, you shall never see again." (Exodus 14:13, ESV)

2. God caused the earth to open up and swallow those who rebelled against Moses and Aaron:

> And as soon as he had finished speaking all these words, the ground under them split apart. And the earth opened its mouth and swallowed them up, with their households and all the people who belonged to Korah and all their goods. (Numbers 16:31–32, ESV)

3. Salvation comes from God alone:

> Behold, God is my salvation; I will trust, and will not be afraid; for the LORD GOD is my strength and my song, and he has become my salvation. (Isaiah 12:2, ESV)

4. For an analysis on the size of the ark, see "How Big Was Noah's Ark?" Ark Encounter, https://arkencounter.com/noahs-ark/size/, (accessed August 15, 2019).

5. The idea that they would plot to destroy the ark and prevent salvation comes from how the religious leaders and elders plotted to destroy Jesus:

> Then the chief priests and the elders of the people gathered in the palace of the high priest, whose name was Caiaphas, and plotted together in order to arrest Jesus by stealth and kill him. (Matthew 26:3–4, ESV)

6. Nobody expected the flood of Genesis because they didn't take God's coming judgment seriously. The same will be true when Jesus returns. Nobody will be expecting it because they do not take God's judgment seriously:

> Therefore you also must be ready, for the Son of Man is coming at an hour you do not expect. (Matthew 24:44, ESV)

7. Jesus is God's only plan for salvation:

> And there is salvation in no one else, for there is no other name under heaven given among men by which we must be saved. (Acts 4:12, ESV)

8. Doing what's right in your own eyes leads to hell:

> There is a way that seems right to a man, but its end is the way to death. (Proverbs 14:12, ESV)

9. The unbeliever has no idea what is in store for them when they reject salvation and continue in their sin:

> And Jesus said, "Father, forgive them, for they know not what they do." And they cast lots to divide his garments. (Luke 23:34, ESV)

Chapter 26—Inside the Ark

1. The Ark Encounter exhibit in Kentucky displays animal enclosures equipped with clay food and water containers each with a continuous feeder bowl. Well within the capabilities of Noah and his family. For more info on the possibilities inside the ark, see Laura Welch, *Inside Noah's Ark: Why it Worked*, (Green Forest, Master Books, 2016), 36–37.

2. The Ark Encounter exhibit in Kentucky shows the possibility of food storage consisting of grains, grasses, seeds, nuts, fruits, and vegetables along with dried fruits and vegetables. Well within the capabilities of Noah and his family. For more info on food storage possibilities inside the ark, see Welch, *Inside Noah's Ark*, 26.

3. The ark had three decks:

   > Make a roof for the ark, and finish it to a cubit above, and set the door of the ark in its side. Make it with lower, second, and third decks. (Genesis 6:16, ESV)

4. There was enough space on the ark for every animal kind, including food storage and supplies. For more info on how it was determined if there was enough room to accommodate all the animals and space for supplies, see Ken Ham, Bodie Hodge, *A Flood of Evidence: 40 Reasons Noah and the Ark Still Matter,* (Green Forest, Master Books, 2016), 209–217.

5. The Ark Encounter exhibit in Kentucky shows that it was very plausible that Noah used a bamboo-piping system to distribute water throughout the Ark. For more info on the how water may have been collected and distributed, see Welch, *Inside Noah's Ark,* 29–35.

6. The Ark Encounter exhibit in Kentucky shows that it was very plausible that Noah stored food in clay vessels throughout the ark. For more info on the how food may have been stored on the ark, see Welch, *Inside Noah's Ark,* 29–35.

7. Although Genesis 6:3 indicates that God gave Noah 120 years as a countdown to the flood, a reasonable analysis would indicate that it took Noah and his family about seventy-five years to build the ark. For a commentary on how long it took to build the ark, see: Bodie Hodge, "How Long Did It Take for Noah to Build the Ark?" last modified May 23, 2018, https://answersingenesis. org/bible-timeline/how-long-did-it-take-for-noah-to-build-the-ark, (accessed August 15, 2019).

8. Many will mistake God's patience as proof that He isn't coming or that He just doesn't exist:

   > knowing this first of all, that scoffers will come in the last days with scoffing, following their own sinful desires. They will say, "Where is the promise of his coming? For ever since the fathers fell asleep, all things are continuing as they were from the beginning of creation." (2 Peter 3:3–4, ESV)

9. Atheist Richard Dawkins attempts to use science to make the case that everyone who believes in God is deluded. For full context, see Turek, *Stealing From God*, xiii.

10. Paraphrased from a quote by atheist Richard Dawkins, "When one person suffers from a delusion, it is called insanity. When many people suffer from a delusion, it is called religion." For full context, see Turek, *Stealing From God*, xiv.

11. Satan blinds the minds of unbelievers so that they reject salvation:

> In their case the god of this world has blinded the minds of the unbelievers, to keep them from seeing the light of the gospel of the glory of Christ, who is the image of God. (2 Corinthians 4:4, ESV)

12. The promise of God to work all things for good is for believers:

> And we know that for those who love God all things work together for good, for those who are called according to his purpose. (Romans 8:28, ESV)

13. They all went into the ark just as the Bible says:

> They and every beast, according to its kind, and all the livestock according to their kinds, and every creeping thing that creeps on the earth, according to its kind, and every bird, according to its kind, every winged creature. They went into the ark with Noah, two and two of all flesh in which there was the breath of life. (Genesis 7:14–15, ESV)

Chapter 27—The Flood

1. Noah and his family and all the animals were in the ark for seven days before the flood came:

> For in seven days I will send rain on the earth forty days and forty nights, and every living thing that I have made I will blot out from the face of the ground. (Genesis 7:4, ESV)

2. God shut them in the ark:

> And those that entered, male and female of all flesh, went in as God had commanded him. And the LORD shut him in. (Genesis 7:16, ESV)

3. Based on underwater volcanic activity around the globe, it is plausible that during the flood global catastrophic eruptions sent subterranean waters into the air and back to earth as rain:

> In the six hundredth year of Noah's life, in the second
> month, on the seventeenth day of the month, on that day
> all the fountains of the great deep burst forth, and the win-
> dows of the heavens were opened. (Genesis 7:11, ESV)

4. The "fountains of the great deep" most likely refers to earthquakes, volcanoes, and geysers of molten lava and scalding water being squeezed out of the earth's crust in a violent, explosive upheaval. For a biblical and scientific commentary of the Genesis flood, see Ken Ham, Tim Lovett, Andrew Snelling, John Whitmore, *A Pocket Guide to the Global Flood: A Biblical and Scientific Look at the Catastrophe That Changed the Earth,* (Petersburg, Answers in Genesis, 2009), 9.

5. Based on the current puzzle-like shapes of the continents, global investigations of the earth's crust reveal a plausible single continent before the flood that broke apart during the flood. Biblical support for a single continent is plausible based on a possible interpretation of Genesis 1:9–10, indicating that all the waters were in one place separate from the land before the flood. For a biblical and scientific commentary on a pre-flood super continent and catastrophic plate tectonics, see Ham, Lovett, Snelling, Whitmore, *A Pocket Guide to the Global Flood,* 75–80.

6. All died in the flood:

> Everything on the dry land in whose nostrils was the breath
> of life died. (Genesis 7:22, ESV)

7. God only spared Noah and his family along with the animals on the ark when He poured out His wrath on the ungodly in a global flood:

> If He did not spare the ancient world, but preserved Noah,
> a herald of righteousness, with seven others, when he
> brought a flood upon the world of the ungodly. (2 Peter
> 2:4, ESV)

8. There are dinosaur footprints all over the earth. For an example of nearly one hundred dinosaur footprints from multiple species discovered in one place, see Katherine Hignett, "Almost 100 Dinosaur Footprints From Multiple Species Discovered After Raging Storms," December 18, 2018, https://www.newsweek.com/dinosaur-footprints-science-dinosaurs-ancient-footprints-geology-paleontology-1263583, (accessed August 16, 2019).

9. Those who refuse to repent and reject God's salvation will not escape the wrath of God:

> For the great day of their wrath has come, and who can
> stand? (Revelation 6:17, ESV)

10. Marine life, plants, and land-dwelling creatures are found buried together all over the earth. For more scientific and biblical commentary on the evidence of a global flood, see Ham, Lovett, Snelling, Whitmore, *A Pocket Guide to the Global Flood,* 38–39.

11. After a global flood we would expect to find billions of dead animals and plants that were buried rapidly and fossilized. For a scientific and biblical commentary of the evidence of a global flood, see Ham, Lovett, Snelling, Whitmore, *A Pocket Guide to The Global Flood,* 37.

12. The flood waters lifted the ark off the earth:

    > The flood continued forty days on the earth. The waters increased and bore up the ark, and it rose high above the earth. (Genesis 7:17, ESV)

13. It rained nonstop for forty days and forty nights:

    > And rain fell upon the earth forty days and forty nights. (Genesis 7:12, ESV)

14. The waters rose until they were approximately twenty-two and a half feet (fifteen cubits) above the mountains:

    > The waters prevailed above the mountains, covering them fifteen cubits deep. (Genesis 7:20, ESV)

15. God made a wind blow:

    > But God remembered Noah and all the beasts and all the livestock that were with him in the ark. And God made a wind blow over the earth, and the waters subsided. (Genesis 8:1, ESV)

16. God closed the fountains of the deep and restrained the rain:

    > The fountains of the deep and the windows of the heavens were closed, the rain from the heavens was restrained. (Genesis 8:2, ESV)

17. The ark rested on the mountains of Ararat:

    > And the waters receded from the earth continually. At the end of 150 days, the waters had abated, and in the seventh month, on the seventeenth day of the month, the ark came to rest on the mountains of Ararat. (Genesis 8:3–4, ESV)

18. The water receded enough to see the tops of the mountains:

    > And the waters continued to abate until the tenth month; in the tenth month, on the first day of the month, the tops of the mountains were seen. (Genesis 8:5, ESV)

19. A plausible explanation as to where the flood waters drained is that the mountains rose and the ocean sank as deep trenches were formed causing the water to

drain into the oceans. For more commentary of where the flood waters drained, see Mike Oard, "How did the waters of Noah's Flood drain off the continents?" July 30, 2015, https://creation.com/how-did-the-waters-of-noahs-flood-drain, (accessed August 16, 2015).

20. Noah sent out a raven, and it flew back and forth, waiting for the earth to dry, but it never returned:

> At the end of forty days Noah opened the window of the ark that he had made and sent forth a raven. It went to and fro until the waters were dried up from the earth. (Genesis 8:6–7, ESV)

21. The raven is a hardy and intelligent bird that can survive on many kinds of foods, even in harsh environments. For more info on ravens, see "Raven," Encyclopaedia Britannica, https://www.britannica.com/animal/raven, (accessed August 16, 2019).

22. Noah sent out a dove, but it returned because the waters were still too high:

> Then he sent forth a dove from him, to see if the waters had subsided from the face of the ground. But the dove found no place to set her foot, and she returned to him to the ark, for the waters were still on the face of the whole earth. So he put out his hand and took her and brought her into the ark with him. (Genesis 8:8–9, ESV)

23. Doves mostly eat seeds. For more info on doves, see "Mourning Dove," All About Birds, https://www.allaboutbirds.org/guide/mourning_dove/lifehistory, (accessed August 16, 2019).

24. This time the dove returned with an olive leaf:

> He waited another seven days, and again he sent forth the dove out of the ark. And the dove came back to him in the evening, and behold, in her mouth was a freshly plucked olive leaf. So Noah knew that the waters had subsided from the earth. (Genesis 8:10–11, ESV)

25. This time the dove did not return:

> Then he waited another seven days and sent forth the dove, and she did not return to him anymore. (Genesis 8:12, ESV)

26. The ground was finally dry:

> In the six hundred and first year, in the first month, the first day of the month, the waters were dried from off the earth. And Noah removed the covering of the ark and looked, and behold, the face of the ground was dry. (Genesis 8:13, ESV)

27. The animals' dream is a paraphrase of what God said to Noah:

> Bring out with you every living thing that is with you of all flesh—birds and animals and every creeping thing that creeps on the earth—that they may swarm on the earth, and be fruitful and multiply on the earth. (Genesis 8:17, ESV)

Chapter 28—The New World

1. Noah and the animals were in the ark approximately 371 days. For an overview of the flood timeline, see Bodie Hodge, "Biblical Overview of the Flood Timeline," August 23, 2010, https://answersingenesis.org/bible-timeline/biblical-overview-of-the-flood-timeline/, (accessed August 17, 2019).
2. God wants godly marriages who produce godly offspring:

> Did he not make them one, with a portion of the Spirit in their union? And what was the one God seeking? Godly offspring. So guard yourselves in your spirit, and let none of you be faithless to the wife of your youth. (Malachi 2:15, ESV)

3. God wants us to teach our children the way of the Lord:

> Fathers, do not provoke your children to anger, but bring them up in the discipline and instruction of the Lord. (Ephesians 6:4, ESV)

4. Continued sinful rebellion against God provokes Him to wrath:

> Remember and do not forget how you provoked the LORD your God to wrath in the wilderness. From the day you came out of the land of Egypt until you came to this place, you have been rebellious against the LORD. (Deuteronomy 9:7, ESV)

5. "Be fruitful and multiply" is God's cultural mandate, which tells us that our original purpose was to create cultures and build civilizations that fear the Lord. For more commentary on the Genesis cultural mandate, see Pearcey, *Total Truth*, 47.
6. Those who forsake the Lord shall be consumed by eternal destruction:

> But rebels and sinners shall be broken together, and those who forsake the LORD shall be consumed. (Isaiah 1:28, ESV)

7. Obeying the cultural mandate is how we participate in God's work in maintaining and caring for His creation. For more commentary on the Genesis cultural mandate, see Pearcey, *Total Truth*, 81.

to remote parts of the Grand Canyon to meet with God and seek His guidance. While he was there God said one thing: "Write." After returning from that trip, Chris spent every spare moment writing this story. All in all, this book took thirteen years to write.

Chris is proof that God uses ordinary people who are devoted to Him to do extraordinary things.

CPSIA information can be obtained
at www.ICGtesting.com
Printed in the USA
LVHW022248300520
656910LV00004B/257